Janice M. Park.
June '69

D1100424

SINCE 1945:

Aspects of Contemporary
World History

Also available

WORLD QUESTIONS: A STUDY GUIDE
General Editor, James L. Henderson, PH.D.

Since 1945

Aspects of Contemporary World History

GENERAL EDITOR

James L. Henderson, Ph.D.

Senior Lecturer in the Teaching of History and International Affairs, University of London Institute of Education

LONDON

METHUEN & CO LTD

First published in 1966 by
Methuen & Co Ltd
11 New Fetter Lane, London EC4
© 1966 Methuen & Co Ltd
Printed in Great Britain by
Butler & Tanner Ltd, Frome

CONTENTS

PREFACE BY THE EDITOR   *page* 9

INTRODUCTION: THE WRITING AND TEACHING
OF CONTEMPORARY HISTORY
The Historian Speaks by Roger Morgan, Ph.D.   11
  *Lecturer in International Relations, University of
  Sussex*

The Teacher Speaks by D. B. Heater, M.A.   24
  Senior Lecturer, Brighton Training College

1 THE WORLD SCENE IN 1945   47
   by Gerald Bailey, M.A.,
   *Lecturer and Writer under the John Rowntree
   Charitable Trust*

2 THE COLD WAR:
   Its Origins by Christopher Seton-Watson, M.A.   64
   Oriel College, Oxford

   Its Continuation by Roger Morgan, Ph.D.   85
   *Lecturer in International Relations, University of
   Sussex*

3 THE SOVIET UNION SINCE 1945   92
   by Jack Lively, M.A.
   Lecturer in Politics, University of Sussex

4 THE UNITED STATES OF AMERICA SINCE 1945   109
   by D. Snowman, Ph.D.
   Assistant Lecturer in Politics, University of Sussex

5 THE EMERGENCE OF MODERN CHINA   137
   by Victor Purcell (*deceased*), C.M.G., Ph.D., D.LITT.
   Emmanuel College, University of Cambridge

Contents

6 THE PHENOMENON OF NATIONALISM IN ASIA:
China, Japan, Indonesia, Pakistan and Ceylon   *page* 154
by Ian Thomson, M.A.
  St Paul's College Cheltenham

India by B. N. Pandey, LL.B., M.A., Ph.D.   163
  *Lecturer in Modern History, School of Oriental and
  African Studies, University of London*

7 THE PHENOMENON OF NATIONALISM IN AFRICA
The Emergence of Nationalism by Colin Legum   176
Commonwealth Correspondent, The Observer

Some Problems of Independence   186
by Robin Hallett, M.A.

8 THE PHENOMENON OF NATIONALISM IN THE
MIDDLE EAST SINCE 1945   195
by Professor E. Kedourie, B.Sc. (ECON.)
  London School of Economics, University of London

9 REVOLUTION AND REFORM IN LATIN AMERICA   210
by Harold Blakemore, Ph.D.
  *Secretary, Institute of Latin American Studies,
  University of London*

10 THE GROWTH OF EUROPEAN UNITY   238
by Russell Lewis, M.A.
  European Communities' Information Service

11 GREAT BRITAIN: RETROSPECT AND PROSPECT   260
by James L. Henderson, Ph.D.
  Institute of Education, University of London

FURTHER READING   273

INDEX   275

PREFACE

The origin of this book was a specific occasion; it now attempts
to meet a general need. Most of the material in it was contained
in a series of lectures given to students in training colleges of
the London University Institute of Education during the Academic Session, 1964–5. For that audience, and for the potentially
far wider audience of readers of this volume, an effort has been
made to answer two questions: What has been happening in
the world since 1945 and what does it signify?

The answers which emerge cannot possibly be complete, and
indeed they are sometimes contradictory, partly due to the
diverse viewpoints of the contributors and partly due to the
paradox of actuality contained in the events themselves. Nevertheless it is hard to read through this sweeping survey without
becoming aware of certain patterns, which the last twenty years
have imposed on history. Three obvious examples are, first the
disintegration of a monolithic world communism to the accom-
paniment at the same time of the proliferation of Communist
states, secondly what Geoffrey Barraclough has named "the
dwarfing of Europe", and thirdly what Dame Edith Sitwell,
referring to the 6th of August 1945, called, "the cloud in the
Heavens shaped like the hand of Man".

THE EDITOR

THE WRITING AND TEACHING OF CONTEMPORARY HISTORY

The Historian Speaks

by Roger Morgan

There are three main problems raised by the question whether contemporary history can really be described as reputable history at all. Many professional academic historians seem to take as their guiding motto the famous last line of that great work of historical philosophy, *1066 and All That*, which went something like this: "After the Great War America became the Top Nation and history came to a . . ." Even though that was written some years ago, many people still seem to think history really stopped in 1918 or even in 1914, and in some universities the great emphasis in the History course is still on the Tudor and Stuart constitutional history of England.

As defenders of the argument that contemporary history really is history, the first argument we have to face is that there is really not enough source-material. How can we presume to interpret what has been happening in the world since 1945 when we cannot look at the documents? The archives are shut up, and the documentary material which after all is the basis of all historical research is just not available. A second argument is that we are all bound to be biased about recent problems. Those who remember the Suez crisis of 1956 or the Cuba crisis of 1962, will know that events of this sort can arouse very strong passions. We felt personally involved in these things; we as citizens had to make up our minds what we thought about them, so how can we say that as historians we are now in the same position to be as objective about them as we hope we are about, say, the problems of James the Second or Magna Carta? This problem of bias in the historian is an accusation to which we have to face up; and thirdly, it seems to me that the most difficult of the problems we have to tackle is the one of perspective. Here we are a year or two on from the Cuba crisis, and we have to try to explain its significance and give an interpretation, in the same way that we claim to give an interpretation of why the First World War happened or why Bismarck treated the Catholic Church as he did. It seems to me that this is perhaps the most difficult problem of the three, the problem of not being far enough away from the events we try to describe to give an objective picture of them, quite apart from any question of bias or lack of documentation.

For the student of the history of the world since 1945 the source-material is in many ways more limited than for the historian who covers the field up to 1945. Up to 1945 reasonably adequate documentation on the foreign policy of the great Powers can be obtained. There is full access to the records of the foreign policies or at least some of them. With a knowledge of German or Japanese, documents that were captured from these Powers after they were defeated in the Second World War are available. In the case of the German archives they were brought to this country and filmed completely, and although the originals have now been given back to Bonn, the copies are still there in the Public Record Office. The historian who can read German can go right through all the diplomatic dealings and most of the military planning of the German Governments up to 1945, and from this material, from documents exchanged by the Germans with the Russians, with the French, with the British, at least some picture can be provided of the foreign policy of these other Powers too. Since 1945, there has not been that sort of war with those sorts of consequences for historians, and so we are limited, in the way of official documents, to what our governments will allow us to read.

There is a problem, then, for the historian who aims to investigate what has happened in the last twenty years, but I think it can be argued that by intelligently using newspapers and other published sources, the information that governments do publish from time to time, it is possible to arrive at a reasonably complete picture of what governments were doing. Any really significant event, any significant decision by any government, leaves some kind of trace in the newspapers, in public statements, at the time: to illustrate this, here is an example of how specialists on Soviet foreign policy have been able to deduce trends in current Soviet policies, even in a country where a fully free press as we understand it does not exist, and where ministers are not in the habit of giving off-the-cuff statements to journalists. This seems to me an interesting example of the way in which the historian deprived of his full documentation can deduce what great Powers are up to.

In 1951, a couple of years before Stalin died, Soviet foreign policy had run into rather a dead end; there was a war going on in Korea which the Soviets had probably not bargained for and which they wanted to stop; their policy in Germany, a policy of trying to take over West Berlin by exerting economic pressure, had been foiled by the Western reaction, the creation of the North Atlantic Treaty in 1949; and Soviet foreign policy in general was moving towards a rather more conciliatory phase, which began quite distinctly a couple of years before Stalin's death, not afterwards. One sign by which historians even in 1951 could see what was happening was this: on 29th April, *Pravda* published a review of the latest volume of Stalin's collected works, which were then coming out. Stalin at that time was of course regarded as one of the classic writers of Marxism–Leninism, and when Volume 13 of his collected works came out at the end of April, there was a tremendously favourable review in *Pravda*. What this review did was to stress all the things in the book which pointed out that conflict between the Communist world and the capitalist world was inevitable, that the final victory of Socialism was a matter of hard struggles, but that sooner or later capitalism would collapse – that conflict, in general, was still a fundamental doctrine of Soviet foreign policy. This was natural, this was the Soviet line at the time. But about two weeks later, on 16th May, *Pravda* rather oddly published a second review of this same volume of Stalin's works. Again, not surprisingly, the reviewer said what a good book it was and what a genius the author was, but this time, instead of stressing all the bits in the book about the conflict between the two social systems and the inevitable overthrow of capitalism, and all the rest of it, the reviewer argued that the real significance of the book lay in its passages about the possibility of peaceful coexistence and the long-term prospects of reducing tension and conflict between the two blocs; the review said practically nothing about war and conflict. This is a small example, and somewhat specialized, but it shows how even in the Soviet press the observant historian can find evidence at the time about decisions being made – in this case, obviously quite important decisions about Soviet policy, since, sure enough, moves were soon afterwards made towards a cease-fire in Korea, and new Soviet proposals for the re-unification of Germany came out early in 1952. Thus this little incident, which struck some observers even at the time as significant, helps us to date a major turning-point in Soviet foreign policy.

It is still true, of course, that we often do not possess as much documentation about recent events as we have about the events of the slightly more remote past: however, the critical sifting of bits of evidence like this and of all the memoirs that are published by statesmen anxious to justify their actions, and of all the piles of propaganda that different governments do put out for their own purposes, should eventually produce, not just an accumulation of lies, but some sort of approximation to the truth; this is the way in which the historian of contemporary affairs, like any other historian, deals with written sources.

In further defence of contemporary history, it may be pointed out that in many ways the contemporary historian has sources not available to his colleague writing about people who died in the Middle Ages. Alan Bullock, for instance, the biographer of Ernest Bevin and Adolf Hitler, has described in an essay on this subject[1] how the writer on contemporary affairs can look at all kinds of raw material which other historians do not have. All the research done now by public opinion polls on people's voting behaviour, for instance, on political attitudes, on the reasons why elections go the way they do, are available, as the result of techniques of historical research which are not available to the historian trying to interpret the elections of the eighteenth century. Again, the historian of the twentieth century has living witnesses to question, which is not true for historians writing, say, about Frederick the Great or Elizabeth I. Bullock describes how he was able to question Lord Attlee on the foreign policy of the British Labour Government just after the war when Ernest Bevin was Foreign Secretary, or to question Dean Acheson, the former American Secretary of State, on why the United States decided to re-arm Western Germany. Even the historian unable to interview his characters in person can listen to tape recordings. For instance, there is a record made by ex-President Harry Truman, answering questions by the American interviewer, Ed Murrow, on why he decided he must sack General McArthur from the command of the United Nations and United States forces in Korea in 1951: Truman, giving into the microphone his personal explanation of why he found McArthur's behaviour impossible is a priceless, living, historical

[1] Alan Bullock, "Is it Possible to Write Contemporary History?" in Max Beloff, ed., *On the Track of Tyranny* (Vallentine, Mitchell 1960), 67–75.

document which the historian of earlier ages simply does not possess.

The final defence of the idea that contemporary history, as regards sources, really *is* history, comes from Professor E. H. Carr, whose brilliant book *What is History?*[1] makes, in a typically mischievous way, the point that really the medieval historian has a much *easier* time than the modern historian, just because most of his sources have been destroyed. This happened by the accident that monasteries were burnt down or that revolutions occurred, or that the documents just got worm-eaten and gradually crumbled away. (Not only that, but also the documents that the medieval historian does work from are somewhat one-sided anyway because all of them are written by monks who had a natural interest in trying to prove that the population was entirely Christian, and so we naturally get an idea that the Middle Ages were a very strongly Christian period, when in fact the people who might have said the contrary, who were not Christians, were not in a position to write and say anything.) As Carr says, the modern historian has a great mass of material which really in some ways sets him a much more difficult task than that of the historian building up a picture of the Middle Ages from the rather fragmentary and polluted sources that may happen to be available. Carr quotes Lytton Strachey's remark, "ignorance is the first requisite of the historian, ignorance which simplifies and clarifies, which selects and omits", and then describes the mass of material available to the contemporary historian in these words:

> When I am tempted, as I sometimes am, to envy the extreme competence of colleagues engaged in writing ancient or medieval history, I find consolation in the reflexion that they are so competent mainly because they are so ignorant of

[1] E. H. Carr, *What is History?* (Macmillan, 1961), 9. (Also available as a Pelican Book.)

their subject. The modern historian enjoys none of the advantages of this built-in ignorance. He must cultivate the necessary ignorance for himself. . . .[1]

By which Carr means the process of selecting what is relevant, what really are the historical facts, from the great mass of printed and other source material which surrounds us. So it *can* even be argued that the contemporary historian is not just a historian, but even a rather better sort of historian, than those who deal with the more remote past.

As an example of how complete documentation is not necessary to write good history, let me briefly mention two accounts of how the Second World War happened. Many historians think that Professor Sir Lewis Namier, when he wrote his book, *Diplomatic Prelude*, which is an account of the diplomacy of the last couple of years before 1939, based very largely on contemporary newspaper accounts (part of this book actually came out during the war), gave a much truer account of why the war happened than his pupil, Mr A. J. P. Taylor, who produced three years ago a very controversial book on *The Origins of the Second World War*.[2] Taylor had access to all the German documents that I mentioned, which he could use as a result of the war, but he yet produced, to my mind, a much more tendentious and less convincing picture of why the war happened than did Namier, writing with very much less in the way of documentation. Let us therefore reject this argument that to write good history, the historian must have full sources, and that if he does have full sources, he necessarily writes good history. There is very much more to history than just having the material there; it has to be properly interpreted.

[1] E H. Carr, *What is History?* (Macmillan, 1961). (Also available as a Pelican Book.)

[2] L. B. Namier, *Diplomatic Prelude, 1938–1939* (Macmillan, 1948); A. J. P. Taylor, *The Origins of the Second World War* (H. Hamilton, 1961, and Penguin Books, 1964).

With regard to the problem of bias, our own feelings about the events that we are describing are certainly there. The main reason, probably, why we are concerned as students or as researchers with contemporary history is because these events have had an impact on our own lives and we personally feel involved with them. But does that necessarily make it impossible for us to come to a fair judgment about why they have happened? Obviously, we may have our own feelings, as individuals or as citizens, about whether the policy of the British government, at the time of Suez, was a good thing. Obviously, we may have feelings about whether the policy of the British Labour Party in the years since the war in refusing to join in Western European institutions has been a good or bad thing. It seems to me that as historians, however, we have the responsibility of trying to put these personal feelings on one side, to steer a path that is free from bias, and to show this path to other students, who are just as liable to be biased as those who try and write or teach this sort of history.

As an example of this, and having mentioned Suez, I am reminded of a lecture I gave once on the Suez crisis where my audience of second-year undergraduates included on the one hand, a young lady who was a Young Conservative and a very strong admirer of Sir Anthony Eden, and on the other hand, a student from Northern Nigeria who was a Muslim and a very strong admirer of President Nasser. I looked from one to the other of these as I went along; every time I said anything that was at all critical of Sir Anthony Eden, the young Conservative lady scowled and the Nigerian beamed, but when a bit later on I said something critical about President Nasser's motives and the implications of his nationalization of the Canal, their expressions were reversed. I felt that so long as they were beaming and scowling in roughly equal proportions, I was probably doing a fairly good job in explaining as a historian why things happened, and whether statesmen's decisions were rational, that is to say, whether Sir Anthony Eden and President Nasser were pursuing policies that took account of implications and realities. This is the job of the historian as a historian, as distinct from saying, as a citizen, that a given policy was good or bad. I agree that this may involve a feat of permanent schizophrenia; but we must at least attempt it.

This difficulty is not one which is peculiar to contemporary history. There is a story told by Marc Bloch, the great French medieval historian, who was killed by the Nazis in the Second World War, but who wrote before he died a magnificent work of contemporary history on the reasons for the French defeat in 1940:[1] he recounted in another book that came out after his death the story of how, when he started as a young history teacher in a French school, his headmaster warned him of certain difficulties which would arise in teaching controversial problems in history: "Here, with the nineteenth century, there is little danger, but when you touch the religious wars of the sixteenth century, you must take great care."[2]

So again, the problems of bias are by no means unique in contemporary history; they may arise very much in the way people argue about the sixteenth century or even earlier periods. As an ideal for us to aim at in this respect, I would like to quote the words of another French writer, Alfred Grosser, who has recently written a book on the foreign policy of France between 1945 and 1958; these were years in which he had been very actively engaged as a journalist, in supporting or attacking certain lines of policy, but he has succeeded in writing an admirably objective account of French foreign policy in these same years.

He says in his introduction: "What I have tried to do is to study with entire sympathy the men and groups whose ideas and actions seemed to me to be bad, and to study with an

---

[1] M. Bloch, *Strange Defeat* (O.U.P., 1949).
[2] Quoted by Bullock, loc. cit., p. 71, on whom I have drawn for large parts of this argument.

ever-vigilant critical sense the men and groups to which I felt myself nearest."[1] This, it seems to me, is an ideal to which we should all, as historians of any period, attempt to remain true.

I have said that the third difficulty, the problem of perspective, is in some ways the most difficult. Can we really be sure that we can identify the fundamental movements now going on in the world, and assess the significance of events that happened just the other day? For an example of a historian who is willing to commit himself quite firmly, let me quote Professor Geoffrey Barraclough, who argues in his recent book, *An Introduction to Contemporary History*, that the years around 1960 and 1961 marked a turning point. This is what he says, talking about a new period in which a turning point occurred and world history entered on a new phase: "The opening of this new period – which is, of course, the period of 'contemporary' history in the strict sense of the word – can be placed with some degree of assurance at the end of 1960 or the beginning of 1961."[2] He gives reasons for arguing that an entirely new period then began: a new generation came into power in the United States in the person of Kennedy; the conflict between the Russians and their Chinese allies became quite open and irreparable; in Africa the dismantling of European colonialism was finally or all-but-finally achieved and the new states of Africa moved very rapidly towards integrating themselves in a new international bloc; in Western Europe, the Rome Treaties of 1957 were beginning to take effect and Western Europe was becoming hardened into an economic and political bloc; and thus Professor Barraclough, for the reasons summarized here, is prepared to commit himself to the view that a radically new era in interna-

[1] A. Grosser, *La Quatrième République et sa Politique Etrangère* (A. Colin, 1961), 11.

[2] G. Barraclough, *An Introduction to Contemporary History* (Watts, 1964), 29–30; this book gives references to further reading on the problems of studying contemporary history.

tional relations has opened. Personally I find it difficult to accept this, and I think perhaps in the year or so since Professor Barraclough wrote there has been a shift back in the other direction: one obvious thing is that the very young generation that seemed to be running American policy has now been replaced, thanks to Kennedy's assassination, by an older generation. I think also that the split between China and the Soviet Union, although it is very acute and very violent, is perhaps not as irrevocable as Barraclough seems to argue, and as for the suggestion that the African states are forming themselves rapidly into a new coherent bloc, I do not really think this is so, any more than I believe that the six Western European countries of the European Economic Community are doing so. Of course my judgment may prove to be quite wrong: by the time any of my words appear in print, it may be possible for someone to say that what Barraclough wrote in 1963 was after all right. This, it really seems to me, is the problem: we can say in general terms what happened, we can chronicle the events, we think we can understand most of the motives, but can we really be sure that the events and trends we pick out as significant really are so? This is an acute problem for the historian who tries to assess events in motion. Anybody writing a history of China, say, in 1947, would have said that there was a civil war going on between the Communists and Chiang Kai-Shek, but from the look of things, Chiang Kai-Shek was obviously going to win. He was getting a lot of aid from the Americans, the Chinese were not getting much help from the Russians, and quite clearly, the Communists were going to be beaten: a number of people did say things to this effect at the time. Yet only two years later, by 1949, the Communists were in power: they won the civil war and Chiang Kai-Shek was forced to flee to the island of Formosa.

There is an account of British foreign policy, written during the last months of 1962, which mentions the negotiations on

British entry into the European Economic Community, always in this form: *when* Britain is a member of the European Economic Community, or *when* current negotiations in Brussels come to a successful end, this, that, and the other will follow. Of course, we all know what happened in January 1963, just after this clearly implied prediction: the outcome of the negotiations was quite different from that predicted, and this sharply illustrates the historian's problem. Yet this does not make the study of contemporary history invalid, and it is a problem that affects other branches of history, too. There is the well-known story of the Chinese historian, who was asked fairly recently his views on the significance of the French Revolution of 1789, and who shook his head very sadly and very wisely and said that surely it was much too soon to come to any sort of judgment about a contemporary event of this sort. A final quotation in defence of contemporary history comes from one of the greatest historians of all: Thucydides, who wrote the history of the Peloponnesian War while it was still going on. He opens his account of it thus: "Thucydides, an Athenian, wrote the history of the war between the Peloponnesians and the Athenians; he began at the moment that it broke out, believing it would be a great war, and more memorable than any that had preceded it."[1]

In conclusion I would like to suggest that four main trends in the world's history since 1945 may be discerned.

The first and most obvious feature is that Europe as a centre of world power has given way to two super-powers. Until quite recently, Europe was the centre of the world. A mere twenty-five years ago, the attention of the world centred on what was going on in Munich, or what was going on in the last negotiations before war broke out in September 1939: Europe was the centre of power politics, even the centre of world politics, and Europe gave orders to the rest of the world. Now two super-

[1] Thucydides, *The History of the Peloponnesian War*, ed. R. W. Livingstone (O.U.P., 1951), 33.

powers from outside have really moved in and taken over what used to be a European monopoly of world power. The Soviet Union and the United States met in Germany in 1945, and Europe can never become again the centre of power in the way that it was.

The second factor is the way in which Europe has been further weakened by the rise of nationalism and successful demands for independence among people who formerly were ruled by the European colonial powers. It is an obvious fact of the modern world, that the number of people, and the amount of territory still held by European States as colonies is now minute compared with what it was before the war, and that the resulting new States are beginning in many ways to play a positive and active part in world affairs, an independent rôle of a kind that they could not have played twenty years ago.

The third factor that I think ought to be mentioned as a main characteristic of our world is the deadlock, in terms of nuclear strength, between the two power-blocs. The Soviet Union and United States are both now capable of annihilating the other: both of them realize this fact of deadlock, and this has a number of effects including the gaining of a little more independence by some of the smaller states that until quite recently lived in the shadow of one or the other of the super-powers.

A fourth and rather paradoxical point is that the states of the world are tending to group themselves into larger units, but only with all sorts of resistances and hesitations. On the one hand, there is a tendency towards integration, towards a bloc or unit much larger than the state. This is reflected at the highest level, the world level, in the United Nations Organization, and at regional levels by all kinds of institutions all reflecting the idea that the old national state is out of date, and must be replaced as the unit of international politics by a bigger grouping. Thus, for instance, we get the movement towards unity in Western Europe; we get military alliances covering the North

Atlantic area, we get military, economic and political groupings run by the Soviet Union in Eastern and Central Europe; and we get, too, the Arab League in the Middle East and new organizations which give expression to the desire for unity among the new states of Africa. However, as well as this phenomenon of states acting together in blocs, co-operating freely with each other in certain of their policies, there is still the contrary tendency of states to re-assert their old national independence. This is illustrated by the way in which General de Gaulle has tried to lead Western Europe into independence of the United States, or the way in which the Rumanians, the Czechs, the Poles, the Hungarians and, of course, the Chinese have been trying to loosen the grip of the Soviet Union. There is a tendency towards what is sometimes called "bloc politics": but the contrary tendency is still very much alive too. These are the kinds of problem which this book explores.

The Teacher Speaks
by D. B. Heater

A proper understanding of the history of the mid-twentieth century surely requires a world perspective. Technological and economic developments have produced such a close interweaving of interests that a teacher of contemporary history would probably find a national or continental approach more difficult in practice than the global scale. The very nature of recent history forces the teacher into world history. Some people, however, argue that history should be studied on a global scale not so much for the sake of historical understanding as for world understanding. For the sake of reducing international tension, it is argued, all history teaching of whatever period should be given in a world perspective. This brings us into the realm of education for international understanding – a separate subject in its own right.[1]

The argument concerning the study and teaching of contemporary history falls fairly naturally into five parts. First, I hope to indicate the widespread interest there exists in the subject. Secondly, I want to suggest that contemporary history is a respectable subject for academic study. In the third place, I wish to show that the subject is a suitable one to be included in a school curriculum. Fourthly, it will be useful to discuss the various methods that may be used in teaching contemporary history. And finally, I should like to sketch various ways in which the teaching of the subject may be more fully developed.

Interest in Recent World History

Although the situation is steadily improving, there are still too many universities, colleges and schools failing to provide adequate courses in contemporary history. The hungry sheep are forced to grub among the tufts of television programmes and paper-backs, thus consuming an unbalanced diet that is only partially satisfying. At best, these young people will acquire in such ways disconnected snippets of information; at worst, they will come to define international affairs as James Bond's cosmopolitan sex-life.

An interest in recent history is surely most natural, certainly at the levels of secondary and higher education. The history of the past two decades has pace, drama, colour and pathos: pace in the rise of Afro-Asian nations and in technological developments; drama in the tensions of the Cold War; colour in personalities like Khrushchev, Castro and Nkrumah; pathos in the Korean refugees, Indians dying of starvation, Hammarskjöld dying in the cause of world co-operation.

Moreover, the intrinsic fascination of the subject is reinforced by the relevance of these issues to the actual world in which the

[1] See especially *The Year Book of Education, 1964.*

pupil or student is living. When one teaches medieval history, for example, much of the charm of the subject and its relevance to the twentieth-century world lies in the fact that the Middle Ages show us so well what our contemporary society is *not*. The relevance is one of contrasts. I would not for one moment conclude that the study of contemporary history should supersede that of more remote periods. The conclusions that can be drawn are that the interests in the two studies are of a different kind: that the relevance of recent history, being of a positive nature, will have a greater impact on the average student; and that consequently greater efforts than are generally being made at the moment should be directed to satisfying this intellectual curiosity.

Television, the cinema and paper-backs can be seen both as satisfying this demand and stimulating the interest; dangerous in highlighting the sensational and in encouraging an uncritical attitude as well as useful in providing teaching aids from which class lessons can develop. It is surely the teacher's duty to emphasize the positive qualities of these media; to foster the interest and develop a critical attitude of mind towards them. A viewing (or reading) of *Dr Strangelove* by a sixth form already prepared by lessons on the arms race and disarmament programmes would be a most valuable exercise in critical thinking on contemporary problems. A similar exercise might be performed at the Secondary Modern fifth-form level by a series of lessons on the Soviet control of Eastern Europe and a critical reading of Dennis Wheatley's *Curtain of Fear*. Sixth-formers will see films like *Dr Strangelove*; 16-year-olds will read paperbacks like *Curtain of Fear*. The interest is there; it should be put to good use.

The pulse of interest from the learners has already, it is true, set up a sympathetic resonance of concern among many teachers; echoes are being heard in the reshaping of curricula and the construction of new examination syllabuses. At the undergraduate level of study the newer universities are giving considerable weight to twentieth-century history. In the training colleges the introduction of the three-year course and the appointment of new staff to meet expansion programmes have been taken as opportunities in a number of colleges to include some aspects of recent history in their curricula. Furthermore, the enthusiastic response to the lectures upon which the present book is based is a further indication of the breadth of interest among students specializing in subjects other than history. Many Grammar School teachers are developing their own and their pupils' interests in the contemporary world in the sixth-form general studies lessons. The Agreement to Broaden the Curriculum campaign has led to the organization of many interesting courses, most of which include a study of twentieth century history. One may note the publication of S. E. Ayling's *Portraits of Power* as one result of a course along these lines.

In many ways teachers are a conservative profession: curricula are changed only reluctantly; and nowhere is this resistance to change more clearly revealed than in examination syllabuses. Yet here, too, contemporary history is edging its way in. The Modern Studies syllabus for the Scottish Leaving Certificate is a particularly interesting venture. In England, the Cambridge Board have the well-established paper at both "A" and "O" levels on *World Affairs since 1919*; London introduced a similar "O" level paper in 1964; while other boards include questions in their normal history syllabuses or in general history papers on the post-1945 world. The introduction of the C.S.E. examination was, of course, an open invitation to teachers to produce new ideas. Most schools preparing candidates for this examination, if not all, have the opportunity of specializing in twentieth-century history if they wish. The Reading Institute of Education has produced a "model syllabus" for the period since 1913 at this level. The popularity of the most modern period in the various C.S.E. options will probably increase when suitable class-books become more readily available.

Children and young people from about 8 to 14 will ask teachers questions and enjoy quizzes on contemporary history; older school pupils will read paper-backs, view TV programmes, take part in classroom discussions and join debating clubs; students will form their own world affairs societies and start to read the weekly reviews. The development of this interest is a great educational opportunity. It is also a great educational challenge, for there are many difficulties. Among the difficulties facing the would-be teacher of contemporary history is the belief sincerely held by many historians that the study of the most recent age cannot be true history in any academically respectable sense.

Contemporary History as an Academic Study

The essence of the academic argument against contemporary history is the belief that by the use of his specialized techniques and ways of thinking the historian can produce a more accurate picture of the sixteenth century, for example, than he could of his own age, or indeed than could a contemporary Tudor observer have done. I do not wish to deny that the historian in the conventional sense of the term has important advantages over the student of the contemporary world; but I do not believe that he holds all the trump cards. And since I am here frankly arguing a case I shall be quite consciously giving greater emphasis to the arguments in favour of the historian of recent events.

The objections to the study of contemporary history as an academic subject resolve themselves into three main arguments: first, there are objections to the nature of the source material; secondly, it is objected that a study of contemporary events must by very definition lack a proper historical perspective;

and finally, it is argued, the historian of the recent past is in danger of introducing bias into his work.

The problem concerning the nature of the material available to the student of contemporary affairs is a two-fold one. It is pointed out that official archives are not open to the researcher; and yet at the same time the enormous volume of material that is available gives him a false sense of the completeness of his evidence. But no period of history is entirely free of its own peculiar source problems.

More serious is the problem of perspective. All history (in the sense of the historian's record) is, of course, generalization. The historian selects the material that he considers significant in the light of the ages surrounding his own special period, both before and after. Thus, Sir John Neale, surveying the comparative impotence of parliament in the 1540's and its revolutionary power in the 1640's, sought out new evidence about the Elizabethan House of Commons that became particularly significant in the light of this comparison. The historian of contemporary affairs, however, lacks half his perspective guidelines: he knows what preceded his period of study; he cannot know what is to follow. His selection of significant facts may, therefore, be distorted. More than that – his judgment may be distorted too. This danger of distorted judgment may be illustrated by the comment of *The Times* on the 1938 Munich Agreement: "Applause for Mr Chamberlain," it declared, "registers a popular judgment that neither politicians nor historians are likely to reverse." Furthermore, it is not only the lack of hindsight that undermines the contemporary historian's perspective. There is a less obvious way in which his selection of material may become distorted. It is probably true to say that an historian working on the 1950's, for example, will be more conscious of the impact of the events of those times on the condition of the world in which the historian is living than will his colleague working on the 1750's. There will be a stronger tendency to select material relevant to the present when working near to the present than when working on a more remote period. "History for the sake of the past," Professor Oakeshott has called the historical past; "history for the sake of understanding the present" he has called the practical past. To the latter he denies the term history: this approach certainly does carry within it serious dangers of anachronistic thinking.

The contemporary historian's involvement in the condition of the world in which he is living raises the third issue of bias. Bias in the writing of recent history may operate at two distinct levels. A government may control the release of documents in order to present itself in a favourable light, or even, as in the case of Soviet Russia, control the actual writing itself. Secondly, the historian himself may distort his material in presenting it, either consciously or unconsciously, so bound up may he be personally with the issues involved. In this whole problem of bias, it is argued, contemporary history, precisely because of its relevance and its high emotional charge, is in greater danger of a distorted presentation than more distant ages. How can one write an unprejudiced history of the Cold War, for example?

Faced with this formidable array of difficulties, the contemporary observer must surely find it impossible to conduct the cool, scientific collection, sifting and ordering of material that would entitle him to assume the name of historian. What, indeed, can be said in his defence?

In the first place, it must not be too readily assumed that the facts, or indeed the interpretation, that an historian of contemporary affairs may produce must of necessity be inferior to those of his colleague working in other fields. We may admit that future research and reinterpretation will necessitate adjustments and that the contemporary observer can therefore produce only a provisional account. But is not the history of every age being constantly revised? Is there not, in the words of Professor Butterfield, "a profound sense in which all histories . . .

are only interim reports"? Each generation has its own particular concerns, which become mirrored in the history that it writes. We no longer today have the optimism of a Lord Acton to believe in the possibility of a definitive history. But, the purist historian may persist, even if conventional history may not be definitive, it will be less open to revision than contemporary history. Yet even this argument may be doubted. The historian of recent times is much less restricted than many of his colleagues in the documentary material that he has at his disposal. It would be ridiculous to suggest, for example, that a more accurate account could be given of the preparations to meet the Anglo-Saxon invasions of the early fifth century than of those made in face of the threatened German attack in 1940. Moreover, not only has the contemporary historian rich documentary sources, but he has the opportunity of interviewing the people involved, and of comparing the written with the verbal evidence.

Thus, the very proximity of the historian to his material, while an admitted danger, can yield advantages. Nor are the advantages confined to the collection of facts. The interpretation provided by the contemporary observer may have a clarity and freshness lacking in the work of his colleagues. Firstly, attitudes of mind and similar intangible factors can be captured when one has lived through the age; they are sometimes elusive to the historian who has to rely on documentary evidence alone. In the second place, the topics of contemporary history have been subjected to less academic debate than at least the more controversial topics of conventional history. And is it too cynical to suggest that some historical debates produce more heat than illumination? How much more understanding do we really possess regarding the economic and social position of the gentry in seventeenth-century England or the political motives of eighteenth-century M.P.s compared with contemporary observers?

Perhaps the most cynical comment ever passed about

31

historical interpretation is the epigram of Dean Inge concerning historians, "to whom is vouchsafed the power, denied to Almighty God, of altering the past". The comment focuses attention, in a brutal way, on the historian's major professional hazard, namely of striving to write history without bias. If his work is to have life, it must be written from a point of view; the historian must become involved with his subject. The search for utter objectivity leads the historian into the path of the matter-of-fact chronicler. And even then bias is not shaken off: it clings to the chronicler in his act of selection. The historian of recent times is in truth prone to the vice of bias; but if he be of good conscience, he can strive to cleanse himself, heartened by the knowledge that his brothers are little more wholesome than he.

Not only is the contemporary historian justified in pursuing his craft, it can be argued that he has a positive academic and social duty to do so. There is considerable demand for his wares, and if the trained and responsible historian does not supply them, less reputable writers will. And these lesser writers are much more likely to produce biased accounts than the academic historian. Consequently if the historian resigned the subject to them alone, not only would present-day readers be deprived of a scholarly account but future historians would be hindered in their search for the truth.

The social responsibility of the historian to provide the public with sound commentary on world affairs is perhaps one of the strongest arguments in favour of the academic study of the subject. Scholarship should be pursued for its own sake, of course, and scholars should be allowed perfect freedom to select their own area of study. But just as no economist or biologist would pass by any part of his subject that had a practical application, so the historian, thus minded, should not be dissuaded from studying recent events most relevant to the problems of his day. It has frequently been noted that the historian's function as a commentator on contemporary affairs has a most honourable tradition: historians who have fulfilled this function have included Thucydides, Tacitus and Clarendon. In an article in *History* in 1941 Dr Gavin Henderson expressed this point of view very forcibly.

> But surely [he declared], the study of the past stultifies itself if it stops just when it is most needed – just when its judgments might be of real use to a distracted world? Are not historians selling their birthright – the birthright won for them by Thucydides – for a mess of pottage? For a quiet academic existence far from the madding crowd, for a reputation of amiability and absentmindedness and general futility?

The Place of Contemporary History in School Curricula

If the historian accepts the social responsibility of providing commentary on contemporary affairs he is undertaking a broadly educative function. And it is to the place of contemporary history in the specific context of education in the school that we must now give our attention. Many of the arguments revolve round the issue of contemporary history as an academic study and are relevant to the school situation, especially the Grammar Schools. The study of a subject at school level, however, raises broader issues also. The school is concerned not only with the personal development of its pupils, but with preparing them for life in society at large. Therefore when one seeks to enquire about the value of a subject in the school curriculum, one is asking a question broader than the issue of the academic or aesthetic worth of the subject. The practical relevance of a subject assumes especial importance in a materialist, competitive world like our own. As the Crowther Report comments, "Today, it seems to us that education is generally thought to be a 'nation-building' investment fully as much as part of the welfare state." If the historian cannot persuade society that his subject is a good investment, it will be in grave danger of being shouldered out of the curriculum to share the fate of the Classics.

The issue of bias, although already discussed, must be touched upon again both because of the particular dangers it presents in a school situation and also because it is perhaps the major cause of reluctance among teachers to tackle the subject. Any intelligent person who studies contemporary affairs, it is argued, will be bound to develop strong views on controversial issues. At worst, an unscrupulous teacher will use his lessons in contemporary history for propaganda purposes, foisting his views on to immature minds insufficiently critical to detect the bias. At best, the responsible teacher will be unable to present a fair picture of both points-of-view in a controversy. Thus, if the teacher's biased teaching goes undetected he will be (guiltily or not) indoctrinating his pupils; if it is detected, strong protests will fall about his head from pupils, head-teacher and parents. In short, it is concluded, contemporary history is sound teaching material neither for its educational value nor for its effect on the teacher's peace of mind.

Yet even the difficulties of wrestling with the problem of bias are not the end of the worries of the teacher who would teach the history of recent times. He needs knowledge of the subject and both time and energy to keep this knowledge constantly up-to-date. For we must not blink the fact that a large proportion of history teachers are woefully ignorant of twentieth-century history, since most university and training-college courses, until recently at any rate, have finished at 1914, or at best 1939. There is also the problem of what might be called the built-in conservation of the history teacher's note-book. A newly-appointed, enthusiastic teacher may compile an admirable set of lesson notes on the history of the modern world chronologically to the year of his appointment. But how many will have the time and energy to revise these notes each year in the light of new events? It is said that an incumbent of an august chair of history, appointed in 1905, was still lecturing on modern history to 1905 when he retired nearly a quarter-of-a-century later!

The teacher, then, is faced with grave difficulties. But so too are his pupils. International affairs, it may be argued, is essentially an adult study: it is concerned with places outside the child's environment and with ideological concepts too abstract for the child to comprehend. What can the average schoolchild understand of, for example, Communism in China? The history and present-day running of his own locality or at the most the story of his own land is all that the pupil of average intelligence can be expected to master.

Again, as with the academic case, we are faced with a formidable array of objections. In marshalling the case for the defence it will be convenient to separate the purely pedagogical arguments from what might be called the social justification for the subject. It may also be noted that since this was one of the topics investigated by the Newsom committee, their findings, set out mainly in the chapter, "The Proper Study of Mankind", will be used to substantiate certain stages of the argument.

Let us take the problem of the teacher's difficulties first of all. The arguments outlined above on the issues of propaganda and the teacher's grasp of the subject are perhaps adverse reflections on the teachers and their training rather than on the subject. The question of propaganda is a question of trust. We trust the teachers of religious education not to abuse their position by indoctrination; and we trust those who feel that they cannot properly handle the subject not to undertake it. Can we not extend a similar trust to teachers of political subjects? The Crowther Report draws upon this analogy. Commenting on the needs of the adolescent it states,

There is no period of life when people more need what the Education Act means when it refers, perhaps rather unhappily, to "religious instruction", and no period when it is more difficult to give. What is true of ethics and philosophy is true also of politics. The fact that politics are controversial – that honest men disagree – makes preparation for citizenship a difficult matter for schools. But it ought to be tackled, and not least for the ordinary boys and girls who now leave school at fifteen and often do not find it easy to see any argument except in personal terms.

In other words, it is the duty of the teacher not to shy away from controversial contemporary issues but to use them as a means of teaching emotionally-disciplined reactions and clear thought. Admittedly such a programme needs a skilful teacher; but then we should be encouraging our teachers to sharpen their skills not blunting them by instilling despondency. So too with the acquisition of sheer factual knowledge, the interested teacher should be given encouragement and help.

The argument was stated above that the complexity of the subject made contemporary history unsuitable for school study. Each of the points may be countered fairly shortly. In the first place, the belief that education must start with the child's environment (if by that term we mean his immediate surroundings) is no longer a valid concept in the age of the cinema, television and increasing foreign travel. And even if the child does have to exercise more imagination in studying contemporary South Africa than contemporary Sussex, the leap is certainly no greater than that required by the study of Roman Sussex, for example. A similar argument may be used in the problem of the abstract nature of many contemporary issues. Is the Reformation any easier for the child to understand than the Cold War? In teaching both we obviously have to suit the material to the ability of the class. It will be perfectly possible to teach the Berlin Airlift to a class quite incapable of comprehending the theory of capitalist encirclement. Rigorous selection of material is also necessary, of course, not only for suitability but because of the sheer bulk of the subject when using a global perspective.

We can, however, go further than the mere answering of doubts and criticisms. There are positive advantages to be gleaned from the study of recent world history.

It may be noted first of all that there is something untidy and unsatisfying in bringing a chronological history course to an end at any point before the year in which the class is being taught. Even if the course proceeds to 1945, much of the present-day world remains mysterious and unexplained – the tension between the U.S.A. and the U.S.S.R., the evolution of the Commonwealth, the position of Communist China, to mention but a few topics. That these questions are of interest to young people has already been indicated. And apart from the intrinsic interest in the subject, there is the appeal to the adolescent of what is an adult study. The adult nature of the subject is used by some as an argument against its introduction into schools; but precisely the opposite conclusion may be drawn. The Newsom Committee has expressed the opinion that "the more any lessons can be given a realistic and adult reference, the better" and urges the investigation of contemporary problems by adolescents so that they may gain experience in "using adult sources of information and becoming involved in a world situation in which they may have a part to play". The 15-year-old, especially in the Modern School, wants perhaps more than anything else to be respected as a near-adult. Any subject that treats him in an adult way or is overtly preparing him for life when he emerges from school will be considered useful and worthy of attention.

The whole problem of the suitability of school subjects, history included, for the vast bulk of school pupils with limited academic interests is one that has been given insufficient attention. It is necessary here therefore to say a few words about contemporary history specifically in the context of our post-1944 ideal of "secondary education for all". In this country certainly during the past generation or so we have been experiencing an educational revolution. This has been a two-fold process of expansion of educational opportunities through the pressure of social attitudes and a revision of what is thought to be the proper nature of education through the impact of new educational theories. A purely academic education, in the Classics for example, while suited to an élite of pupils from educated families, is seen to be quite unfit for the education of the majority of children especially when educational theorists are insisting on the function of education as a process of social training. We have reached a position, therefore, where we recognize that the Victorian system of elementary instruction in the 3 R's for the masses does not go far enough, while the Victorian secondary curriculum of the Public Schools is inappropriate. The traditional subjects of the Secondary School curriculum must therefore be partly shaped, if they are to meet these conditions of widespread education, so as to be relevant to the life for which the pupil in school is preparing.

The function of history in this context is clearly as a training in citizenship. And in order to discharge this heavy responsibility effectively the school must surely provide education in world affairs. The school owes this to the democratic society of which it is a part. In the words of the Newsom Report, "A man who is ignorant of the society in which he lives, who knows nothing of its place in the world and who has not thought about his place in it, is not a free man even though he has a vote." We might carry the idea to its ultimate conclusion and say, with Aristotle, that a man who is not consciously integrated with the society in which he lives is not only not free but not a properly developed man. It should further be noticed that civic education today cannot stop short at instruction in the country's constitution. Every nation-state is now part of a complex network of

38

global relationships. Civic education must consequently be interpreted as education in the condition of the world and an understanding of how this condition arose; in short, recent world history.

Methods of Teaching the Subject

The subject is clearly most suited to the fourth and fifth-form level of the Secondary School. Three advantages will be derived from arranging the syllabus in this way. First, such a course would bring a chronological study of history to a natural conclusion; secondly, the subject would develop naturally from the adolescent's maturing interest in political and world affairs; and finally, it would be an appropriate study for pupils about to leave school. The development of "O" level and especially C.S.E. syllabuses in recent world history is therefore to be applauded.

It must not, however, be thought that the subject is out of place with other age ranges. In the Junior School, stories of famous people and Topic work could well draw upon this material; the lives of Hammarskjöld and Kennedy being obvious choices in the first category and modern Africa, Russia and China in the second. In *The Living Past*, the editor of the present volume has pointed out the importance of the history teaching in the lower age ranges being in sympathy with – providing an "underpinning" for – the work to be undertaken at the adolescent level. In particular, the reiteration of national myths may build up a distorted view of other peoples that could hinder the systematic study of recent world history at a more mature age.

At the other end of the pupil's or student's career, in the sixth form and in institutions of higher education, contemporary history should be available either as a major study or for general educational purposes.

If one defines recent world history as the period since 1945 (as in the present volume), the subject can be viewed in two distinct perspectives and therefore as having two different functions. It may be considered as bringing the study of history chronologically up-to-date or as a background to current events. Nor is the distinction a purely academic one; for if the teacher views it in the first light, the subject becomes an integral part of the history syllabus; if in the second, it may form part of separate current affairs lessons. In deciding which arrangement is preferable a number of considerations should be kept in mind.

Three main arguments may be put forward in favour of current affairs lessons separate from the normal history syllabus. In the first place, this arrangement would satisfy the purists who believe that events so recent that they cannot be viewed in a proper historical perspective should be excluded from the history syllabus altogether. History and current affairs, it may be argued, are separate disciplines and therefore require separate treatment. They may even be taught by different members of staff; and this is the second argument. The history specialist is most frequently to be found responsible for civics or current affairs lessons. Nevertheless, a strong case can be made out for the work being undertaken by someone else. This case rests on the fact that there is no necessary correlation between an interest in the remoter periods of history and an interest in contemporary affairs. The history teacher may have a specialist interest in prehistoric archaeology, medieval architecture or the Industrial Revolution and may be able to fire his pupils with enthusiasm for his particular field of study. But this will not necessarily make him an effective teacher of contemporary affairs; and since it is a subject requiring skill and delicacy in its handling, it may be better for a specialist in another discipline to undertake the work if he is equipped to do so. The third argument for separate current affairs lessons is flexibility. "Strike while the iron is hot" is one of the hoariest of "tips for teachers". It is none the less valid for that. Incidents can be chosen each week for their topicality, so that while the press, radio and television are keeping the public's attention on the visit of a head of state or the latest international incident, the teacher in his current affairs lessons can paint in the historical background and develop the theme with a freshness that will be lacking if the incident has to await its turn in a properly formulated contemporary history syllabus.

The decision between contemporary history and current affairs may easily depend on the circumstances in the individual school; though, all things being equal, I think a weightier case can be made out for integrating the study of recent events into the normal history syllabus. We may recall here certain points already used to justify the subject in general. Firstly, there is the artificiality of bringing a chronological syllabus to an end before reaching the present day. Secondly, the utilitarian value of history will be reduced in the eyes of the unacademic pupil if the study of "useful" current affairs is divorced from history. History which does not lead to the present cannot appear to lead to the future, the dimension of time that interests the adolescent. Thirdly, the difficult problem of bias is eased if the contemporary world is fitted firmly into an historical context. To say, "this is what is" sounds so much more dogmatic than, "this is how it came about". The teacher, moreover, may be led to a greater respect for objectivity if he can view the present as part of history rather than as a subject that has special emotional significance. One may also add two further considerations of a very practical nature. Past and present can very profitably be made to illuminate each other if they are both treated as being part of the same flow of events and if they are both taught by the same member of staff. Constant cross reference makes for lively teaching, highlights the relevance of all history and keeps contemporary affairs in proper perspective. Finally, the teacher can always prepare his material adequately and present it in an orderly manner if he is working to a previously planned syllabus of contemporary history. The weekly current affairs lesson, on the other hand, is so frequently an unsatisfactory affair, ill-prepared because of sheer lack of time. How many teachers have been faced with the impossible task of an international crisis blowing up in the papers on Tuesday, the fifth form's essays to be marked on Tuesday evening and a fourth-form current affairs lesson first thing Wednesday morning?

It may still be objected by the teacher wishing to undertake contemporary history that there are insufficient teaching aids and that he feels poorly equipped personally to tackle an admittedly difficult subject. It is probably true to say that great advantages would be derived from the adoption, in suitably modified forms, of Junior School teaching methods in Secondary Schools of all types, but especially the Secondary Modern. The Junior School Topic approach to learning is particularly suitable for the teaching of contemporary history. No attempt should be made to cover the whole area of possible study, but certain "patches" should receive special attention. These patches might be selected either for their intrinsic importance or because of their topical interest; because of some special interest the class may have, or because of the relevance of a particular aspect to work in other subjects (especially geography). These patches should be studied in depth with as much reference to documentary and illustrative material as may be available; they may be studied by the whole class or separate patches may be worked on simultaneously by the class organized in groups. Wall space should be used as much as possible for maps, pictures and newspaper cuttings to keep the class abreast with the latest developments in the various parts of the world. With the less able children it may be necessary to restrict the topics chosen to the histories of individual countries; though I am not so sure that with the aid of time charts, other visual aids and the stimulus of the more dramatic incidents attempts could not be made on some aspects of international affairs. The complexity of coping with a number of countries at the same time will make formal class teaching more necessary here.

Both teachers and pupils need books for reference and reading. This, in fact, is a double problem. At the moment there is a shortage of good class books. However, this shortage is a temporary problem until the publishers can make them available. A constant difficulty is the fact that no book can be absolutely up-to-date even on the day of publication. Teachers and pupils therefore need sources of information both to make good the lack of books and to keep up-to-date even when they are published. Useful yearly publications include *The Annual Register* and the *Encyclopaedia Britannica Yearbooks*. More frequent in publication are *The British Survey*, published monthly by the British Society for International Understanding and the four-monthly *The World and the School* published by the associated Atlantic Information Centre for Teachers. Weekly summaries of events can be obtained from *Keesing's Archives* and *The Observer's* special information service.

Conclusions

"That most of the new teachers are only one step ahead of their pupils in comprehension of world affairs should surprise no one. Nor do we yet know how to teach trainees the methods for handling the topics of world affairs, for these techniques do not yet exist." These sobering words were recently written by the Director of the University of Chicago Comparative Education Center. And although he clearly has the American situation in the forefront of his mind, we should not perhaps too readily assume that conditions in this country are any better. The need for research into the best teaching methods and better training and aids for teachers implied in this statement, are both urgent requirements in England.

The Newsom Committee discovered resistance to the subject in many schools, but concluded, "Optimism is possible. The important thing is to discover and apply the means by which it can be justified." What is the best organization for the subject? What are the most effective teaching aids? Are boys more interested in the subject than girls? The wide divergence of success and failure discovered by the Newsom Committee suggest that there are positive answers to questions such as these. It would therefore be of the greatest value to have them systematically investigated and the conclusions made available.

The Newsom Report also calls attention to the need to equip our teachers more effectively for their work: "There is need for a review of what history . . . is taught in higher education. There is certainly need for a large programme of in-service training." The immediate need, of course, is to help the practising teacher. Vacation and evening courses are being provided, and so are books; but more are needed. However, the greatest need is for more imaginative audio-visual aids. More recordings of famous speeches could surely be made available, perhaps on tape and specially edited with commentary for school use. And there must be an enormous wealth of documentary film and other photographic material that could be used for educational films and film-strips; for the teacher's needs in this field have scarcely begun to be met.

The long-term needs of the subject can, however, only be met by the training colleges and ultimately the universities. The influences that make up the total pattern of education are closely interwoven strands and much of the reality is lost if we try to distinguish the individual fibres. But we perhaps do not distort the training college course too seriously if we discern three main threads, namely personal, professional and academic; while most university undergraduate courses do not include the professional element.

Let us consider the part that contemporary history might play in each of these aspects of education. Writing, it is true, not of contemporary history as such but of the allied field of international understanding, Dr Strong has declared that "it ought to form an integral part of any teacher's education"; for he considers it "a vital matter which, in the light of the world situation today, no course of teacher's training, if it is to be considered adequate, can ignore". A grounding in world affairs should surely be part of the mental equipment of any educated person. And we surely hope that our teachers are roundly educated people. A general acquaintance with the subject is necessary for the teacher also in order to cope with questions that any child might raise, stimulated perhaps by a television programme or adult conversation. Such a situation might arise at almost any age level. It might be argued that students' societies, voluntary evening lectures and intelligent reading of the press can prepare the teacher adequately in this respect, though many would like to see something more substantial provided.

Ad hoc arrangements can also do something for the students' professional training: encouragement by the tutor to undertake the teaching of the subject, and experimentation with different techniques jointly with the tutor.

But how much more satisfactory all this would be if it could be backed, in the courses of some students at least, with a sound academic training! Again, something can be achieved, indeed is being achieved, by the adjustment of present history syllabuses. A much more radical approach is, however, necessary: and with the re-thinking of courses in preparation for the B.Ed. degree a fresh approach is possible. What our schools need are specialists in current affairs; not just historians, geographers and economists who happen to have an interest in the subject. A training-college course in modern studies similar to the Oxford P.P.E. syllabus would be an admirable addition to the choice of subjects available to the training-college candidate. Modern History, Economics, Comparative Government, Political Theory might all feature in such a course. It would be a course to meet the needs of the student interested in political-historical studies but who has little interest in, for example, local or medieval history. The training of such students would provide the schools with their current affairs specialists.

The problem is now raised, of course: who is to teach the teachers of the teachers? How many training-college tutors are equipped to provide such a course? The situation is a vicious circle. There must be sufficient faith and courage to break through it. Some training colleges should take the initiative, and universities must give more attention to this field of study. If a major break-through is to be achieved in this important field of education, it is the universities that must give the lead: only they can provide the fundamental education upon which the teachers in the Grammar Schools and the lecturers in the colleges and departments of education can base their work.

The position of recent world history in the curricula of English schools does not compare very favourably with the situation in neighbouring countries. The report of the fourth Atlantic Study Conference on Education in 1962 commented on the progress that had been made since their first conference in 1956, though at the same time admitted that, "In English schools discussion of 'current affairs' mostly depended, as it still does, on the interest of individual teachers." English teachers are very fortunate in the liberty they enjoy in arranging the content of their lessons. But liberty implies a comparable sense of duty to use this liberty in a responsible way. In the subject of contemporary history, teachers are presented with fine possibilities for an education that is relevant and stimulating. The lectures in this volume have been made available in the hope that these possibilities will in the future be more fully exploited.

CHAPTER I

THE WORLD SCENE IN 1945

by Gerald Bailey

All times, it has been said, are times of transition. But the term applies perhaps with peculiar aptness to 1945 as a year of both war and peace. Even the ending of hostilities came in two significantly separated stages, the first in Europe and the West, the second in the Far East. Already in the summer of 1944, the Allied landings on the coast of Normandy followed by the stage-by-stage reconquest of France, had broken the military and strategic stalemate in the West and begun to foreshadow the certain ultimate defeat of Hitler and the Nazi cause. Eleven months were to intervene, it is true, before the Allied victory was assured but in this period the Germans were pressed back relentlessly from the West while the Soviet armies drove in from the East. At the end of April 1945, Hitler committed suicide in authentic Wagnerian style in the ruins of Berlin, and within a week Germany had unconditionally surrendered to the Allied Powers. The destruction of the Third Reich was complete.

Even so three months were to elapse before hostilites against Japan ended in the Eastern theatres of war. After the momentous battles of the Coral Sea and of Midway, fought in the summer of 1942, American sea and air power gradually overcame the Japanese and began the progressive and immensely costly recapture of the key islands of the Pacific. By the time of the German surrender in April 1945, massive air attacks and naval bombardments were already being directed against the mainland territory of Japan. On the 6th and 9th of August respectively the first – and to date the last – atomic bombs to be used in war were dropped on the Japanese cities of Hiroshima and Nagasaki, killing and injuring, it is estimated, 160,000 Japanese in the one city and 120,000 in the other. On the eve of the dropping of the second bomb, Russia fulfilling undertakings given at the Yalta Conference six months earlier declared war on Japan. Five days later Japan had unconditionally surrendered and within three weeks the Second World War was over six years and a day after its "phoney" inception in Western Europe in September 1939.

The military struggle, then, was over, the bombs had ceased to fall and the guns were silent – to remain silent by and large for five years or more. The world lay shocked and bleeding; much of it literally in ruins and facing unprecedented tasks of rehabilitation and reconstruction. Almost all the major cities of Germany were mere heaps of rubble, as were the industrial plant and equipment of the Ruhr valley. Extensive physical damage had been inflicted similarly on many of the countries of Western Europe, notably Italy and Holland. In France, to be specific, 55,000 factories and business houses, 135,000 agricultural buildings, over 2 million dwellings and more than 7,000 kilometres of railways and 7,500 bridges had been destroyed. In Britain the centre of many of her great industrial cities, as well as large areas of the metropolis, had been reduced to ruins and more significant still for her economic future, more than a thousand million pounds of her foreign investments had been sold to pay for the war. In the Soviet Union, Hitler's armies had destroyed or partly destroyed and burned 1,710 towns and over 70,000 villages and made 25 million people homeless. They had destroyed or damaged 31,000 industrial enterprises employing 4 million people and 98,000 collective farms. According to figures given by Mr Molotov, then Foreign Minister in November 1945, the Nazis had killed or stolen

48

7 million horses, 17 million cattle and tens of millions of pigs and sheep. In addition, creating a problem scarcely completely resolved even today, millions of people were either homeless or in exile in foreign lands – fugitives from war and enemy occupation or from political tyranny and persecution. Millions of prisoners of war were in foreign hands; 10 million or more conscripted workers who had been taken to Nazi Germany to work in its fields and factories had to be moved back to France, Italy and elsewhere. No less real in its effects was the damage – much more difficult to measure and to remedy – to the whole fabric of social relations and the organizational framework for all the international life of the world.

War had brought to the victor nations [as Hugh Seton-Watson has written],[1] both terrible losses and unbounded hopes. In countries liberated from German or Japanese rule the sufferings had been greater and the hopes were perhaps even higher. Foreign occupation had in many cases deepened the old divisions of class and ideology and resistance had promoted social revolution or led to civil war. Where European colonial rule had been overthrown by Japan, plans for national independence had been made which lost none of their force when Japan was defeated. The two greatest victorious Powers stood each for a different answer to the general demand for a new deal for the world. America offered liberal democracy but insisted that this was not possible without private capitalism and the pursuit of business profit. Russia offered what it called "Socialism" but maintained that this could be achieved only through the one-party State which forcibly suppresses all critics of its policies. On the Elbe and the Rhodope, in the jungles of Tonkin and along the 38th Parallel of Korea, were already present the class

[1] Hugh Seton-Watson, *Neither War nor Peace*, 1960, 20.

conflicts, nationalist movements and ideological claims that shaped the post-war world.

The working-out of these conflicts and the tensions they created is the substance of the history of the last twenty years. Our concern here is with the immediate aftermath of the fighting and the immense tasks of salvage and of reconstruction made urgently necessary by the collapse in many places of orderly government and the world-wide physical and moral effects of six years of destruction. The war had to end at least in Europe before reconstruction could be taken up in earnest but a good deal of inter-allied machinery set up during the war years primarily to meet the war-time needs of the governments concerned was used even before the fighting stopped to lay the foundations of post-war reconstruction and to form in many cases the framework of the agencies of international co-operation later to be permanently established under the United Nations system. The International Bank for Reconstruction and Development and the International Monetary Fund, which were created to bring stability and order to international banking transactions and to facilitate national schemes of reconstruction and development, were originally planned at the Bretton Woods Conference held in the United States in July 1944 though they did not begin to operate effectively until 1946. The World Food and Agriculture Organization, commonly known as FAO, which was established in 1945 and initially had the task of allotting surpluses of scarce foods to countries most urgently needing them, had been planned originally as early as 1943 at a Conference called by President Roosevelt and held also in the United States at a place named Hot Springs. The international organization later to be known conveniently as UNESCO and concerned "to contribute to peace and security by promoting international collaboration in the fields of education, science and culture", can be said to have had its first origins at a Council of Ministers of Education of the Allied Countries held here in London in the dark days of 1942. In November 1943, there had been established the United Nations Relief and Rehabilitation Administration (UNRRA) which between 1944 and the end of 1947 was to provide aid on a massive scale – once described as "the biggest piece of first-aid work in history" – for the war-devastated countries, saving in the process whole populations from starvation and disease. And in numerous other ways, machinery and organization established to serve the more efficient prosecution of the war or to deal with the urgent problems which war created, was being adapted and extended throughout 1945 to meet the emergency needs of a world returning fitfully and laboriously to peace.

So much for the initial beginnings of reconstruction in the financial and economic and social fields, dictated and demanded by pressing human needs. No less pressing and certainly no less complex were the political and administrative decisions to be taken or confirmed by the victors to deal with the defeated enemies, the future of their frontiers and the interim governance of their territories. These problems had already been faced in anticipation, and in confident expectation of victory, by the leaders of the three great powers on the Allied side – the United States, the Soviet Union and the United Kingdom – at meetings held in various parts of the world while the war was still undecided in any final sense. At Teheran in November 1943, Roosevelt, Stalin and Churchill had discussed and agreed upon their peace aims in broad and general terms. In 1944, there was a meeting at Dumbarton Oaks in the United States to discuss the shape and purpose of the new world organization that was later to become the United Nations. During that same autumn of 1944, agreements had been reached in London about the zones of military occupation for which the three powers (later to be joined by France) would be responsible when the allied military forces entered Germany. In February 1945, when victory over Germany seemed not only certain but imminent, the three leaders met at Yalta in the Crimea to confirm decisions on the major political questions involved in the ending of the war and the making of at least a provisional peace settlement. Six months later and two months after the collapse of Germany, they met again – in the first strictly post-war Conference – at Berlin in what became known as the Potsdam Conference to confirm agreements on the treatment of Germany and the delimitation of her frontiers and to consolidate as they hoped their collaboration in the after-war years now that the menace of Hitlerism had been destroyed and the most complete victory in modern times had been placed in their hands. At Berlin, if not earlier at Yalta, it was patent that the post-war era had begun.

Before turning to the problems which confronted the statesmen at Yalta and Potsdam, it may be useful to note the relative strengths and weaknesses of the three great powers who were now virtually assuming "the directorate of the world" and whose actions and inter-actions were to shape the peace. The stupendous increase in American production for the prosecution of the war – America had been for four years in Roosevelt's phrase "the arsenal of the democracies"—had made the United States far and away the greatest industrial power in the world. Moreover, an unlimited American intervention in the war together with the inescapable commitment to share in the rebuilding of a shattered world, had put an end at least for the foreseeable future to the traditional isolationism of the United States and obliged her peoples to confront squarely the responsibilities of being the world's greatest power. In the then exclusive possession of the atom bomb and its secrets America held, and held alone, a supreme weapon against which there was – and still is – no known means of defence. In principle the Big Three were to be equal partners in settling the peace as in principle, at least since 1941, they had been equal partners in waging the war. In fact, this colossus across the Atlantic was, to adapt George

Orwell's quip, infinitely more equal than the rest. Seen in relation to the overwhelming power of the United States, the United Kingdom and the U.S.S.R. looked a good deal more "like poor relations than equal allies".

For Britain the situation was almost exactly reversed. Far from stimulating and increasing its wealth the United Kingdom had stripped itself of its wealth to win the war – a war it had waged for two years virtually without allies. Britain could no longer rely on income from vast foreign investments to help pay for imports of food and raw materials as in the time-honoured past. Her naval power no longer "ruled the waves" and though her colonial Empire was still largely intact politically when the war ended it was clearly destined for early liquidation. Meanwhile it was manifest that for the time being at least the United Kingdom must continue to be dependent substantially in economic terms on the resources of the United States.

As for the Soviet Union, reactions there to the ending of the war and the responsibilities of the peace were bound to be ambivalent and confused. The Russians had won epic military victories at Stalingrad and elsewhere; they believed themselves erroneously though not without some justification, to be in effect the sole architects of victory over the common enemy. They had added 24 million people to the Soviet Union by the annexation of the Baltic States, the Eastern territories of Poland, Bessarabia and Northern Bukovina, parts of Finland and part of the former East Prussia. Through the use of the Red Army, they had established a control over the whole of Eastern Europe which in large part they maintain to this day. And their Communist revolution had emerged if anything reinforced by nearly four years of military struggle. On the other hand they had suffered losses of man-power and material possessions and of productive capacity far in excess of those inflicted on their allies and they faced in terms of size a problem of reconstruction immeasurably greater than either Britain or the United

States. And over all in these early stages of the peace lay for them the shadow of the exclusive American possession of the atomic bomb – the unique weapon developed by their allies in secrecy and by processes still to be withheld from them. Where and how were they to find the security repeatedly threatened and breached in their history and put in the gravest jeopardy by Hitler's invasion of the recent past? Where and how were they to find the productive capacity, the capital equipment needed to replace the stupendous losses of machinery and man-power incurred in the war? These were the fundamental questions the Russians brought to the meetings of the Big Three. These were the considerations that lay behind the statesmen as they sat down together to liquidate the war and to fashion the peace.

The meeting of Stalin, Roosevelt and Churchill at Yalta in the Crimea in February 1945 has been described as "the curtain-raiser to the post-war age". The discussions ranged widely over the international problems jointly and severally confronting the major Powers, but three questions in particular were of out-standing importance. In respect of the new world organization to be set up in place of the former League of Nations, certain agreements had been reached in earlier war-time meetings of the Allies. At Yalta, two notable decisions in this field were taken, both of which helped to preserve the unity which it was a major purpose of Yalta to maintain. Stalin who had earlier demanded a separate seat for each of the sixteen republics in the Union of Socialist Soviet Republics, yielded to Western opposition and agreed to content himself with places for Byelo-Russia and the Ukraine in addition to the Soviet Union itself. On American insistence, though with the ready concurrence of Britain and the Soviet Union, the great powers were given a veto in the proceedings of the proposed Security Council of the world organization through the requirement that every major decision must have the concurring votes of the Big Four – that is of

Britain, the United States, the Soviet Union and China, later to be joined by France.

Nor did the question of Germany's future raise any seriously divisive problems at this stage. In earlier war-time exchanges it had already been agreed that the defeated Germany was for the foreseeable future to be administered by the Allies themselves in three zones of approximately equal size. At Yalta, Stalin was persuaded to abandon his opposition to French participation in the inter-allied control of Germany, and France was thereupon given a zone to administer carved out of the American and British zones and conceded an equal place on the Control Commission. On the question of reparations from Germany where significant differences of attitude emerged, Stalin yielded to Western and particularly British opposition to inordinate Soviet demands and it was agreed that the possibilities of moderate and attainable reparations should be referred to a special commission to meet in Moscow.

It was in the consideration of the Polish question that the first serious differences emerged between the Big Three on the conditions of a post-war settlement and both at Yalta and subsequently in the Berlin Conference, much time had to be given to the future status of Poland. Here the issue was the character of the new government of Poland and the precise delineation of her frontiers. For Stalin it was clear that the Provisional Government should be the Soviet-approved "Lublin Committee", as it was styled, which was largely the creation of the Polish Communists and the Russians themselves. The Western allies insisted that if this body was to become even the Provisional Government of Poland it must be supplemented by the inclusion of democratic leaders from other parties including members of the exiled Polish Government in London. The point was conceded by Stalin at Yalta but later, in fact, the Western governments withdrew recognition from the Polish Government in London and recognized the Lublin Committee on the understanding that Mr Mikolajzyk, leader of the Polish Peasant Party, would be included in it. It was agreed also that the Provisional Government should hold free elections on the basis of universal suffrage at the earliest possible moment which could be, said Stalin at Yalta, "within a month". In the event, the Soviet Government delayed by every possible means the effective participation of non-Communist leaders in the Provisional Government and two years elapsed before the elections were held – under conditions that were in no sense "free".[1]

On the question of the future frontiers of Poland there was broad agreement at Yalta that the Soviet Union should be given the former areas of Poland east of the so-called Curzon Line and that Poland should be compensated for the loss of territory by the cession to her of German lands in East Prussia and in the west. But how far west was this new Polish frontier to run? Stalin again had no doubt about the answer. It should run from Stettin in the north, along the length of the Oder and the western Neisse rivers down to the Czech frontier. This would not only restore to Poland the territories annexed by Hitler in 1939 but give her control over Pomerania and Silesia including the ancient German city of Breslau. For Roosevelt in particular, these were excessive demands and though Stalin's proposals were tentatively accepted it was understood that the final determination of the Polish German frontier should be left to an ultimate Peace Conference. The Potsdam discussions six months later failed to resolve these allied differences and though it was agreed that meanwhile the Western territories, as they were to be called, should be under Polish administration, it was confirmed that "the final delimitation should await the peace settlement". The frontier still awaits this formal definition twenty years later, though no one doubts today that it has very little likelihood of being changed save in a mutually inconceivable war.

[1] See Chapter 2 for further treatment of this complex theme (Ed).

The Yalta Conference was also the occasion for an agreement, not to be disclosed until much later, under which Roosevelt and Stalin made concessions significantly extending Soviet influence in the Far East. Japan was still undefeated and to secure Russian help in encompassing her defeat in the shortest possible time and a Russian promise to declare war on Japan within a short period after the German surrender, the Western allies secretly agreed that as the outcome of victory the Soviet Union should be given southern Sakhalin and the string of the Kurile Islands, should have its suzerainty over Outer Mongolia recognized and should have restored to it in Manchuria the privileges broadly that Czarist Russia had had in this area before its defeat by Japan in 1905 – agreements which in so far as they concerned China were to be ratified in a treaty signed by President Chiang Kai-Shek and the Soviet Government in August 1945. Thus was confirmed Russia's position as an Asian power and as a dominant influence in the North-eastern Pacific.

Despite its general harmony, Yalta had already begun to reveal the tensions and undercurrents which were ultimately to destroy the solidarity of the war-time allies and the unity which, though precariously, they had achieved in face of the common enemy. At Potsdam where the Big Three met again in July 1945, the strains facing the alliance were intensified though outward unity was maintained. Here the major business was the future treatment of Germany and the issues it posed were urgent and inescapable; Hitler was dead and the defeat of his military forces complete; Germany itself was in a state of virtually total collapse. Could the major allies find solutions on which they could agree or would the alliance founder "in the devastated and demoralized heart of Europe itself"?

Again the broad objectives of policy were not in dispute. Clearly Germany must be disarmed and demilitarized; equally clearly she must be denazified and, if possible, every last trace of Nazism removed. Obviously there was no immediate possibility of her ruling herself and the necessity of a long period of joint allied control while the re-education and the re-establishment of democracy in the German state and the German people proceeded, was taken to be axiomatic as it had been through all the preliminary discussions in the war years themselves. It was relatively easy for the Big Three (now Stalin, Truman and Attlee, since Truman had succeeded Roosevelt, removed by death, and Attlee had succeeded Churchill, removed by the vagaries of a British general election) to agree in Berlin that no central German government could or should be established and that the administration of affairs in Germany should be based on the decentralization of the political structure and the development of local responsibility. It was not too difficult to agree that despite the division of Germany into four zones of military occupation and four regional military administrations, certain matters, such as finance and transport, were to be handled centrally for the whole of the country under the direction of a Control Council comprised of British, Soviet, American and French representatives. It was not even impossibly difficult to reach agreements in principle on the problem of reparations where disparity in the economic resources of the zones from which each of the four powers were authorized to draw their reparations was to be rectified by the right of the Russians to draw additional reparations from the Western zones.

The Big Three could attain therefore, and did attain, a fair measure of agreement on the principles of action and the construction of the machinery to implement them. A unified Four-power control of the defeated enemy on the basis of a theoretically undivided Germany was established. This unity was not to survive however the failure to define the generalities – such as the necessity to create a true democracy in Germany – which were allowed to obscure fundamental differences of ideology and political purpose. It was not to survive the strains already created by differences over Poland, nor the suspicions engendered by the unilateral and clandestine Western development of the atom bomb, only disclosed to the Russians as the Potsdam Conference closed. But at Potsdam in the summer of 1945 the alliance still held, even if precariously. And nearly three years were to elapse before the formal Four-power governance of Germany came to an end, the two separate German States were established and the partition of Germany fulfilled.

Meanwhile an event of more encouraging significance had been taking place in San Francisco where on 26th June 1945, fifty-one founder members signed the international treaty which three months later brought into being the United Nations. This was the culminating act in a series of declarations and conferences – the Atlantic Charter of 1941, the Washington Declaration of 1942, the Moscow Declaration of 1943, the Dumbarton Oaks Conference of 1944 and the San Francisco Conference itself – in which the Western allies either alone or in company with the Soviet Union had formulated the aims for which they were fighting, the nature of the peace they sought to establish and the means whereby the future peace and stability of themselves and the world at large was to be assured.

The task of the San Francisco Conference was to finalize the discussions on major questions concerning the new world organization which had taken place earlier at Dumbarton Oaks and elsewhere, to adopt the Charter as the constitution and directive of the United Nations and to establish the Preparatory Commission which was to arrange the first sessions of the constituent organs through which the United Nations would carry out its purposes. It was at San Francisco also that decisions were taken to deny membership of the new organization to the defeated enemies – to make indeed active participation in the war against Hitler and the Japanese the indispensable criterion of the right to founder-membership – and to define the powers of discussion and recommendation that were to belong to the General Assembly in the new organization. The first meeting of the Executive Committee of the Preparatory Commission was held on 9th August, three days after the first atomic bomb fell on Hiroshima. The Preparatory Commission itself met in London on 24th November, completing arrangements for the first General Assembly which opened in London on 10th January 1946. "The birth pangs of the new world order" were over; the sequence of triumphs and tribulations which were to beset its early years were still to come.

Contemplating the world-wide range of the membership of the United Nations today with its one hundred and fifteen States – half or more than half of its members drawn from the African and Asian continents – and contemplating, too, the radical shift in the balance of forces that has taken place in the General Assembly in recent years, it is pertinent to recall the strikingly different composition of this first United Nations that came into being simultaneously with the first epoch-making detonation of the atom bomb. Even then, though Africa and Asia were still largely unrepresented, it was not by any means preponderantly or exclusively a European body as had been its Genevan predecessor, the League of Nations. As we have seen, no former enemy countries were allowed in; there were of course no neutrals either (they were admitted later and in various stages); there was no representative from Poland. There were indeed only eight countries besides Great Britain and the Soviet Union, neither of them wholly European, to represent the European scene. Overwhelming these numerically, were twenty-one Latin American Republics, all the States of the Middle East, Liberia, Ethiopia, the Union of South Africa, India (not yet fully independent), China and the Philippines. Nevertheless the hegemony of the Western great powers and especially of the United States within the organization, was virtually complete – the voice of Washington being reinforced constantly and faithfully by the collective voices of the Latin-American governments. The Soviet bloc was in a tiny minority.

The invasion from the new Africa and the new Asia was yet to come.

In these early days of the United Nations there was little of the excitement and unrestrained optimism which characterized the founding of the League of Nations in 1919. There was no one at San Francisco bold enough to quote, as Lord Curzon did a quarter of a century earlier, the chorus from Shelley's *Hellas*: "the world's great age begins anew, the golden years return". Much had been learnt in the travail of the Second World War and the tragic interludes after 1919 which served to make that war inevitable. Hopes for the future were sober and restrained. Mr Bevin, the British Foreign Secretary, speaking at San Francisco, said that no one would claim that an unbreakable guarantee of peace had been created but they had forged the means whereby peace could be attained if only men were ready to make sacrifices. Mr Gromyko, speaking for Russia, said that co-operation had been essential for the defeat of Hitler's Germany; co-operation was no less necessary to preserve the peace. General Smuts, an architect also of the first League of Nations, was sure that the Charter though not perfect was a very real advance on all previous plans for security against war. These were moderate and reasonable assessments and expectations. Later the reader will be able to judge for himself how far they have been realized.

Even if there had been any disposition in the summer of 1945 to indulge extravagant hopes for the world that was to emerge from the war, the mood could scarcely have outlived the release of the first atomic bombs over Japan on those fateful days in early August. These were events that were seen even then to have changed the course of history and to make 1945 perhaps the most momentous year since history began. Twenty years later we have of necessity learnt – maybe with dangerous ease – "to live with the bomb" and to recognize that its perils, though now greater and still ever-present, have already served to discourage more reckless actions on the part of statesmen and of nations and, perhaps, to ensure that the second world-wide Armageddon was the last. But in those latter months of 1945, the shock of the bomb was too vivid and too immediate to permit, at least to the ordinary person, any clear perception of what its meaning was to be. True the statesmen of the West were under no illusions as to the awful responsibility they had assumed in making and using the new weapon. In a broadcast from Washington on the day the bomb was dropped on Nagasaki, President Truman was already urging Western leaders and peoples to constitute themselves trustees of this new force, to prevent its misuse and turn it into channels of service to mankind. In less than four months and in implementation of this pledge, the President of the United States and the Prime Ministers of Great Britain and Canada, meeting in Washington, were offering just as soon as effective enforceable safeguards against the use of atomic energy for destructive purposes could be devised, to share information on the practical industrial application of the new forms of energy and proposing the setting-up of a Commission under the United Nations to work out plans for the international control of atomic energy and the limitation of its use to peaceful ends.

Nor at this time was there any dearth of sombre warnings from the statesmen as to what the cost of failure might be. "This revelation of the secrets of nature," said the former Prime Minister in characteristic Churchillian, though by no means unfitting language, "long mercifully withheld from man, should arouse the most solemn reflections in the mind and conscience of every human being capable of comprehension." "We must indeed pray," he added, "that these awful agencies will be made to conduce to peace among the nations and that instead of wreaking measureless havoc upon the entire globe they may become a perennial fountain of world prosperity." Less than a month after the devastation of Hiroshima and Nagasaki, the new British Prime Minister Mr Attlee, in a broadcast to the nation, was saying that though a great victory had been gained the triumph would be short-lived if they did not take to heart the lessons that their suffering had taught them and the heavy responsibility that their victory entailed. Unless they could set against the incalculable losses of the war a faith in the progress of the human spirit and in the growth of a new conception of human society, those losses would have been in vain. Their rejoicings, therefore, must be tempered with the gravity of the problems which confronted them in the new era.

CHAPTER 2

THE COLD WAR

Its Origins

by Christopher Seton-Watson

The purpose of my theme can best be served by beginning with five quotations. The first is from the broadcast which Winston Churchill made to the British nation on the 22nd June 1941, the evening of the day that Hitler attacked the Soviet Union. He said:

> The past, with its crimes, its follies and its tragedies flashes away. . . . Any man or state who fights on against Nazidom will have our aid. . . . The Russian danger is our danger, just as the cause of any Russian fighting for his hearth and home is the cause of free men and free peoples in every quarter of the globe.[1]

This public announcement that Britain welcomed the Soviet Union as an ally in the war against Hitler was made at a dramatic moment. For the past year Britain, with the Commonwealth, had been fighting alone, and it had been hard to see how victory was to be achieved. Now Britain had an ally, and a great ally, once again, and victory ceased to be just a matter of faith.

The second quotation is from the public communiqué issued by Roosevelt, Churchill and Stalin at the end of the Yalta Conference in February 1945, as the war in Europe was nearing its end. This communiqué read: "Our meeting here in the Crimea has reaffirmed our determination to maintain and strengthen in the peace to come that unity of purpose and of action which has

[1] Churchill, *The Second World War*, III, 332–3.

made victory possible." This is the high-water mark of the Grand Alliance. Unity of purpose and action has been achieved in war; the three leaders of the Alliance pledged themselves to maintain their unity in peace.

My third quotation is from Winston Churchill again, a little bit later, 29th April 1945. The war in Europe was only ten days off its end. In a private letter to Stalin, he wrote:

> There is not much comfort in looking into a future where you and the countries you dominate, plus the Communist Parties in many other States, are all drawn up on one side, and those who rally to the English-speaking nations . . . are on the other. It is quite obvious that their quarrel would tear the world to pieces and that all of us leading men on either side who had anything to do with that would be shamed before history.[1]

This was a gloomy foreboding of what has to come; Churchill saw that the future of the Grand Alliance was in doubt even before the war in Europe was over.

My next quotation is from President Truman – a private letter of January 1946 to his Secretary of State, Byrnes: "Unless Russia is faced with an iron fist and strong language, another war is in the making. Only one language do they understand – 'how many divisions have you?' I do not think we should play compromise any longer. . . . I'm tired of babying the Soviets."[2] This letter shows how far President Truman had travelled in the eight months since the war in Europe ended. The United States was, in fact, pretty slow to adjust itself to the changed situation, and went on trying for many months to collaborate with the Soviet Union and to maintain the Grand Alliance. But already by January 1946 there had been moments of exasperation, and this letter of Truman to Byrnes is an example of one

---

[1] Churchill, *The Second World War*, VI, 433.
[2] Truman, *Memoirs*, I, 492–3.

of them. Private exasperation, however; such things were not
yet said in public.

My last quotation is again from Winston Churchill, from the
speech he made in March 1946, when leader of the Conservative Opposition, in the presence of President Truman at Fulton,
Missouri. On that occasion he appealed to the American people
to tighten the political and military links between Britain and
America in order to stand up to the Soviet Union. Churchill
said:

> From Stettin in the Baltic to Trieste in the Adriatic an Iron
> Curtain has descended across the continent. . . . Whatever
> conclusions may be drawn from these facts – and facts they
> are – this is certainly not the liberated Europe we fought to
> build up. Nor is it one that contains the essentials of per-
> manent peace. . . . From what I have seen of our Russian
> friends and allies during the war, I am convinced that there
> is nothing they admire so much as strength, and there is noth-
> ing for which they have less respect than weakness, especially
> military weakness.

This speech, with its tacit assumption that the Grand Alliance
was dead, made a great stir. It has been called the first shot in
the Cold War: it certainly used Cold War language. Shortly
afterwards Stalin made this comment upon it: "To all intents
and purposes Mr Churchill now takes his stand among the
warmongers. A point to be noted is that in this respect Mr
Churchill and his friends bear a striking resemblance to Hitler
and his friends."[1]

Four of these five quotations fall within the span of thirteen
months, and they illustrate the rapidity of the change, the extent of the upheaval that took place in the world in 1945 and

[1] Survey of International Affairs 1939–1946, McNeill, *America,
Britain and Russia*, 657–8.

1946. Churchill gave the title of "Triumph and Tragedy" to the last volume of his *Second World War*: the triumph of the Grand Alliance over Hitler and Japan, and the tragedy of the break-up of that Alliance almost before victory had been won. Between 1945 and 1947 the high hopes that the Grand Alliance would continue into peace were shattered; in their place came reluctant acceptance of mutual hostility and a divided world, reluctant acceptance of a Cold War.

Our search for the origins of the Cold War must start in the Grand Alliance itself; and in order to understand the strength and weakness of that Alliance, we must consider both the legacy of all the years since the Russian Revolution in 1917 and the more immediate legacy of the years 1939–41.

First, the remoter legacy. Since 1917 Soviet Governments had been preaching world revolution, thereby provoking fear and hostility throughout the rest of the world. It was not easy to forget that entirely. Churchill might say "the past with its crimes, its follies and its tragedies flashes away"; but it didn't quite flash away. And look at it from the Soviet point of view. We cannot understand Soviet foreign policy and Soviet attitudes towards the rest of the world unless we realize how firmly embedded in Soviet thinking was the concept of capitalist encirclement. A hostile capitalist world, the Soviet leaders assumed, was out for the destruction of the one socialist state in the world. That assumption dates from the very early days of 1918–20, the days of British, French, American and Japanese intervention on the side of the enemies of the Bolshevik Government. The events of those years seem to have created a trauma in the minds of the rulers of the Soviet Union. Certainly in the years leading up to the second war, it was their constant fear that the international crisis would end in an agreement between all the capitalist powers, in a British and French deal with Hitler at the Soviet Union's expense. So much for the legacy of fear, hostility and suspicion dating from 1917.

More important for what came after was the legacy of the years 1939–41. Successive Soviet Governments, faced as they saw it with encirclement, tried to split the capitalist powers and so prevent them ganging up on the Soviet Union. Immediately before the outbreak of war in 1939, negotiations were going on in Moscow between the British and French on one side, and the Soviet Government on the other, for an alliance to resist Hitler. While these were actually in progress, Stalin began secret negotiations with Germany. In the end, in August 1939, he made his choice of a pact with Hitler. This was an outstanding success, from the Soviet Union's point of view, for the policy of splitting the capitalist world by making a temporary agreement with one part of it. Stalin must have known that his pact with Hitler made war between Germany on the one side, and Britain and France on the other, inevitable. He counted on being able to sit back and watch the two halves of the capitalist world tearing themselves to pieces. And who would gain from that process? The Soviet Union.

The pact with Hitler was immediately followed by the partition of Poland, with Hitler invading from one side and the Soviet Union from the other, and the Soviet Union annexing a large piece of eastern Poland. Between 1939 and 1941 the three independent Baltic States (Esthonia, Latvia and Lithuania) were also annexed, together with a piece of Rumania down on the Black Sea. There was a great westward thrust of Soviet power in those two years, followed, of course, by all the apparatus of the Communist police state.

In that same period the Soviet Union attacked and defeated Finland in the winter war of 1939–40. Nor did even that represent the limit of its ambition. Soviet eyes turned towards Turkey, the Straits and the Persian Gulf, the traditional targets of Russian expansion, and in November 1940 the Soviet Foreign Minister, Molotov, went to Berlin to confront Hitler with his country's claim to domination of those areas. All this time, too, the Soviet Government was giving Hitler considerable economic and even a little indirect military help.

That then was the legacy which the Grand Alliance had to live down after June 1941; and, of course, it did not live it down entirely. Mutual suspicion survived. Three examples of this may be given. First, the fact that the British and Americans did not pass on to Stalin, their ally, information about the development of the atomic bomb; this was a very big limitation to the Alliance: secondly, while a vast amount of economic and material help was given to the Soviet Union, there was not, looking at it from the Soviet point of view, much military collaboration. When Churchill, in the summer of 1941, asked Stalin what he wanted the British to do, he got this answer: land your troops in Western Europe and relieve the pressure upon us. Nobody in Stalin's position could have given any other answer. But what about the second front? It did not come in 1941, nor in 1942, nor in 1943. All the correspondence, often acrimonious, between the British and Americans on one side and Stalin on the other, must be read in the light of this failure, as the Russians saw it, of the Western powers, right up to June 1944, to make a proper military effort in Western Europe. There is no doubt that Stalin had the suspicion that this was not *inability* but *unwillingness* to launch the second front. He must often have asked himself, were not the British and Americans sitting back and watching, just as he had sat back and watched between September 1939 and June 1941?

A third example of this mutual suspicion was the fear on both sides, at different periods of the war, that the other would make, or try to make, a separate peace. In the very last month of the war, in the spring of 1945, Stalin accused the British and Americans of negotiating with the enemy behind his back and of trying to arrange a surrender of the Germans in the West, which would allow the British and American armies to move rapidly eastwards and halt the Red Army's advance. There was not one scrap of truth in this accusation, but Stalin made it, and very bitter words passed.

These were some of the weaknesses of the Grand Alliance. What about the credit side? What kept the Grand Alliance together in the face of the legacy of the past and these continuing suspicions? First, clearly, the common interest in the defeat of Germany and of Japan. The Soviet Union did not fight the Japanese until right at the end in August 1945, but the British and Americans counted on Soviet help to hasten victory in the Far East. This in itself was a powerful reason for strengthening the Alliance. It was a formidable task to defeat Hitler and his allies, and the combined strength of all was necessary. The main architects of the Grand Alliance, therefore, were Hitler and the Japanese.

But as the months went by, in addition to the bond of common interest, there also developed strong bonds of sympathy between the Allies. This is something we tend to forget today. In Britain and America and all over the free world there was a growing admiration of Russian heroism, a growing recognition that the Red Army was saving millions of British and American lives (again something we too often forget), a growing sympathy with the terrible sufferings of the Soviet people in their war of national defence and liberation from the invader. Indeed the Soviet Government called it the Great Patriotic War, and to galvanize popular resistance, it made appeal after appeal to national pride, even to Russian history. Little was heard of communism or world revolution during the war, and the Comintern (or Communist International) went into total eclipse. The Comintern, founded in 1919, was an association of all the Communist parties in the world with its headquarters in Moscow, and its job was to direct the world revolutionary movement. In 1943 Stalin dissolved it. This act deepened British and American sympathy for the Soviet Union and gave rise to great hopes, which are echoed in another passage of that same letter of

Churchill to Stalin of 29th April 1945. In it he writes of the "very warm and deep desire to be friends on equal and honourable terms with the mighty Russian Soviet Republic and to work with you, making allowances for our different systems of thought and government, in long and bright years for all the world which we three Powers alone can make together".[1]

The questions that people in the West were asking themselves at the end of the war were: Has the Soviet Union changed as a result of the war? Have its leaders really put world revolution and the spread of communism behind them? Will Stalin continue to act and talk as a Russian rather than as a Communist? If so, in spite of our different systems of government, is there hope that the Grand Alliance will continue, that we and the Russians will grow together and thereby ensure lasting peace?

Now were people justified in hoping this? As we look back, I think we can say, No. Though if we make allowances for the stress and anxiety of the time, we can see why people did hope, why they indulged, if you like, in wishful thinking. Why do I say their hopes were unjustified? Because if one examines carefully the war aims of the Grand Alliance, one can already find in them the seeds of the subsequent cold war. Look first at the Atlantic Charter of August 1941, published at a time when the United States was not yet in the war. In it Churchill and Roosevelt declared that their countries sought no aggrandizement, territorial or other; they desired to see no territorial changes which did not accord with the freely expressed wishes of the people concerned; and they respected the right of all peoples to choose the form of government under which they would live. This was a democratic declaration of faith in the principle of self-determination, which the Soviet Union subsequently accepted as a statement of Allied war aims.

The second statement that deserves scrutiny is the Declaration on Liberated Europe published at the end of the Yalta

[1] Churchill, *The Second World War*, VI, 431–2.

Conference in February 1945. In that document the three Great Powers pledged themselves to assist the liberated peoples of Europe "to create democratic institutions of their own choice", by establishing provisional governments "broadly representative of all democratic elements in the population" and by facilitating free elections which would lead to the formation of permanent democratic governments. That was a declaration to which Stalin put his name, as well as Churchill and Roosevelt.

The long tragic story of how all these promises came to nothing can be told in terms of Poland, because Poland was in many respects the crux of the Grand Alliance. There were two problems about Poland. First, what frontiers should it have after the war; and second, what form of government?

The British position with regard to Poland was this: that in 1939 Britain and France went to war because Hitler attacked Poland, with which they had signed a military alliance. As Churchill told Stalin at Yalta, the British interest in Poland was one of honour.[1] In that same letter to Stalin of 29th April 1945 he wrote, "They [the British] can never feel this war will have ended rightly unless Poland has a fair deal in the full sense of sovereignty, independence and freedom, on the basis of friendship with Russia."[2] Note the last phrase, "friendship with Russia". Nobody challenged the right of the Soviet Union to ask that the post-war government of Poland should be friendly; this was considered a reasonable demand. But what did the Soviet Union mean by a friendly government? Here lay the crux.

In 1939 Poland had been partitioned. The Soviet Government had annexed the eastern third of Poland (which had a mainly non-Polish population) and showed every sign that it intended to keep it. Indeed, almost immediately after Hitler's invasion in June 1941, one of the first requests that the Soviet Government made to London was to recognize the new fron-

[1] Churchill, *The Second World War*, VI, 322.   [2] ibid., 431.

tiers of the Soviet Union, the annexation of this one-third of Poland. So right from the beginning, from 1941, Poland was a bone of contention.

In the autumn of 1941, when Russia was hard pressed and the Germans were at the gates of Moscow, an agreement was signed between Stalin and the Polish Government in exile in London. This was the high-water mark of harmony on the Polish issue inside the Grand Alliance. Two years later that harmony, always precarious, was shattered. By then the tide of war was turning, the Red Army was advancing; the Soviet Government was less in the mood to be conciliatory to Poland. In the spring of 1943 the Germans announced they had discovered, in the Russian territory under their control, the mass grave of many thousands of Polish officers who, they alleged, had been taken prisoner by the Red Army in 1939 and subsequently massacred. When the Germans suggested that the International Red Cross should conduct an impartial investigation, the Polish Government in London associated itself with this demand. The Soviet Government took this as a hostile act and broke off diplomatic relations.

The situation worsened early in January 1944 when the Red Army crossed the pre-1939 frontier of the Soviet Union and advanced on to what had been Polish soil. In September 1944 occurred the great insurrection of the Polish Home Army in Warsaw. Because the Home Army owed its allegiance to the Polish Government in London, which the Soviet Government had ceased to recognize, the Red Army stood by and watched while the Germans crushed the rising. (Even if a more charitable interpretation is put on Soviet actions, even if one admits that it was militarily difficult for the Red Army to help, why was it also made so exceedingly difficult for the British and American Air Forces to help?)

The dispute over Poland dragged on throughout 1944-5. By the end of the war the American and British Governments had agreed that the Soviet Union should keep the part of Poland it had taken in 1939 and that the Poles should be compensated by annexing part of Germany. But the amount of compensation to which they proceeded, with Soviet support, to help themselves was much greater than the British and Americans had ever contemplated. In consequence the frontier of Poland now runs far to the west, along the Oder–Neisse line, and about 5 million Germans have been expelled from what was purely German soil. That frontier is a violation of the principles of the Atlantic Charter, because the 5 million Germans were never given an opportunity to determine their own future. They were forcibly expelled, and the British and American Governments acquiesced, not without protest but because they believed, as indeed was the case, that they had no alternative.

So much for the frontiers. The second point at issue, the form of Poland's government, proved even more intractable. In the summer of 1944 the Soviet Government set up a Polish Committee of National Liberation, composed mainly of Communists, to which it entrusted the civil administration of Polish territory as it was liberated by the Red Army. Early in 1945 the Soviet Union recognized the Committee as the provisional government of Poland. There were now two Polish governments: one in London, the ally of Britain and the U.S.A., the other at Lublin in Poland, the ally of the Soviet Union. In July 1945, after laborious negotiations, the two governments were fused into a democratic coalition. But its life was brief and troubled. The real ruler of Poland was the Red Army, and under its protection the Polish Communist Party was assured effective power. As time went on it became quite clear that the Soviet demand to have a friendly government in Poland was in fact a demand to have a Communist government, and that the Soviet promise to allow the Poles "to create democratic institutions of their own choice" was a hollow mockery.

Poland, then, was the crux of the Grand Alliance. But similar events were taking place in other countries liberated by the Red Army, so that by the end of the war the British and Americans were confronted with a fearful dilemma. What were they to do in the face of this kind of action by the Soviet Union? Were they to resist, or were they to appease, to compromise, to go on trying to be friendly?

Winston Churchill saw the danger earlier than the Americans. By May 1945 he was quite clear in his mind that Britain and America should resist, should use their great military strength to stand up to the Soviet Union and call a check. The opportunity offered itself at the end of the war. It had been agreed that Germany should be divided into American, British and Soviet zones of military occupation, and the boundaries of those zones had been drawn on the map. In fact, when the fighting ceased, the British and American armies were well to the east of the line that the Red Army was supposed to reach. Churchill said, let us stay where we are and refuse to withdraw to the agreed line until we have forced Stalin to carry out his promises and make a fair settlement for the whole of Europe. But quick action was needed, because he knew that Britain and America were going to demobilize and would in a year or so be weak. Now was the time to stand firm, before the armies of democracy melted away. But President Truman did not see it that way and insisted that the American and British armies should withdraw into the agreed zones. Churchill tells us that Truman's reply "struck a knell in my breast but I had no choice but to submit".[1] No choice but to submit because by the end of the war Britain had long ceased to be the equal of the U.S.A. in military or economic strength. From now on the protagonists of the Cold War were the United States and the Soviet Union, with Britain playing only a secondary rôle.

This brings us to the Cold War itself. Two periods may be distinguished: the first from 1945 to 1947, which can be called

[1] Churchill, *The Second World War*, VI, 525.

the transitional period, during which the Grand Alliance broke down; the second from 1947 to 1949, during which the Cold War reached its peak. In the first period, four features of Soviet policy stand out. First, the Soviet Union pushed its frontiers even farther west than in 1939–41, making an addition of 21 million people to its pre-1939 population. The second feature was the Soviet Union's determination to obtain security on its western frontiers by controlling the countries of Eastern Europe with their 100 million inhabitants. This was done by a process of progressive communization, by what the leading Communist of Hungary called "salami tactics". Eastern Europe was swallowed one slice at a time, in the calculation that, if each slice was thin enough, Britain and America would not resist. Already by the end of 1945, Rumania, Bulgaria, Yugoslavia and Albania were ruled by Communists. In 1947 Hungary and Poland, after a brief transition, followed the same way. That left Czechoslovakia as the only democratic country in the Soviet sphere.

The third feature of Soviet policy was the exaction of maximum reparation from Germany, to repair the havoc that Hitler's aggression had caused. The fourth could be called the return to communism. In August 1945, quite soon after the end of the war, Kalinin, the President of the Soviet Union, made this significant speech: "Even now, after the greatest victory known to history, we cannot for one minute forget the basic fact that our country remains the one socialist state in the world. . . . Victory does not mean that all dangers have disappeared. Only the most concrete, most immediate danger, which threatened us from Hitlerite Germany, has disappeared."[1] Back, then, to capitalist encirclement, back to the five-year plans with their emphasis on heavy industry and armaments. At once the all-out effort began to catch up the West in the manufacture of nuclear weapons. Once again belts and minds were to be tightened. Con-

[1] Survey of International Affairs 1939–1946, McNeill, *America, Britain and Russia*, 653.

tacts with the West were severed and indoctrination of the Russian people with the harsh faith of communism was resumed.

Turning to American policy in this transitional period, two of its component elements deserve emphasis: first, the desire to return to normality as soon as possible; second, the attempt to create permanent international machinery through which peace could be preserved. The desire for normality appeared most clearly in the military sphere. At Yalta and on other occasions, Roosevelt had said that no American Government would be able to keep American troops in Europe for more than two years after the end of the war. Events were of course to prove him wrong. Nevertheless demobilization went ahead at a frantic pace. In June 1945, the Americans had 12·1 million men in uniform. A year later they had 3 million and a year after that, in June 1947, 1·6 million. The armies of democracy did indeed melt away, as Churchill had foreseen. In the economic sphere, too, a quick return to normality was intended. The Americans believed that after a brief transitional period, during which massive emergency relief would have to be given to Europe, the world would revert to normal trade and normal financial relations between states. A third way of getting back to normality was to complete the peace treaties quickly. In the course of 1947 four treaties were signed, with Italy, Rumania, Bulgaria and Hungary, the minor allies of Germany. That was the first stage, and the Americans expected a treaty with Germany to follow close behind. But here the Cold War caught up with them. Today, in 1965, the peace treaty with Germany has still not been signed.

The American desire to create machinery for the preservation of peace found its main expression in the United Nations. During the war Stalin had agreed that the Soviet Union should be a sponsor of that organization and become one of its leading members. At the time this agreement had seemed one of the greatest triumphs of the Grand Alliance. So when peace came, the United States was not thinking in terms of frontiers or power politics or spheres of influence or, least of all, cold war; it was working for a new world order based on a continuation of the wartime Alliance within the framework of the United Nations. Americans looked to the Soviet Union as a partner in the task of "winning the peace".

Between 1945 and 1947 those hopes were dashed. The United Nations failed to provide the framework for a peacetime Grand Alliance, and was instead riven by bitter quarrels and rendered impotent by the Soviet Union's repeated use of its right of veto. Gradually the United States abandoned its attempt to maintain the Alliance and accepted the fact of a divided world. And all along the lines where the armies had stopped when the fighting ceased, tension and friction grew. There was tension in Persia, where the Soviet Government delayed for many months the promised evacuation of its wartime garrisons and appeared to be creating a Communist state in the area under its control; tension on the frontier of Turkey, caused by a blunt Soviet demand for the cession of territory and control of the Straits; tension in northern Greece, where the monarchist government, backed by Britain, fought a civil war against Communist guerillas based on Bulgaria, Yugoslavia and Albania; tension at Trieste between Communist Yugoslavia and anti-Communist Italy; and most important of all, tension all down the demarcation line in Germany, to which we must now turn.

It is a curious thing that when the war ended, the Allies had no clear policy for Germany. They had agreed to divide the whole country into zones of military occupation, but after that their ideas were exceedingly confused. At the Potsdam Conference in July 1945 it was decided that Germany should preserve its unity, under the joint control of America, Britain and Russia, but be disarmed and deprived of its heavy industry so that it could never again become a threat to peace. This decision assumed the continuation of the Grand Alliance. The unity of the Allies and the unity of Germany under their joint control were therefore inseparably linked. As soon as the first broke down, the second broke down also.

The Grand Alliance lasted in Germany only until the spring of 1946. The Allies set up a Control Commission in Berlin, which was to be the instrument of joint control. The Americans, in particular, made great efforts to get on with the Russians. General Eisenhower, the first U.S. representative on the Control Commission, later wrote in his memoirs, "Berlin, we were convinced, was an experimental laboratory for the development of international accord. . . Overshadowing all goals for us Americans was the contribution we locally might make to establishing a working partnership between the United States and Russia."[1] The high-water mark of collaboration was reached in March 1946 with an agreement on the level of industry to be permitted in Germany. Once that was settled, all industrial plant and equipment above the permitted level became available as reparations, mainly for the Soviet Union.

Reparations dominated the German scene for the next two months. Most of the plant which the Soviet Union claimed had inevitably to come from the British and American zones, where the bulk of German industry lay. The Americans and British expected that their zones would in exchange receive food from the Soviet zone, where Germany's richest agricultural land was situated. This was the reason why the preservation of German economic unity was so important. But right from the beginning that unity existed only on paper. The Soviet Government acted in its own zone exactly as it pleased, just as it had acted in the rest of Eastern Europe. It helped itself to reparations without informing the Control Commission, stripped East Germany of its industry and much else besides, and made no effort to send food to the West. This situation soon became intolerable.

[1] Eisenhower, *Crusade in Europe*, 500.

79

The population of West Germany had to eat; and if no food came from the East, it had to be supplied and paid for by the U.S.A. and Britain. As the Labour Chancellor of the Exchequer, Dalton, observed in his budget speech in April, "The British taxpayer cannot much longer be expected to go on paying what are, in effect, reparations to Germany."[1] So on 3rd May 1946 General Clay, Eisenhower's deputy on the Control Commission, announced that no more reparations would be sent from the western zones until the Soviet Union had agreed to restore the economic unity of Germany and effective joint control.

This was the first serious breach between the United States and the Soviet Union. It was an important moment. May 1946 was the start of a long period during which, under the pressure of events and without any preconceived design, the present rigid division of Germany took shape step by step. The Americans, British and French dug their toes in on one side, the Russians on the other. On both sides the will to control Germany grew weaker, the desire to win the Germans as allies (and later to rearm them) grew stronger. In September 1946 the American Secretary of State, Byrnes, declared at Stuttgart, "We are not withdrawing, we are staying here", and announced his country's intention to "help the German people to win their way back to an honourable place among the free and peaceloving nations of the world".[2] The grim winter of 1946–7 accelerated the change in Western opinion. Firstly, consciences were roused by the misery and degradation that defeat had inflicted upon the Germans. Secondly, it became apparent that the economic revival of Germany was essential to the recovery of Western Europe, and that if Germany did not revive, if the attempt to restrict the German economy was not abandoned, communism had good prospects of conquering the West as well

[1] Dalton, *High Tide and After*, 113.

[2] Survey of International Affairs 1939–1946, McNeill, *America, Britain and Russia*, 732.

as the East. So, gradually, fear of communism and the Soviet Union eclipsed the old fear of Germany. In the western zones there began the process of building from the bottom a democratic system of government; in the eastern zone the pace of communization quickened. By 1947 the political and economic division of Germany was a fact. A big step had been taken along the road leading to the present situation, in which there are two sovereign German governments, one in the West allied with the U.S.A., one in the East allied with the Soviet Union; a situation in which the boundaries between the zones, which had been drawn merely for the administrative convenience of the Allied armies of occupation, have become the frontiers between East and West, between the democratic and Communist worlds.

Two events of 1947 brought the post-war period of transition to an end and ushered in the second, climactic phase of the Cold War. These were the proclamation of the Truman Doctrine and the launching of the Marshall Plan.

In March 1947 the British Government decided it could no longer supply arms and finance to the Greek Government in its civil war with the Communists. The British economy was under great strain; Dalton insisted that "our endless dribble of British taxpayers' money to the Greeks" must cease.[1] The American Government was informed and at once saw great danger. If the British withdrew their support from the Greek Government, what was likely to happen? The Communists would win the civil war and Communist power would erupt into the Mediterranean. President Truman accepted the challenge. In a speech to Congress asking for 400 million dollars of aid for Greece and Turkey, he declared, "I believe it must be the policy of the United States to support free peoples who are resisting attempted subjugation by armed minorities or by

---

[1] Dalton, *High Tide and After*, 206.

outside pressures."[1] This Truman Doctrine was not popular at first in the U.S.A. But in the end, in spite of doubts and hesitations, the American people followed their President. March 1947 is therefore a turning point in American history. Not only was it a revolutionary break with the old tradition of isolation; it was also the end of the post-war dream of a return to normality and of the illusion that the United Nations would be sufficient in itself to preserve peace. Here was the United States taking on direct and perilous commitments (the first of many) in two far-off countries and shouldering a financial and military burden which the British were now no longer strong enough to bear. As Truman later wrote in his *Memoirs*, "America had served notice that the march of communism would not be allowed to succeed by default" and had aligned itself clearly at the head of the free world.[2]

The Marshall Plan followed within a few months. General Marshall, whom Truman had recently appointed as his Secretary of State, became convinced that unless immediate action was taken to revive its economy, Western Europe might lapse into chaos. As he put it, "the patient is sinking while the doctors deliberate". In his great speech at Harvard on 5th June, he promised that, while the initiative must come from Europe, if the European nations could get together and work out a joint programme for economic recovery, the American Government would back that programme generously. The British and French took him at his word and a conference was quickly called in Paris to start work on the plan.

The offer made at Harvard was open to Eastern as well as to Western Europe. But the Soviet Foreign Minister, Molotov, soon announced that the Soviet Union would have no truck with the plan, which he denounced as dollar imperialism and an attempt to interfere in the domestic affairs of independent

[1] *Documents on International Affairs 1947–1948*, 6.
[2] Truman, *Memoirs*, II, 107–14.

nations. Not only did the Soviet Union refuse to attend the Paris conference; it also ordered all the governments of Eastern Europe to stay away as well, and even forced the Czechs, who had originally accepted Marshall's offer, to cancel their acceptance. And so the split between East and West widened yet further. The Soviet Union's reaction to the Marshall Plan was bitter and uncompromising. In the autumn of 1947 it created an organization called the Cominform, which was the Comintern in a new dress. Orders went out to the Communist parties of Western Europe to abandon the moderation they had practised in the years of the Grand Alliance, and instead to stage strikes and riots, even, if possible, insurrections. Elsewhere, in Malaya, Burma, Indonesia, Indochina, Communist guerillas took to the jungle. In many parts of the world the Cold War turned very warm.

One of the most dramatic events of this second phase of the Cold War was the Czechoslovak coup of February 1948. Czechoslovakia was the only country in the Soviet sphere that was still democratic at the end of 1947. The outstanding feature of post-war Czech Governments had been that, while democratic in our sense, they were also determined to be on the closest possible terms with the Soviet Union. Indeed it was the proud boast of Czech democrats at that time that their country could act as a bridge between East and West. If the Soviet Union was justified in demanding friendly governments in neighbouring countries, Czechoslovakia *had* a friendly government. But that was not enough. In February 1948 the Czech Communists, at Soviet bidding, carried out a coup and installed a purely Communist régime.

Later in the spring of 1948 there followed, of course, the Berlin blockade, the most critical moment yet of the Cold War. This was an attempt by the Soviet Union to force the Western garrisons out of Berlin and extinguish the vigorous outpost of democracy which had flourished under their protection. If the Russians had succeeded, they would have inflicted upon the

West not only a humiliating physical withdrawal but also a shattering psychological defeat. General Clay summed up the situation in these words: "When Berlin falls, Western Germany will be next. If we mean to hold Europe against Communism, we must not budge."[1] The Americans, British and French did not budge, and $2\frac{1}{4}$ million inhabitants of Berlin were supplied by air for the best part of a year, till the Soviet Government lifted the blockade and conceded victory to the West.

One further event of 1948 must be mentioned. In June Tito broke with Stalin and Yugoslavia was expelled from the Communist community. This was, for the West, a radiant break in the thickening gloom. In the perspective of 1964 we can understand its immense significance. It meant that, even at the outset of the Cold War, there were currents flowing which, five years later, were to help bring on the thaw.

By the middle of 1949, when the Berlin blockade ended, Europe had settled into the mould that we know today. The Cold War was at its peak, with the opposing armies lined up along the demarcation lines, glowering at each other, and the nuclear armaments race in full swing. Under the threat of communism, the first steps had been taken towards West European union, and the United States, Canada, Britain and the leading nations of Western Europe had drawn together in a military alliance, the North Atlantic Treaty Organization. Meanwhile the Marshall Plan was laying the foundation of West European recovery and the future "economic miracle". Since 1949 in Europe frontiers and forms of government have remained unchanged and there has been no significant alteration in the balance of power between East and West. But that, of course, has not meant the end of the Cold War. Having reached stalemate in Europe, it overflowed into the rest of the world, above all into Asia where, in that same year of 1949, the Communists won the civil war in China and almost at once plunged their

[1] Clay, *Decision in Germany*, 361.

84

vast country into the world struggle. That was the beginning of the third phase of the Cold War, which was to be even more critical than the first two.

Its Continuation

by Roger Morgan

The history of the Cold War, once the events of 1948–9 had drawn the lines firmly across Europe, can be divided very broadly into three periods: the early 1950's, when open conflict occurred chiefly in the Far East; the later 1950's, when it was the turn of the Middle East to become the main – though by no means the only – theatre of action; and finally the first half of the 1960's, which saw the spread of the Cold War into new continents with the Congo and Cuban crisis (as well as its revival over Berlin and Indo-China), but at the same time a number of East–West agreements signifying a growing readiness to coexist.

The People's Republic of China, established in October 1949 after the Communist victory in the Civil War, fitted uneasily into the international pattern of the Far East. Britain, it is true, recognized the new régime early in 1950, as did the recently-independent India; France, however, refused to establish relations with a régime that was giving ever-increasing aid to the nationalist Viet-Minh rebels in Indo-China; while in the United States, despite preparations by Secretary of State Acheson to recognize the People's Republic, there was bitter public disappointment at the collapse of the Chiang Kai-Shek régime which had been regarded as stable and pro-American, and the question of recognition was postponed – like that of China's seat in the U.N. – until after the Congressional Election of November 1950.

In June of that year, however, the situation was changed by the outbreak of the Korean War. Korea, liberated in 1945 after thirty-five years of Japanese rule, had been divided, like Germany, into Soviet and United States zones of occupation, and these zones had hardened, as in Germany, into two hostile states. Korea was strategically very significant for her neighbours, Russia, Japan and China; the United States, too, increasingly prominent as a Far Eastern power because of the eclipse of Japan, had an interest in Korea's fate, and rushed forces from nearby Japan to repulse the attack launched by Communist North Korea on 25th June 1950. Although this U.S. action received the official backing of the United Nations, and although Britain and other U.N. members gave general support, 90% of the U.N. war effort in Korea came from the U.S.A.

The Korean fighting, which caused heavy casualties, was dramatic in its reversals of fortune: in September the U.N. forces advanced across the 38th parallel into North Korean territory; then, as predicted in warnings from India, this provoked the intervention of China in October, and further crushing victories for the Northern side; during the winter of 1950–1 the U.N. troops slowly fought their way back to roughly the 38th parallel, but General McArthur, their American commander, argued that a decisive victory over the Chinese forces could only be won by bombing their supply-lines inside China itself; this led to disagreement between President Truman and the General, and to the latter's dismissal in April 1951; as recounted elsewhere in this volume,[1] the Soviet Government was also ready for a compromise, and armistice negotiations began in the summer of 1951, though they failed to produce a final cease-fire until July 1953.

An international conference at Geneva in 1954 failed to turn the Korean cease-fire into a real peace, and in fact had to devote

[1] See p. 121.

most of its attention to the burning problem of Indo-China, where fighting between the former French colonial rulers and a Communist-led nationalist movement had continued since December 1946. Originally a straightforward struggle between these two parties, the fighting developed wider Cold War implications after 1949, when the Communist victory in the Chinese Civil War allowed increased Chinese intervention in Indo-China, as in Korea. American aid on the French side was also very considerable, but it stopped short of the atomic bombing which some French and American military leaders saw as the only thing that would have saved the desperate military situation leading to the loss of the key fortress of Dien-Bien-Phu in May 1954, and to peace in July; this peace was therefore made on terms which left the Viet-Minh (Communist) forces dominant in North Viet-Nam and well placed to exert further pressure on the South.

Although the United States Government had negotiated with Communist China at the Geneva Conference it refused either to recognize China officially or to sign the Geneva agreement providing for elections to reunify Viet-Nam by 1956. In fact, U.S. support for the extreme Right-Wing government of President Diem in South Viet-Nam, combined with further Communist pressure on this state and on the other Indo-Chinese states of Laos and Cambodia, were to cause recurrent crises even when the main Cold War focus shifted elsewhere.

By the year 1955, when both the U.S.A. and the U.S.S.R. possessed thermonuclear weapons, and when the risks of any attempt to upset the balance had been underlined not only by the 1948-9 confrontation on Berlin but also by the more alarming crises in the Far East, signs of a détente began to appear. Stalin's death (March 1953) had led to a milder Soviet tone towards the West and to a reconciliation with the heretical Yugoslavs, and by May 1955 agreement on the evacuation and neutralization of Austria was at last reached by the four Powers.

Despite this and the succeeding "summit" conferences, however, the impossibility of agreement on major issues such as Germany was shown by the Western decision to carry out West German rearmament (proposed during the Korean crisis of 1950 but postponed so as not to block possible reunification), and by the Soviet creation of the Warsaw Pact (May 1955).

The year 1955 also saw the return of the Cold War to the Middle East, an area from which it had been absent since the days of Soviet pressure on Turkey and Iran in 1945–6. An anti-Soviet defence alliance created by these states and by Iraq during 1955, and known from its headquarters in Iraq as the Baghdad Pact, provoked Soviet protests; and when Britain joined the pact in April 1955, and seemed to be developing it as an anti-Egyptian rather than an anti-Soviet organization, Egypt turned increasingly to the Soviet bloc for aid. The Cold War was only one factor in the chain of events leading to the Suez crisis of 1956 – others were the Israeli-Egyptian dispute, France's troubles in Algeria, and Anglo-American doubts about Egypt's financial soundness and the legality of her nationalization of the Suez Canal; however, one strand in the tangled story was the Soviet success in "leaping over" the barrier of the Baghdad Pact and establishing influence in states like Egypt to the south of it, and the consequent Anglo-French attempts to persuade the U.S.A. that North Africa was being opened up to Communist infiltration. When the crisis came, this argument failed to induce the U.S.A. to support the Anglo-French attack on Egypt (Oct.–Nov. 1956), and the Soviet threat to bombard the invading states with rockets came only when it was clear that their Egyptian operations were in any case going to be ended by U.S. financial pressure and world condemnation; yet the Suez crisis, like the later chain of Levantine upheavals set off by the Iraqi revolution of July 1958, indicated that this was a period when the parties to the Cold War, having run into deadlock both in Europe and in the Far East, might find themselves fighting out their differences as a result of involvement in local conflicts in the Middle Eastern theatre lying in between.

By the end of the 1950's other shifts in the balance had seemed likely, yet in the end failed to come about: the Polish and Hungarian revolts of 1956 had shown the disunity of the Soviet bloc, yet the West had been no more able to act than when the East Germans had rebelled in 1953; at the same time the spectacular Soviet advance in rocket techniques shown by the 1957 Sputnik, and soon followed by the West, underlined that the balance of power had indeed become a balance of terror.

Such factors, and perhaps also the departure of the intransigent John Foster Dulles from the American Secretaryship of State in 1959, led to renewed attempts at reconciliation between the two sides: Khrushchev's talks with Eisenhower at Camp David in America in September 1959 seemed to augur well for the success of the general "summit" conference planned for Paris in May 1960, to which even de Gaulle and Adenauer, who had acquired a reputation for being "difficult" over East–West relations, had agreed. The conference itself turned into a fiasco – Eisenhower refused to apologize for the American action in sending U2 reconnaissance aircraft over Soviet territory, one of which had been shot down, while Khrushchev, possibly under pressure from "tough" elements in the U.S.S.R. and from the increasingly militant Chinese, refused to continue the conference unless this apology were made.

It was in any case doubtful whether summit diplomacy would have brought the two sides closer on fundamentals, especially as President Eisenhower was due to be replaced within a few months (in the event by the youthful and dynamic Kennedy), and the 1960's soon characterized themselves as a period when the Cold War conflict spread to new continents, Africa and Latin America.

In the new states of Africa, where Soviet economic aid and

political example had exercised at least some influence over the more anti-Western leaders, notably Dr Nkrumah of Ghana and President Sekou Touré of Guinea, a major irruption of Cold War politics was threatened by the crisis in the Congo. In the breakdown of public order following the sudden Belgian granting of independence (July 1960), it seemed for a time as though direct Soviet influence would be established over the Lumumba-Gizenga régime in Stanleyville. However, the U.N. action to preserve the unity of the Congo, strongly backed by the U.S.A. and by the majority of the U.N.'s new African member-states, appears to have frustrated this potential Soviet foothold in West Africa; and an apparent Communist advance in East Africa, the People's Republic of Zanzibar proclaimed after a revolution in January 1964, seems at the time of writing (January 1965) to have been "contained" by Zanzibar's union with the more moderate Tanganyika.

More dramatic than the Cold War's spread into Africa was its development in Latin America. Fidel Castro's socialist régime in Cuba, set up after the overthrow of the dictator Batista in 1959, accepted increasing dependence on the Communist bloc both because of Castro's Marxist convictions and because of the U.S.A.'s economic boycott and support for the attempted invasion by Cuban émigrés in April 1961. The Soviet move in November 1962 to install nuclear weapons in Cuba – no doubt an act legitimate in international law, but in substance a provocative challenge to American supremacy in the Caribbean – led to a moment when catastrophe appeared inevitable, but a compromise was reached by which Khrushchev's rockets were removed in return for a formal undertaking by Kennedy not to invade Cuba.

The two world leaders, clearly shaken by this experience of "brinkmanship", explored during 1963 the possibilities of agreement on a number of issues: better mutual communications to prevent war by misunderstanding were established by the

Washington–Moscow "hot line" of June 1963; the Test Ban Treaty was signed in Moscow in August, opening the way to possible agreements on disarmament or at least arms control; and even on Germany – which had been the subject of renewed alarms since 1958, culminating when the Berlin wall was built in August 1961 – possibilities of compromise were being explored by 1964.

This pattern of East–West détente forced on both sides by the "pax ballistica" was confused by other phenomena: continuing conflict in Viet-Nam and the Congo; revolts against the U.S.A. and the U.S.S.R. led respectively by a nationalistic France and a militaristic China; and changes, between November 1963 and October 1964, in the political leadership of America, West Germany, India, Britain and the Soviet Union.

However, the underlying pattern remained one of responsible attempts by the two super-powers to overcome their ideological mistrust in the interests of co-existence, even though either or both of them might still be tempted into making a move against the other in the local crises repeatedly developing in a highly unstable and potentially still explosive world.

CHAPTER 3

THE SOVIET UNION SINCE 1945

by Jack Lively

If we compare the Soviet Union in 1945 with the Soviet Union today, we can have no doubt that many far-reaching changes have taken place, changes which can in part, but by no means wholly, be ascribed to the Russian recovery from war-time dislocation. Some of the tension and much of the terror have gone from the lives of ordinary citizens; the power of the political police has been severely curtailed; there have been changes in the legal system; the structure of economic administration has been remodelled; production has been expanded, even if economic progress has been uneven; and this expansion has been reflected in greater availability of consumer goods.

Many of these changes have been accompanied by an explicit repudiation by Soviet leaders of many of the central features of Stalinist rule. In 1945, Stalin had been hailed as a latter-day Messiah, the builder of communism and the winner of the war. Since 1956, he has been criticized for his "flagrant mis-use of power", his "brutal wilfulness", his "self-deification", to quote only some of Khrushchev's own charges, put forward in his famous secret speech to the twentieth party Congress in 1956.

The changes seem considerable, and what I wish to do in this chapter is to describe them and assess their extent. In making this kind of assessment, there has been some disagreement amongst historians and commentators on the Soviet Union. To some, these changes indicate and exemplify a gradual movement towards democratization which is accompanying, as indeed it must accompany, the growth of industrialization. To others, they have not been changes in fundamentals, and the structure of totalitarian government has been untouched by them. However, before we can assess the significance of the changes, we must see what they have been.

The most obvious feature of Stalinist rule at the end of the war was the extent to which power in the Soviet Union had been concentrated in Stalin's own hands. Stalin had achieved this position of solitary eminence largely through his control of the party machinery. In the years immediately after the Bolshevik revolution of 1917, all opposition parties had been crushed in Russia. But the subduing of opposition to leadership and the elimination of opposing factions did not stop here. It extended to the party itself. Even before Lenin's death, opposition groups within the party were attacked and disbanded, and party discipline was becoming increasingly rigid. However, the whole process was speeded up by the power struggles within the party during the 1920's, the struggle first between Stalin and the Left Opposition and then between Stalin and the Right Opposition. By the end of the twenties, Stalin had emerged victorious. The basis of his victory was his control, as general secretary of the party, over the permanent officials of the party. Indeed, for most of his period of rule, Stalin held no position within the Soviet state, being merely (if that is the appropriate word) a party official. However, since both ideological expectations and political necessities decreed the control of the state by the party, and since Stalin could control the higher organs of the party through his hold over its full-time officials, his position as general secretary was sufficient to ensure him victory over rival leaders whose interests had lain in state policy rather than party organization. His monopoly of power was strengthened by the mass purges of the thirties, one of whose effects was to strip the party almost wholly of its Old Bolsheviks, the pre-revolutionary Bolsheviks, who might have produced a rival to Stalin. Despite Stalin's dependence on the party in his rise to power, by 1945 he was virtually free from any limitation by the party. By this time, he had effective alternative instruments of power, such as the security forces, and was not faced with open debate, still less criticism, in even the highest party organs.

The power struggles of the twenties had naturally involved conflicts over policy. Stalin's own course was by no means straightforward, but by the end of the twenties, he had emerged as the advocate of the rapid industrialization of the Soviet economy. This programme, which was embarked on in the first five-year plan in 1929 was based on two major planks, preference for heavy producer industry and collectivization of agriculture. In effect, the policy demanded the financing of industrial expansion by the restriction of peasant consumption.

During the war, the efforts of the Russian population were sustained partly by an appeal to Russian patriotism and also by the raising of hopes of relaxation in the post-war period. But, in the event, the period between 1945 and the death of Stalin in 1953 was to show that Stalin was bent on restoring the policies and the methods of rule of the 1930's. This can best be illustrated by looking at particular aspects of Soviet politics – economic policy, the régime's attitude towards intellectuals and the power structure.

Economic recovery in the Soviet Union after the war was uneven. In industry, there was some measure of success, but in agriculture the achievement was much less marked. By the end of the 1940's, pre-war industrial capacity had been broadly restored and by the last years of Stalin's rule had been exceeded. But the balance of expansion was still dictated by the preference for heavy producer industry. By 1952, production of producer goods was roughly two and a half times that of 1940, but consumer goods production had been expanded only one and a half times. This politically decided balance is important to notice, for it meant that the industrial expansion was not clearly reflected in a rise of living standards.

Agricultural recovery after the war was much less pronounced. The problem of agricultural production has been and is the most difficult in the Soviet economy. During the N.E.P. period of the twenties the solution had been to leave the land in the hands of the peasantry. But the decision to embark on rapid industrialization, which demanded that the countryside should assume the burden of financing the expansion, required in consequence the strengthening of the economy's agricultural base. The first five-year plan attempted to do this through taking the land out of private hands and putting it into communal and state ownership. Two types of organization, the collective farm and the state farm, were created to do this. The collective farm was in theory communally owned and communally managed. In fact it has been tightly controlled by the state or the party and had very heavy demands laid on it in the way of compulsory deliveries to the state. Not all the land of the peasants who joined collective farms, voluntarily or otherwise, was collectivized. Small plots of land were retained by collective farmers and, although they constitute a constant offence to the régime, they have remained as an example of private ownership of the means of production. In contrast to the collective farm, the land of the state farm was owned by the state and its workers were state employees. This type of farm was moreover controlled directly by governmental organs. Although this type of farm was more in harmony with Communist ideology than the collective, the extension of the state farm sector was halted after 1934 and many of the state farms, which had usually been much larger than the ordinary collective, were split up into smaller units.

This was the pattern of agricultural organization at the outbreak of war. During the war, much of the richest land in the Soviet Union fell into German hands. The occupying forces preserved the collective system as the most effective way of collecting farm produce. Nevertheless, during the chaos of war and the retreat of the German armies, the collective farmers in many cases managed to enlarge their private holdings at the expense of the collectives. In the immediate post-war situation, therefore, the perennial difficulties in agriculture were compounded by the dislocation of occupation. The first response of the régime was to try to recover the land filched by the peasantry, and by September 1947 it could be claimed that 14 million acres had been restored to the collectives. As a longer term measure, the attempt was made to strengthen party representation in the countryside by stepping up recruitment to the party in the collectives, distributing party members so as to form party cells in the maximum number of farms, and strengthening the Communist element in the machine tractor stations. In 1950 a start was made on cutting down the number of collectives and so building them up into larger units as an aid to mechanization and party control. This policy was carried through by Khrushchev who had been transferred from the Ukraine to Moscow in 1949. It resulted in a reduction in the number of collective farms by about two-thirds between 1950 and 1953. Khrushchev put forward another proposal in 1951 for agro-towns, huge state farms centred around a large community of agricultural workers exploiting the land largely by mechanical means. This proposal was shelved but was to be revived by Khrushchev after Stalin's death. By these means, agricultural production was raised to its pre-war level, but stagnated at that level. In 1952, production was barely above the 1940 level whilst industrial production had doubled.

From this brief sketch of post-war development it can be seen that the general trends in economic policy were largely a reflection of those of the thirties. In industry, the emphasis was laid on producer goods; in agriculture, the régime was primarily concerned with strengthening governmental and party control and transferring income from the rural to the urban population.

In his attitudes towards intellectuals Stalin again showed that there was to be little divergence from the pattern of his earlier rule. His criticisms were of course directed towards the old enemies – creative writers, philosophers and economists; but Stalin also turned his attention to other fields such as genetics and linguistics. The objects of his attacks were thus fairly diverse, but generally they can be seen as being aimed at frustrating the spread of Western ideas or ideas not ideologically acceptable to the régime and reasserting party control over literature and the universities.

Again in terms of the power structure, the pre-war pattern reasserted itself. Stalin emerged from the war in a personally impregnable position. He had risen to power through his control of the party machinery, but by this time he was in absolute control of the governmental machinery and the security services as well as of the party. The result of this concentration of power in Stalin's hands was the relative decline in the position of the party, which had in any case been weakened by the decimation of its upper ranks during the purges. Indications of this were that no party Congress was held between 1939 and 1952 although the party rules stipulated that Congress should meet at least every four years, that the Central Committee seldom met in the last years of Stalin, whilst even the Politburo (what was to become the Praesidium of the party and was its ruling body) became little more than a rubber stamp for Stalin's decisions. In this situation, no one could question Stalin's own supremacy, but below him there was a constant struggle for power, a continual manœuvring for his favour and for the position as heir-apparent.

Inevitably, in such a system of court politics, questions of policy became intertwined with questions of personalities. The obvious heir-apparent after the war was Malenkov, but the return of Zhdanov to Moscow seemed to threaten his position. The competition between the two men was revealed in the dispute over the dismantling of German industries as war reparations, a policy which had been carried through by Malenkov. Malenkov's position of pre-eminence under Stalin was restored

G

in 1948 with the mysterious death of Zhdanov, but a new rival was to appear with Khrushchev's arrival in Moscow. Again, personal rivalry was translated into conflicts over policy, this time in the area of agriculture. It seems likely that Malenkov was one of those responsible for the blocking of Khrushchev's agro-town proposal.

However, these were conflicts between princes not challenges to the king. The dominance of Stalin was shown by the adulation which was showered on him at the nineteenth party Congress held at the end of 1952. This Congress and the events immediately after it seemed to foreshadow a revival of all the fear and terror of the purges of the thirties. The Praesidium, as the Politburo was now renamed, was swollen in numbers and new blood was brought into it. This was a favourite Stalinist tactic for weakening any party body and had already been used against both the Congress and the Central Committee. Nor did the policy declarations of the Congress promise any softening of the régime's harshness. The discussions were dominated by Stalin's *Economic Problems of Socialism in the U.S.S.R.*, published just before the Congress, and this could raise no hopes for relaxation, either at home or abroad. More significantly perhaps, at the beginning of 1953 the discovery was announced of a secret conspiracy by a group of nine eminent Soviet doctors, who were accused of murdering Zhdanov and of being American agents. This announcement had been preceded by increasingly sharp calls for the reassertion of party discipline and the need for vigilance in the population. All this bore the hallmark of the treason trials of the thirties and seemed to be the prelude to an attack upon the party leadership and perhaps also to a wholesale purge of the party government and industry. Certainly, Khrushchev was later to claim that the former was true.

At this point, in March 1953, Stalin died, perhaps fortunately for the other party leaders; and his death marked a turning-point in post-war Soviet history. In many important respects, post-war Russia had returned to the policies and atmosphere of the thirties, and the régime seemed about to revert to the most hated of its pre-war features, the purge. The death of Stalin was the signal for changes which ended in the explicit repudiation of the late Stalinist régime.

The immediate problem was to fill the vacuum in leadership that Stalin's death had caused. In a system which concentrates power so much, the problem of succession is bound to be acute. That the party's leaders themselves realized this was shown by their prompt calls on the population to remain calm. Immediately after the announcement of Stalin's death, Malenkov emerged as head of both the governmental and party machines. He was senior secretary of the party and was named as Chairman of the Council of Ministers. This isolated eminence was short-lived, for within a week he was relieved of his party post and Khrushchev took this position over from him. Thus, two powerful leaders emerged at the head of different hierarchies in Soviet society, and the whole emphasis of party propaganda was now laid on "collective leadership".

The immediate concern of the new leadership was to end the apparent threat of a revival of wholesale purges. Even before the announcement of Stalin's death, there had been an abrupt end to the mounting vigilance campaign in the press. After the announcement, there was an immediate reduction in the size of the Praesidium and an amnesty was declared for many prisoners. Within four weeks, it was announced that the Kremlin doctors had been released and that they had in fact been illegally arrested, an announcement which made it plain that the danger of a purge on the Stalinist pattern had passed. In July Beria, the head of the State Security Service and one of the top party leaders, was arrested and in December was tried and executed. Although some of the charges brought against him were no more plausible than those his own security officers had brought against others, his fall indicated that the security services would no longer hold that privileged position, even that dominant position, they had achieved in the last years of Stalin's rule. It was a reassertion of the power of government and party officials against the police. The change of mood was also illustrated by a relaxation in the control of intellectuals, although the party was to reimpose discipline in 1954. The thaw in literature was one sign amongst many that there was general agreement among the new leadership that there must be a halt to the rigidity and terror of the Stalinist régime.

The balance of power that emerged on Stalin's death set the stage for a new struggle for leadership. And once again personality and policy conflicts became intertwined. The competition between Malenkov and Khrushchev centred on disagreements about economic policy and more particularly about industrial policy. In August 1953, Malenkov announced a new consumer goods policy. This did not attack the principle of priority for heavy industry, but it was based on the assumption that the Soviet Union had now a sufficiently strong industrial base to expand the production of consumer goods. This policy, which was an important retreat from Stalin's principles, was grafted on to the 1951–5 Five Year Plan. The success of the new programme depended in part on the ability and willingness of factory managers to abandon long-established priorities and to prefer consumer production to the production of producer goods demanded by the existing plan. It depended too on an expansion of agricultural production. By early in 1954, it seemed that this agricultural expansion depended in turn on the crash programme to open up new land in Siberia and Kazakhstan, the virgin lands programme. However, this resurrected the problem of industrial priorities for it required the considerable expansion of the agricultural machine industry and the consequent diversion of resources from consumer production. This policy conflict resolved itself into a clash between Malenkov, backed largely by state officials, and Khrushchev, who had initiated the virgin lands programme and was backed largely by party officials. The struggle continued over 1954, but had probably been decided by August in Khrushchev's favour. In any event Malenkov resigned as Prime Minister in February 1955 and was replaced by Bulganin.

The next dispute within the leadership was over foreign policy, more specifically over relations with Yugoslavia. Since the 1948 Yugoslav-Soviet split, the position of this maverick Communist state had been one of the thorniest of Russian problems. Khrushchev had shown himself eager to heal this wound and in May 1955 he headed a Soviet delegation to Belgrade which subscribed to a joint declaration insisting on the right of different Communist states to follow their different roads to socialism. A significant omission from the delegation was the foreign minister, Molotov, who had opposed all along the resumption of negotiations with Yugoslavia. Again Khrushchev's view prevailed, and Molotov was forced to repudiate his views in July before the Central Committee.

Thus, considerable changes had taken place by the time the twentieth party Congress met in February of 1956. Some of the tension in Soviet society had been relaxed since Stalin's death; there had been signs of willingness to experiment in the economic and administrative fields; there had been softening of the previously rigid attitudes towards foreign Communist parties; and there had been a continued insistence on collective leadership, even though Khrushchev had emerged victorious when crossed by other Soviet leaders. The twentieth party Congress was to set the seal on many of these trends. In its open sessions, the most significant pronouncements were about foreign policy. The policy of different roads to socialism was reaffirmed and the theory of coexistence, the theory that war between the Imperialist and the Socialist worlds was not inevitable, was set forward. Yet the most sensational part of the Congress was Khrushchev's speech at the secret session, in which he conducted a violent attack on Stalinism and the cult of personality, an attack that stripped away the veil from the Stalinist dictatorship. It is important to notice, however, that Khrushchev's assault had its limits. There was, for instance, little criticism of Stalin's work before 1934; no rehabilitation was granted to his opponents during the twenties, whilst there was praise for his achievements during this time – the creation of a unified party, industrialization and collectivization. It was the post-1934 Stalin who was criticized, the Stalin who attacked the party itself and who decimated its top leadership. It is significant too that Khrushchev attributed all the faults of Stalin's later years to Stalin's own personality and not to any defects in the party or the régime itself.

The twentieth party Congress was to have momentous repercussions and these repercussions were to shake Khrushchev's position at least momentarily. It gave an immense shock to the whole Communist world. Even in Russia itself, it had effects more violent than the party leadership can have foreseen, but the reaction in Poland and Hungary was more obvious and more far reaching. The response in Poland stopped short of revolution, but in Hungary it culminated in the October Revolution. This revolt and the subsequent intervention by the Red Army in Hungary marked the beginning of a partial retreat from the policy positions outlined by the Congress. There followed a hardening of relations with Yugoslavia, a cessation of attacks upon Stalin, attempts to bring foreign parties into line with Soviet policies and a revival of the internal campaign for constant vigilance against bourgeois ideology and the enemies of socialism.

Despite this retreat on the political front, Khrushchev was not deterred from advancing reforms in other areas. In February 1957, he proposed a new and radical reform of the economic administration. This involved a complete recasting of its structure and a considerable decentralization of responsibility. I shall go into detail on this later but it is sufficient to say here that there was considerable opposition to the plan not only amongst the top leadership of the party but also amongst those considerable sections of Soviet society who were to be affected by the changes, for example officials in the central Moscow ministries.

This controversy was the background for a new conflict between Khrushchev and his critics on the Praesidium, led by Molotov and Malenkov. Khrushchev survived this crisis by appealing from the Praesidium to the Central Committee of the party, dominated as it was by party officials loyal to him as party secretary. He was however also dependent on the support of Zhukov and the army. By these means, he was able to expel what was labelled "the Anti-Party Group" from the top leadership of the party. He further consolidated his position by having Zhukov dismissed in October and then in March of 1958 by taking over from Bulganin as Prime Minister.

So, by mid-1958, Khrushchev had established himself as sole leader, and had done this largely by his control over the party apparatus. In a sense, this was a reversion to the past, a reassertion of the old position of hegemony of the party and the party secretary. But in other fields, Khrushchev had shown and was to show himself willing to break with the past.

This is revealed clearly enough if we look at his reorganization of the administration. Traditionally, Soviet economic administration was highly centralized. Khrushchev's scheme, put forward at the beginning of 1957, recast the economic structure on a territorial rather than a functional basis. Broadly, it took away industrial management powers from the central Moscow ministries and placed them in the hands of local bodies. The country was divided into a large number of economic-administrative regions, under separate councils of the national economy; many ministries, both of the All-Union and Union-Republic type, were abolished and their functions transferred to these councils. By these means, it was hoped to increase managerial efficiency by bringing management closer to production, and to make economic planning more realistic by shaping it to local needs and capacities. Hard on the heels of this reform of the economic structure came a change in economic policy. In October 1959 a new programme for expansion of consumer goods production was announced, whilst in August 1960 changes were made in the trading system to render it more responsive to consumer demand. The satisfaction of consumer demands has been the burden of the régime's plans and promises ever since. The aim of catching up with the United States in terms of industrial production and the transition to communism promised in the 1961 programme of the Communist party of the Soviet Union are both pledges to the Russian population that the raising of living standards will be a priority for the régime.

Again, this pledge can only be redeemed if the agricultural problem is solved. In this field too, Khrushchev has shown himself willing to experiment. The campaign, launched in 1954, to produce grain from the hitherto untilled areas of the Soviet Union, the virgin lands, has already been mentioned. In addition, there have been under Khrushchev extensive changes in the organization of the collective farm and the position of the collective farmer. In sum, the general effects of these changes have been to decentralize agricultural planning and to give a much greater initiative to the collective farm, to transfer control over farm machinery from the machine tractor stations to the collectives, to replace compulsory deliveries of agricultural produce from the farms to the state by state purchase and to introduce a system of wage payments to collective farmers which has generally benefited them and brought them into line with the workers on state farms. These changes have been accompanied by a tightening of party control over the collectives, but nevertheless they do constitute a very real break with the past in the degree of autonomy which they allowed the collectives.

In the legal sphere too, willingness to change has been

apparent. In December 1958, the Supreme Soviet passed a number of laws recasting the judicial system. This was the culmination of a series of reforms since the death of Stalin. I have already described the immediate reaction to Stalin's death which ended in the execution of Beria. The limitations then imposed on the security services have since been extended. The continual trials of many leading state security officials have been accompanied by an extensive reorganization of the institutions controlled by the security forces. The number of concentration camps was quickly cut down; by May 1957 for example two-thirds of the labour camps in Siberia had been dissolved. In October 1956, two types of deprivation of liberty were established – ordinary prisons and labour colonies. Conditions in the latter were improved and put under the Ministry of the Interior not under the security services. The vast economic enterprises using prison labour and controlled by the security services were also stripped away from them and passed to normal economic organs. Legal reform has not, however, stopped at restricting the power of the security forces. In 1955, the Procuracy was re-formed with the stated intention of insuring that all breaches of law should be brought before the courts, no matter who committed them. In 1958 came important changes in penal law which, at least formally, give greater legal guarantees to the individual. Some indefinite charges like "counter-revolutionary activities" have been eliminated; reprisals against whole groups or classes are condemned; verdicts must rest on evidence before the court and not simply on a confession; punishments can be imposed only by properly constituted courts. Provisions such as these mark a big step forward from Stalin's day, if in fact they are applied. But there are limitations to be noticed about these impressive-sounding reforms. Any form of political opposition is still heavily punished; many vague and uncertain offences are still part of penal law; the citizens courts set up under the "Parasite Laws" have wide powers and indefinite procedures;

above all, the view of law as a political instrument has not been repudiated and in consequence the position of the party above the law has not been challenged.

These changes in industrial organization, in agriculture and in law are indicative of a mood which has affected many other areas of Soviet thought and action – attitudes towards intellectuals, questions of economic theory, educational policy and so on. They point to a few broad features of Soviet government under Khrushchev's direction. His rule has been flexible and has been based on a willingness to adapt institutions to political, social and economic needs regardless of ideology. Efficiency rather than ideological purity has been the criterion of success. It has, moreover, aimed at a relaxation of the terror of Stalinist days. Although it would not be institutionally difficult to restore the instruments of terror, Khrushchev's régime has created an atmosphere and expectations which would make such restoration difficult. Lastly, his government has shown a much greater responsiveness to the wishes of the population, to its demand for consumer goods for example, than ever was the case in Stalinist times. Yet, despite all these changes, the basic political system has not been affected; or rather, so far as there have been political changes, their effect has been to expunge the political developments of the later years of Stalin's life and to revert to the political system of his early years. Their effect has been, in other words, to reassert the dominant rôle of the party in Soviet government and in Soviet life. Khrushchev rose to power, as did Stalin before him, through his control of the party bureaucracy. On this base, he defeated those whose power rested on control of the army, the security services, and the governmental machine. The rejection of Stalinism, which was so much the personal work of Khrushchev, was a rejection of that period of Stalin's rule when he had turned on the party itself. It was a rejection, not only of terror as an instrument of power, but also of the subordinate position in which Stalin had thrust the party.

It was a reassumption of the party's right to direct and control the machinery and the power of the state. It is possible that further changes might take place which would lessen the tension of ordinary life in the Soviet Union. But the route to political power in Russia still seems to lie through the party, and it is difficult to see how the party can relax its monopoly on power without losing its hold altogether. Liberalization there has been, and it may well be that this liberalization has created hopes and expectations which would be difficult now to deny. However, it would be a mistake to my mind to view this liberalization, even if it is a continuous process, as a move towards any sort of democratic régime in our sense of the term. Khrushchev is not a personal dictator, as was Stalin, but this is not because democratic controls have been established, it is because the party as a whole has resumed its long-claimed function as the guide and director of Soviet life.

Postscript

It is the fate of all who write about the Soviet Union to be overtaken by events. On Friday, 16th October 1964, it was announced officially to the Soviet people that the Central Committee of the CPSU and the Praesidium of the Supreme Soviet had "granted N. S. Khrushchev's request that he be relieved of duties in view of advanced age and deterioration of health". The day before, the news of Khrushchev's deposition had broken on an unsuspecting Western world. Brezhnev, a deputy party secretary, succeeded him in the top party post, whilst Kosygin took over as Prime Minister.

It is difficult, if not impossible, at this point to disentangle the reasons for his fall or even in detail the method of his overthrow. The charges brought against him, of "harebrained scheming, bragging phrase-mongering, armchair methods", seem personal rather than substantial criticisms of his policy. It seems likely that misgivings about the directions in which Khrushchev was leading the country were also important. Internally, the régime faced serious economic difficulties, despite Khrushchev's forecast of a good harvest in 1964, and he had not succeeded in making any considerable cuts in defence expenditure. Probably more important was his determination to formalize the split with China at the meeting in December of the world Communist parties. Whatever the reasons for his fall, the manner of his fall was significant. As in 1957, he lost control of the Praesidium, and again the dispute came before the Central Committee. This time, absent from Moscow at a crucial point, he was unable to carry the Central Committee. The fact that a Soviet leader has been peacefully deposed is new; but that he fell through his failure to retain the loyalty of the top echelons of the party suggests that he had been only too successful in his task of restoring the party to its position of pre-eminence in the Soviet state.

CHAPTER 4

THE UNITED STATES OF AMERICA SINCE 1945

by D. Snowman

It was the best of times, it was the worst of times . . . it was the season of Light, it was the season of Darkness, it was the spring of hope, it was the winter of despair, we had everything before us, we had nothing before us, we were all going direct to Heaven, we were all going direct the other way.

Dickens was writing about Paris and London in the late eighteenth century, but his words could well have been penned with the United States of America, 1945, in mind. That year, 1945, caught the American people in their most exuberantly happy mood at one moment and, at the next, at their most despondent. On the one hand, it was the year that witnessed the triumphant end of the most abhorrent war in history. Before the year was out, vast and speedy demobilization was in full swing and millions of families were reunited for the first time in years; many of the war-time food controls were relaxed; the basic elements of what later became known as the "Fair Deal" were announced by President Truman to Congress. On the other hand, 1945 was also the year in which Franklin Roosevelt – almost a second father to so many Americans – passed from the scene; it was the year that began with Yalta and ended with a series of crippling strikes. It was the year of Hiroshima.

1945 was above all a pivotal year, a watershed in American history. After the First World War, the United States had tried to turn the clock back and act as though a global conflict had not occurred. Tariffs were pushed up and immigration quotas down. International co-operation and assistance were dismissed by Congress as the ravings of a handful of unpatriotic idealists. America, comfortably insulated from the rest of the world, moved towards a state of precarious "normalcy". A decade later, she found herself bewildered by the most devastating depression in her history. Harry Truman, a keen student of the American past, decided, when he became President in 1945, that under no circumstances should the United States repeat the faults of the 1920's. He was anxious to do all he could to discourage the unbridled economic disparities and the self-righteous xenophobia of the days of Harding and Coolidge from reappearing now. On the contrary, the new President wanted to increase the prosperity of *all* Americans within the framework of an *ordered* economy; and he wanted to keep the United States irrevocably committed to the struggle to make the world as a whole a safer and a better place.

He knew what he wanted, but he was not sure that he knew quite how to get it. He had never yearned for the Presidency, and the news of Roosevelt's sudden death on 12th April 1945, thrust him into a state of dumbfounded shock. One of his first biographers has a chapter describing the days that immediately followed Truman's succession; he calls the chapter "President in the Dark". James F. Byrnes, later to be appointed to the Secretaryship of State by Truman, has written that the new President was "overwhelmed by the task that had devolved so suddenly upon him". Truman's first full day in office was, as fate would have it, Friday the Thirteenth. To a group of reporters he said:

Boys, if you ever pray, pray for me now. I don't know whether you fellows ever had a load of hay fall on you, but when they told me yesterday what had happened, I felt like the moon, the stars, and all the planets had fallen on me. I've got the most terribly responsible job a man ever had.

The job was more awe-inspiring to its new incumbent than, in all likelihood, it had ever appeared to any previous President. Only six times before in the history of the United States had a Vice-President been called upon to fill the shoes of a President who had died in office; not for eighty years had the White House been occupied by a man whose home was in a Southern or border State; few other Presidents-to-be (and they were mostly of the dubious character of Chester A. Arthur or Warren G. Harding) had managed to reach their fiftieth birthday largely unknown outside their own States. Before 1945, no President had ever come from Missouri; and no change of President had ever occurred, by either accident or design, during the course of a major war.

Truman knew that his very presence in the White House was shattering any number of traditions. Before his time there was up, he was to break a great many more. By 1952, when he retired from the Presidency, Truman's dream of wholehearted and irrevocable American involvement in the cause of a more peaceful, prosperous and free world was becoming a reality. Greece and Turkey had, as he saw it, been saved from communism by the "Truman Doctrine"; Western Europe was beginning to enjoy a period of economic recovery thanks, in large measure, to the Marshall Plan sponsored by the Administration; and developing nations in many parts of the globe were benefiting from American generosity under the "Point Four" programme. Communist advances had been sharply countered in Berlin and Korea, and democratic self-government had been achieved in India, Israel and a host of other nations in the far reaches of the world. Truman's domestic achievements were not to be quite so studded with success; yet, by the time he left office, much of the welfare policy and economic planning that had first been introduced under the stress of emergency circumstances by Franklin Roosevelt had become widely accepted as part of the permanent economic landscape. Prior to the end of the Second World War, many people assumed that Roosevelt's flirtations with Keynesian economics would prove to have been temporary; 1945 saw the beginning of a sustained effort by the Truman Administration to perpetuate the economic experiments of the Roosevelt years.

The year that Truman took over the Presidency was clearly a pivotal year as far as American foreign policy was concerned; everybody who lived through the year could see that. But in domestic affairs, the President found his ambitious path greatly hindered right from the start. Truman was faced with the vast problems that were inevitably washed in by the wake of a long and costly war. The nation's industries had to be converted to the requirements of a peace-time economy; jobs had somehow to be found for several million demobilized soldiers; the galloping war-time inflation had to be brought under control; food and housing shortages had to be ended. While he was trying to grapple with these problems, the President found himself beset with a string of labour difficulties. Wages had not gone up with prices during the war; many union leaders felt that they should begin to do so now. The United Automobile Workers began a three-and-a-half-month strike in November 1945. Soon after the auto workers went back to the factories, John L. Lewis took nearly half-a-million coal-miners out on strike. The railwaymen, too, came out on strike and only went back when Truman threatened to draft them all into the armed services.

Almost all elements of the American population had economic grievances of one sort or another at this period. Any stable adjustment to the economics of peace-time was bound to take a considerable period of time. Nevertheless, the disappointments and frustrations of millions of disillusioned Americans became focused on the Democratic Administration of President Truman. In the mid-term elections of November 1946, the Republicans wrested control of both the House of Representatives and the Senate from the Democrats. As far as domestic policy was concerned, Mr Truman spent the next two years asking the notoriously conservative Eightieth Congress to do things that they simply refused to do, or furiously vetoing measures that, despite his known opposition, they had passed. There were some very famous showdowns – all lost by the President. Congress, by a two-thirds majority in both Houses, passed, over Truman's veto, a labour law (the Taft-Hartley Act) that severely restricted the power of unions, and a tax bill that gave 40% of its tax relief to the 5% of the working population who earned over $5,000 per annum.

The legislative wheels of the American government seemed sometimes to be grinding to a halt. The frustrated President continued to be the butt of conservative anger and liberal sarcasm. The only people Harry Truman could look upon with certainty as his appreciative friends were the French or the British, the Greeks or the Turks. But none of these people had a vote – and an American Presidential election was looming in the uncomfortably near future.

It was widely assumed in 1948 by the professional pollsters and the voting public alike that Harry Truman would, if renominated by the Democratic Party, lose the November Presidential election. To make matters worse, he insisted that a strong Civil Rights plank be inserted into the platform of his Party. Truman's firm commitment to the cause of equal rights for all Americans, regardless of race, colour or creed, caused the political leaders of a number of Southern States (led by Strom Thurmond, then Governor of South Carolina) ostentatiously to desert the Democratic Party and set up a separate right-wing "Dixiecrat" Party of their own. But the moderates of the Democratic Party were also faced with a split on the left wing of their party. Henry Wallace, the former Secretary of Agriculture and Vice President, had, as Truman's Secretary of Commerce, expressed views in public that were critical of the Administration's foreign policy. Specifically, he felt that a warm and generous approach to the Soviets would be more productive than the suspicious caution that was then characteristic of American foreign policy. He resigned from the Cabinet in September 1946, and, by 1948, was heading a new "Progressive" Party the chief aim of which was to try and maintain peace through understanding with the Soviets. Although (or, possibly, because) 1948 was the year of the Communist coup in Czechoslovakia and the Berlin blockade, Wallace's ideas attracted an enthusiastic following – particularly in the large, liberal, urban areas of the north-east.

Truman, "the little man in the big job", had never exuded from the White House any of the demagogic self-confidence so often displayed by his illustrious predecessor. A self-consciously small-time politician with an undiplomatically sharp if folksy turn of phrase, Truman hardly inspired the unquestioned respect of the Democratic professionals. To them the "Dixiecrat" and "Progressive" defections merely made a gloomy situation worse. Although no incumbent President this century had ever been refused the renomination of his party, the party "pros" were frankly sceptical about Truman's chances of retaining the White House for the Democrats. Some of them, casting about for a more promising candidate, approached General Eisenhower, offering him their support if only he would consent to run as a dark horse candidate. He would not.

With an eye to cutting their losses, the loyal delegates at the Democratic National Convention in Philadelphia renominated Truman for the Presidency. The Republicans, meanwhile, had renominated their 1944 candidate, Governor Thomas E. Dewey of New York, a former Wall Street lawyer, and as respectable and efficient a candidate as ever there was. Truman's running-mate was Senate Minority Leader Alban Barkley of Kentucky, a hard-working Democratic war-horse; the Republican Vice-Presidential nominee was Governor Earl Warren of California, later the Chief Justice of the United States Supreme Court.

The 1948 campaign began on Labour Day, early in September. Dewey's train, the "Victory Special", took the Republican candidate all over the country, but he was careful to avoid too strenuous a schedule. His speeches featured the rather paternalistic hope that, in the few months remaining to the Truman Administration, the President would refrain from doing any serious harm to the nation. Between engagements, Dewey relaxed on the campaign train and mulled over in his mind the Cabinet appointments that he expected soon to be making.

Meanwhile, President Truman, his back against the wall, chased around the country trying to make more speeches to more people on more subjects than any Presidential candidate had ever dreamed of before. He blasted away at the "no good do-nothing Eightieth Congress" and implied that its inertia was Dewey's fault. He kissed babies, tried on cowboy hats, and introduced his wife and daughter to his audiences. The crowds liked his salty anecdotes and forgave him his bad grammar. Truman made himself particularly popular among some of the less fortunate elements in American society, notably the small farmers of the Middle West and the Negroes of Harlem. As the weeks went by, Truman's tub-thumping cliché-ridden campaign picked up steam. Increasing numbers of people felt much the same way as a low-income farmer from traditionally Republican Ohio who was later to say:

I kept reading about that Dewey fellow, and the more I read the more he reminded me of one of those slick ads trying to get money out of my pocket. Now Harry Truman, running around and yipping and falling all over his feet – I had the feeling he could understand the kind of fixes I get into.

The *Chicago Tribune* announced the result a short while before the final votes were counted. "Dewey Defeats Truman" blazed its headlines. Then came the biggest political upset in American history. Truman's whirlwind campaign had kept him in the White House with votes to spare; and his "give 'em hell" onslaught against the Eightieth Congress had produced a Democratic majority in both Houses of Congress. As for Thurmond and Wallace, they had polled a mere $1\frac{1}{2}$ million votes apiece.

If Truman thought that his new mandate would enable him to concentrate on the job of making the United States a better place in which to live, he was soon – and painfully – disillusioned. Within a few months of his return to power, China had fallen to Mao, and the Soviets had exploded an atomic bomb. Truman was once again preoccupied with the details of foreign policy.

Many Americans, stunned by the dramatic Communist successes, began to look for scapegoats. America must have been betrayed by Reds at home, they reasoned, otherwise the avowed aims of her foreign policy could not have failed so dismally. After all, everything she had ever wanted to do before she had just gone ahead and done. This simple-minded belief in American omnipotence comforted many people in 1949; those who held it considered that their views were amply justified by the increasingly hair-raising revelations of the Hiss Case. Alger Hiss, a man of impeccable Harvard–New Deal pedigree, was, for many years, a high-ranking State Department official. Early in 1947, he had left the State Department to become the President of the august Carnegie Endowment for International Peace. In August 1948, he was accused by Whittaker Chambers, a self-confessed ex-Communist, of having given American secrets to the Russians in the 1930's. The charges and the denials came thick and fast. At first, many Washington officials tended to dismiss the accusations as absurd. But in time, Chambers began to adduce evidence that made the case for the defence look very flimsy. Hiss changed his mind, denied previous admissions, and remembered previously forgotten facts. Chambers, equally inconsistent, hammered away mercilessly. The Statute of Limitations prevented Hiss from being indicted for treason. But, after two trials, he was found guilty of perjury in January 1950. His conviction was later upheld by the Supreme Court.

A few days after Hiss' conviction, President Truman announced that work was to go ahead with the so-called "hydrogen or super-bomb". If this announcement was supposed to appease the Red-baiters, it failed. They had had their appetites whetted by the Hiss Case, and were in no mood to stop now. Four days after the hydrogen bomb announcement, the British released the news that Klaus Fuchs, one of her most brilliant war-time atomic scientists, had confessed that he had systematically betrayed atomic secrets to the Russians. The Red-baiters howled long and loud. Not only could America not trust her own leaders but her allies, too, were tainted by Communist subversion. Out of this vindictive and suspicious atmosphere crawled Senator McCarthy.

Under normal circumstances, the inarticulate ravings of the Republican Senator from Wisconsin against alleged (but generally unnamed) Communists in high government posts would have gone unheeded. But McCarthy, in his desire to get national prominence, had hit upon the perfect issue at the perfect time. His first sally was to use a Lincoln Day rally in February 1950, as an opportunity of accusing the State Department of knowingly harbouring Communists and fellow-travellers. When he was asked by a special Senatorial subcommittee under Senator Tydings of Maryland to produce some names, McCarthy proved evasive. He would mention a name but deny that he was making a formal charge, he would ask for more time to collect evidence, or he would, under pretence of a more important engagement, simply not turn up to a scheduled hearing. In July, the Tydings Committee issued a lengthy report which cast a very dim light on Senator McCarthy. In official Washington and among the nation's intellectuals, McCarthy's wild and often unsubstantiated accusations tended to be belittled somewhat scornfully.

But in the far reaches of the nation McCarthy was becoming big news. Unsolicited funds poured into his office from admiring patriotic organizations throughout the country. "McCarthy Clubs" sprang up in all sorts of places. And – a sure sign that the man had "arrived" – McCarthy press conferences were always eagerly attended by hordes of scoop-hungry journalists. It was becoming clear, as the months lengthened into years, that he had become the focus of a small but hysterically vociferous right-wing element in American politics and that, as a potentially influential figurehead, his antics could no longer be dismissed with a casual shrug. For all their dislike of him, many liberals and moderates began to fear him. The Senator was riding high.

Alas for his ego, McCarthy found that the Korean War and, in 1952, the Presidential election were getting most of the big headlines. He did what he could to keep on the front page. He issued a stinging attack on a man regarded by President Truman as "the greatest living American", General George Marshall. Marshall, the war-time Chief of Staff, later Truman's second Secretary of State, father of the European Recovery Programme and, at the time of McCarthy's smear, Secretary of Defence, was deeply respected by most of his countrymen, and by none more so than his former comrade-in-arms, General Eisenhower. Yet such was the sinuous influence of McCarthy that Presidential candidate Eisenhower, when whistle-stopping through Wisconsin in 1952, felt constrained to endorse the Senator's candidature for re-election and to delete a flattering reference to Marshall from one of his own speeches.

"Ike" the popular hero easily defeated the Democratic candidate, Governor Adlai E. Stevenson of Illinois, for the Presidency. His speeches had bristled with indignation at the Truman record on what became known as K_1C_2 – the Korean War, administrative corruption, and, above all, internal communism. The Republican Party won not only the White House but also both Houses of Congress. McCarthy's party was now dominant and he himself was assigned the chairmanship of the Senate Committee on Government Operations. Generally, this chairmanship was not considered one of the most powerful jobs on Capitol Hill. Indeed, Senate Majority Leader Taft had engineered this particular appointment in order to try and bottle McCarthy up in a Committee whose chief job was to scrutinize the intricacies of government spending.

But, in the words of Richard Rovere, "Taft's bottle for McCarthy had never been corked; McCarthy simply poured himself out". He put himself at the head of his Committee's Permanent Subcommittee on Investigations and, ignoring the dull but important work of the parent Committee, carried right on with the Red-hunting that had brought him to national and, indeed, international attention in the previous three years. Although his party now controlled both the executive and the legislative branches of government, McCarthy was relentless in his accusations of disloyalty against personnel in the Department of State and other governmental establishments. He hired a couple of henchmen, Roy Cohn and David Schine, and sent them galavanting around Europe investigating "subversion" in American governmental institutions there. When Schine was drafted into the Army, Cohn did all he could to try and obtain preferential treatment for him; when this failed, McCarthy's Subcommittee proceeded to investigate the United States Army on the grounds that some of its leaders (such, for example, as those who had refused to grant special favours to Schine) were playing into the hands of the Communist conspiracy. The Army-McCarthy hearings of May–June 1954 lasted for thirty-five days and were given nation-wide television coverage. Everybody from the Secretary of the Army down to the humblest mess orderly seemed to be called upon to testify at one stage or other in the proceedings. McCarthy knew that the eyes of the nation (upwards of 20 million pairs of eyes, to be precise) were upon him, and revelled in his own importance. But if millions of people saw him bullying government officials and reprimanding Army Generals, they also saw him raising great numbers of ludicrously fastidious points of order and snarling cruelly at innocent victims. They saw him scowling and fidgeting with obvious boredom whenever it was somebody else's turn to speak. They saw him turn on members of his own Committee and accuse them of trying to hinder his efforts. And they saw the Army counsel, Joseph Welch, looking sadly but unflinchingly down upon McCarthy and saying: "If it were in my power to forgive you for your reckless cruelty, I would do so. I like to think that I am a gentle man, but your forgiveness will have to come from someone other than me."

The Army hearings gave Senator McCarthy more publicity than he had ever, in his wildest dreams, expected to obtain. The whole nation stopped what it was doing (or so he fancied) in order to look at him. But the hearings were also the beginning of the end. His most unattractive characteristics had been exposed for all to see. By December 1954, more than two-thirds of his colleagues were voting for a resolution stating that he had: ". . . acted contrary to Senatorial ethics and tended to bring the Senate into dishonor and disrepute, to obstruct the constitutional processes of the Senate, and to impair its dignity". "Such conduct", the resolution concluded, "is hereby condemned". Three years later, McCarthy was dead.

McCarthyism was one of the more unpalatable episodes that Americans had had to live through during the early fifties. But there were many others. The stresses and strains of the Korean War had caused President Truman to become increasingly high-handed in the performance of his duties. In April 1951 he had, as Commander-in-Chief of the American forces, taken it upon himself to dismiss one of the most revered generals in American history, Douglas MacArthur, for repeatedly expressing views at variance with Administration policy regarding Korea. Truman's unpopularity after this action sank to abysmal depths. His standing in the country was not helped when, a year later, in order to forestall a strike in the nation's steel mills (which were making armaments for Korea), he ordered his Secretary of Commerce to seize the mills and, for the time being at least, run them as a nationalized industry. (The President's strong decision was countered by a 6 : 3 decision by the Supreme Court.) Nothing Truman could do seemed to bring the end of the Korean War any closer. Soldiers came home on leave bringing with them tales of fantastic oriental methods of brainwashing and torture. What they came home to was not a great deal more elevating. They found a country in which larger-than-life gangsters were being exposed in alarming numbers by a Committee headed by Senator Kefauver, and, interminably, innocent and conscientious civil servants and soldiers were being browbeaten by a Committee headed by Senator McCarthy.

By the end of 1954, things at last looked brighter. Korea was a thing of the past; McCarthy had done his worst and been censured by his colleagues. Eisenhower's Cabinet, his business-oriented "team", was busily trying to reduce Federal expenditure, eliminate corruption in government, and tighten up the nation's defences. Eisenhower characterized his political philosophy as "conservative" on economic and governmental matters and "liberal" on social and international ones.

While this formula was attractive to many of his countrymen, the President found, to his eternal annoyance, that he could not please all the people all the time. The conservative in him succeeded in obtaining for certain of the Gulf States the control over (but also, as his "big government" colleagues pointed out in vain, the profits from!) the oil deposits a few miles out from their shores. The liberal in Eisenhower was responsible for the formation of the cumbrously named (and, by conservatives, bitterly criticized) Department of Health, Education and Welfare. The internationalist in him led to the establishment (with the fearfully reluctant acquiescence of Congress) of the St Lawrence Seaway Project. On occasion, the President's schizophrenic political personality would result in terrifying mismanagement. "Ike" the liberal humanitarian was anxious to accede to the pleas of the people of Memphis, Tennessee, that they be given more electrical power. Although the obvious way of increasing power in that area would have been to build up the federally organized Tennessee Valley Authority, "Ike" the doctrinaire conservative gave the necessary contracts to two privately-owned, profit-conscious firms headed, respectively, by Mr E. H. Dixon and Mr E. Yates. The disappointed citizens of Memphis later decided to build their own generator – and Eisenhower was thereupon forced to cancel the Dixon-Yates contracts.

If Presidential initiative in domestic affairs was sometimes a little blunted by Eisenhower's uncertainty of purpose, the administration did, at any rate, present an image of benign, respectable and well-meaning government – something that struck a grateful response in an America that had become saturated with sensationalism and anti-Communist hysteria.

So saturated had it become, indeed, that the nation (though possibly not the Secretary of State, John Foster Dulles) looked on with approval as Eisenhower made increasingly friendly gestures towards the Russians. Stalin had died in 1953 and the new Soviet régime was making unmistakable efforts to thaw the Cold War. By 1954, Eisenhower had obtained the defeat in the Senate of the "Bricker Amendment" (an attempt to wrest considerable control over foreign policy from the President); with his hands now free he set to work with a will on his "crusade" to make the world a safer place. He met with the leaders of Britain, France and the Soviet Union at Geneva in July 1955 and, while no actual agreements were reached, it was widely felt that the meeting (and the famous "Open Skies" proposal which Eisenhower put forward) did contribute to the relaxing of world tensions.

It was at this juncture – and only a year away from the 1956 Presidential election – that Eisenhower had a heart attack. Despite the President's absence from the centre of things, the Administration, energetically led by Vice President Nixon, continued to function with remarkable efficiency. Authorities are divided as to whether this indicates the brilliance with which Eisenhower had organized the government or whether, on the contrary, it indicates that the really important work had always been delegated by the President to other people who now simply continued doing the jobs for which they were already responsible. To be sure, nothing of importance happened during the autumn and winter months when Eisenhower was recovering, but, on the principle that no news is good news, political commentators counted their blessings and wished the President a full recovery.

He was sufficiently recovered by the end of February to announce to an eagerly awaiting nation that he intended to run again for the Presidency. His Democratic opponent was again Governor Stevenson of Illinois. The election came immediately after the revolt in Hungary and the Suez debacle. These events did not particularly help Eisenhower; but they assuredly did harm to the cause of the liberal, internationalist Stevenson. The election, even more than that of 1952, was almost a walkover for Eisenhower. Perhaps the only distinction that could be claimed for the 1956 Presidential election was that it was the first time since 1848 that a party had won the White House and yet lost both Houses of Congress.

Eisenhower's second term as President was to prove far more

tempestuous than his first. The cautious "standpattism" of the first term was not to be repeated; but there was no indication of the storms to come as Eisenhower took the Presidential oath of office for the second time, in January 1957.

Eisenhower's second Inauguration found many Americans basking in unselfconscious materialism. Three families out of four owned a car (emblazoned, in all likelihood, with a pair of vast and gaudy tail-fins); four out of five had easy access to a television set. Credit cards and Billy Graham were all the rage. It is true that some writers were prompted by all this to take up de Tocqueville's thesis that America was too conformist a society (Whyte's "Organization Man" appeared at this period). But most Americans found life comfortable the way it was, and, as they looked around the world, they thought they saw Uncle Sam everywhere in the ascendant. As Eisenhower's enormous popular vote had shown, they viewed with equanimity the prospect of four more years of the same.

They were not destined to get four more years of the same. American prestige abroad was to spend four years rocking unpredictably this way and that. Eisenhower's second term saw revolutions in Cuba, Lebanon and elsewhere. It saw Khrushchev, sometimes jovially arrogant (as when "Sputnik" was launched), sometimes conciliatory (as when he visited "Ike" in 1959), and sometimes downright furious (as when he wrecked the Paris Summit Conference). The Americans – especially in the person of Secretary of State Dulles – could, in their turn, be menacing too, on occasions. But within less than a year of Dulles' death in 1959, Eisenhower, in a burst of idealistic fervour, undertook to present personally the olive branch of American friendship to eleven nations in Asia and Europe. His genial globe-trotting did wonders for American popularity abroad. But, only a few weeks later, the goodwill produced by Eisenhower's trip was somewhat blurred by his bungling uncertainty regarding the U-2 incident and by the humiliating failure of the Paris Summit Conference.

Back home, American and world opinion was shocked a few months after Eisenhower's second Inauguration by the school desegregation crisis at Little Rock, Arkansas; a matter of days later, on 5th October 1957, the Soviets gave America the only inferiority complex she had ever suffered in her history by launching "Sputnik I". Jolts like these were hard to take, and America entered a period of radical and rather gloomy introspection.

Little Rock was a sign for all who cared to read that the Negro demand for equality of opportunity could not maintain its air of courteous respectability much longer. In many parts of the country, but particularly in the Old Confederacy States of the Deep South, Negroes had long been refused many of the rights enjoyed by white people. They were prevented from voting (or even registering to vote) by a bunch of dubious subterfuges like the notorious "literacy tests" and the (recently abolished) poll tax; they were sent to manifestly inferior schools as a result of gerrymandered school districts and rigged entrance requirements. In most of the South, Negroes were systematically excluded from jury service and, consequently, no Negro had any chance of legal redress if robbed or fired or evicted by a white man. In the early decades of this century, literally thousands of Southern Negroes were lynched. Yet so subservient was the black man forced to be that he tended to view any organized attempt to demand equality with the white man as not only dangerous but even, perhaps, somewhat presumptuous.

During the World Wars, Negroes fought and died with their fellow Americans. Presidents Roosevelt and Truman took steps to eliminate glaring racial inequities from the armed forces, yet the demobilized Negro often came home to a community where, except among his coloured friends, he was scarcely more welcome than if he had been a craven malingerer. The stark contrast between the rôle that Negroes had played on the international stage and the one they were reduced to playing in the more benighted communities of their own nation produced among the 20 million American Negroes an unprecedented degree of frustration. In their search for better wages and living conditions, many of them began to move from the rural South to the urban North; in their anxiety to obtain better education for their children, they were brazen enough to request that the latter be admitted to hitherto all-white schools. If the bigoted Southern "redneck" was happy enough to see thousands of Negroes fleeing Northwards, he was most disturbed by the determination of those who remained to enable their children to participate in his exclusive education system. The white Southerner had one valuable card to play: he could quote the 1896 Supreme Court decision (*Plessy v. Ferguson*) which upheld the principle of "separate but equal" facilities for Negroes. In the face of this argument, the onus was on the Negro to prove to an all-white court (if he could so much as gain admission to one) that his separate schools were inferior to the white ones.

The Negro was, however, in no mood to wait any longer. Organized Negro movements began, for the first time, to spring up in large numbers all over the country. Some of these movements were predominantly religious, some were concerned with political rights. Some believed in non-violent social action, some in appealing to the courts. By far the oldest of these movements, the National Association for the Advancement of Coloured People and its (now separate) Legal Defence and Education Fund, had been trying for many years to ameliorate the lot of the downtrodden American Negro through decisions in the Federal Courts. Against overwhelming odds, the NAACP had achieved an odd truce here and a paltry victory there. But its finest hour came in May 1954, when the United States Supreme Court issued its famous desegregation decision in *Brown v. Board of Education of Topeka*. In *Brown*, the Court (in a unanimous decision written by the new Chief Justice, Eisenhower appointee Earl Warren) declared, in part:

> To separate them [Negro children] from others of similar age and qualifications solely because of their race generates a feeling of inferiority as to their status in the community that may affect their hearts and minds in a way unlikely ever to be undone. . . . We conclude that in the field of public education the doctrine of "separate but equal" has no place. Separate educational facilities are inherently unequal.

A year and a half later, segregated seating in the buses of Montgomery, Alabama, was abolished as the result of a Negro bus boycott organized by the Reverend Martin Luther King. The Negro revolt was beginning to become organized and it was showing tangible signs of success.

But a Court decision and a successful bus boycott, while they did wonders for Negro morale, did little to improve the harsh social conditions to which the Southern Negro was subjected. The *Brown* decision was to be implemented not immediately, but "with all deliberate speed" – a phrase which gave a loophole to diehard segregationists. Many of them clung on desperately to this vague phrase and succeeded (and still succeed in some more remote areas) in preventing the integration of educational facilities. No Court decision is any use until it is successfully implemented. At the beginning of the 1957 school year, in September, the Little Rock school board, in compliance with the 1954 decision, decided to admit seventeen specially chosen Negro students to the hitherto all-white Central High School. Governor Faubus, in defiance of Federal law, stationed the Arkansas National Guard outside the school ostensibly "to prevent racial violence" but, in effect, keeping the Negro students from entering the school. After an inconclusive meeting with President Eisenhower and nearly two weeks of national prominence, the Governor removed the National Guard from outside Central High and the Negro students were, at last, admitted to the school. Three hours later, they were sent home for their own safety for, as Faubus had predicted, a huge, angry, segregationist mob had collected outside the school building and was threatening to do violence to the Negro children. There was some evidence that no such mob would have materialized had Faubus quietly let the children enter Central High when they were originally supposed to have done so; the relatively liberal Mayor of Little Rock claimed (with, no doubt, a healthy combination of factual accuracy and civic dignity) that the more unruly elements among the rioting crowds were "professional agitators" imported for the occasion from elsewhere. Whatever the causes of the Little Rock riots, they placed Eisenhower in what was, for him, perhaps the cruellest dilemma of his Presidency. A staunch believer in states rights and a man adamantly opposed, for all his military training, to the use of force, the President was faced with a situation that cried out for strong action from the White House. Eventually, he took a series of actions that, while he felt them to be necessary, were most repugnant to him. Not only did he federalize the Arkansas National Guard (i.e. he put it directly under his own command and out of Faubus's), but, more important, he sent a thousand paratroopers into Little Rock to enforce the law of the land for the duration of the school year.

Little Rock shocked the nation. Liberals were horrified at this graphic example of the strength of segregationist feeling in the South; conservatives throughout the nation were disgusted by the sight of a President mobilizing troops in order to enforce Federal law. Educationalists were disturbed when they heard stories about the miserable schools to which the overwhelming majority of Southern Negroes were still condemned. And millions of Africans and Asians – and, inevitably, Russians – smirked with smug satisfaction when they saw America, the obnoxiously self-righteous "land of the free", struggling against enormous odds to obtain equal educational opportunities for some of her own little citizens.

Americans were deeply sensitive to these foreign criticisms; they were particularly embarrassed by the grievous deficiencies in their education system that all the world now knew about. Their doubts about their education system were reinforced with crushing effect when, on 5th October 1957, the Soviets launched the first artificial earth satellite, "Sputnik I". The Space Age had begun, and the Americans were taken by surprise. A month later came the far heavier "Sputnik II". American self-esteem took a sharp turn for the worse. The most confident nation in the world became the most introspective. Some people feared an imminent Russian invasion, others let out their frustrations by turning savagely upon any available scapegoat (alleged Communists in the State Department and the like). Even some mature and thinking Americans considered "Sputniks I and II" as clear signs that American civilization was doomed to go under to the inexorable and ghastly tide of Soviet communism. It was hard to keep level-headed at such a time. The only phlegmatic thing to do – to congratulate the Russians on a fine achievement, and then get on with the business of the day – was clearly out of the question. After all, the "Sputniks" were not only superb propaganda for the Communists; they also constituted a potential military threat.

The Administration decided to speed up its own space programme. At a deeper level, its chief concern was how best to improve the American educational system. In Washington, facts and figures were quoted with impressive gravity about the number of trained scientists the Soviets were producing, the number of women who were getting degrees in Russia, or the proportion of applied scientists to theoretical ones and of scientists to arts students at Moscow University. Within months, Congress had passed the National Defence Education Act which, among other things, appropriated money for what were popularly dubbed

"Sputnik Scholarships". These were to be given to young Americans studying physics, mathematics, foreign languages, political science – anything remotely related to the problems of national defence. Large government grants to university physics departments and greatly increased Defence Department contracts also followed in the nervous months following the Russian "Sputniks", as did the creation of a new White House body the President's Science Advisory Committee.

Little Rock and "Sputnik" shocked Americans. These two incidents that occurred in the autumn of 1957 combined to set the United States upon a course from which there was no turning back. For it was clear that it would be a long time before Americans would be able to sit back and preen themselves on the justice and stability of their social and educational systems, and, perhaps, they would never again be in a position to moralize about the deficiencies of those parts of the globe that were not under American influence. At home, the Negro now knew that he had not only the sympathy of the Federal Courts but also the might of the Federal Army behind him. As for foreign relations, all but the most sceptical were forced to admit for the first time that, while the Russians might be evil, they were not necessarily as inefficient or as uneducated as they had traditionally been pictured.

The Negro revolt had gone from strength to strength. Café "sit-ins" were organized in 1960 – and a number of café-owners were obliged either to serve Negroes or to shut their doors entirely; a year later, the Congress of Racial Equality arranged a series of "freedom rides" – and, after much hatred and some blood had been spent, all facilities connected with interstate buses were desegregated; in September 1962, after a series of incidents reminiscent of Little Rock, the University of Mississippi ("Ole Miss") admitted a Negro student. Just under a year after the "Ole Miss" crisis, in August 1963, a quarter of a million people representing a great number of civil rights groups met at a giant rally in Washington to register their eloquent and moving plea for the many rights that were still denied to American Negroes. President Kennedy listened to their plight with a sympathetic ear and recommended to Congress the strongest civil rights measure the country had ever seen. Within a year (helped, no doubt, by the great tide of pro-Kennedy sentiment that swept the country in the months after the President's assassination and, of course, by the political wizardry of his successor, Lyndon B. Johnson) that bill had been passed in largely unaltered form by an otherwise rather reactionary Congress. Today, integrated civil rights organizations are operating in many parts of the country (but particularly in the South), and their activities are most varied. Some of them send groups of Whites and Negroes to previously all-white hotels or restaurants; by these actions, they test the degree to which the "public accommodations" clause of the 1964 Civil Rights Act is being implemented. Others devote their energies to the attempt to encourage voter registration and political education among Negro communities. There are also a number of bodies concerned with urban renewal, slum clearance, and better educational and medical facilities for Negroes.

Much remains to be done. Only a minute fraction of Southern Negroes are yet able to vote or get a schooling approaching the standards given automatically to their white neighbours. Violence and bloodshed against Negroes, particularly in the South, are still not uncommon. Indeed, the very fact that the Negro is so vehemently demanding rights where he has long been denied them causes social tensions and violence that would probably not otherwise occur. But the movement begun by *Brown v. Board* and Little Rock is on the offensive and is showing results. The Negroes are more confident than ever before that, in the words of the hymn they sing as a sort of rallying cry: "We shall overcome".

The effects of "Sputnik" are harder to assess. America entered the "Space Race" with the grim determination to overtake the Russians. She has, to date, sent fewer men for fewer hours into space than they have. But most Americans, in the years following "Sputnik", took comfort from the fact that (notably under the Kennedy-Johnson Secretary of Defence, Robert MacNamara) the entire defence structure of the nation was thoroughly reviewed and rationalized such as greatly to reduce any serious threat of nuclear annihilation at the hand of the Soviets. Popular American attitudes towards the Soviet Union began, after "Sputnik", to come to grips with the idea that not all Communists were necessarily the irresponsible and ignorant war-mongers they had frequently been depicted as being prior to October 1957. This popular misconception tended, gradually, to give way to the considerably less dangerous one that, behind the Kremlinological personality struggles, the U.S.S.R. was really run by a bunch of computer-like technological geniuses.

"Sputnik" had its effect, too, on those more sophisticated Americans responsible for the formulation of American foreign policy. In the years following 1957, they tended increasingly to eschew any "total" solutions to the problems of East–West relations. The world has seen, instead, a series of hesitant, groping steps towards some sort of *détente* between the two superpowers. Sometimes (the Cuba crisis of October 1962 was such a time), even this seemed too much to ask. On other occasions – helped by Russian differences with China and some of the European satellites – a real Russo-American breakthrough seemed imminent. The great lesson that American policy-makers learned in the years following "Sputnik" was to afford to the Russians a mature and ungrudging respect. The Test Ban Treaty of 1963, the greatest achievement of the Kennedy administration, would have been impossible without that respect.

The Eisenhower years ended and America embarked upon a new and uncharted course. She watched, with not a little scep-

ticism, as her youngest elected President (and the first Catholic
ever to hold that office) took over the toughest job in the world.
At his Inauguration in January 1961, John F. Kennedy struck
a noble and hopeful note. He expressed his urgent desire that,
under his Presidency, the nations of the world would come together and, in joint harness, "explore the stars, conquer the
deserts, eradicate disease, tap the ocean depths, and encourage
the arts and commerce". In his sanguine anxiety to get on at
once with the new job, Kennedy added, with words that have
taken on a new and tragic twist: "All this will not be finished in
the first one hundred days. Nor will it be finished in the first one
thousand days, nor in the life of this Administration, nor even
perhaps in our lifetime on this planet. But let us begin."

President Kennedy did not have time to do much more than
begin. Thirty-four months after his Inauguration, he was dead.
But in the short time that he was President, he left his mark
indelibly upon the office that he had held and the nation that he
had led.

From the first, he was anxious to continue the dialogue with
the Soviet Union. He even dared in his Inaugural Address, to
hope that both sides would be able to "formulate serious and
precise proposals for the inspection and control of arms – and
bring the absolute power to destroy other nations, under the
absolute control of all nations".

The Administration did not get off to a good start. The in-
decisive "Bay of Pigs" invasion of Cuba brought down much
criticism upon the head of the bewildered President. But he
grew in his job. When the supreme test came, Kennedy did not
falter. He faced the Cuba missile crisis of October 1962 with
cold firmness and, perhaps more remarkably, showed patient
magnanimity to Khrushchev in the months following the latter's
humiliation. This understanding approach led to the Test Ban
Treaty and to a host of smaller events all suggestive of a real
thaw in the Cold War.

Kennedy's accomplishments on the domestic front were somewhat less impressive. Elected President by a hairbreadth over former Vice President Nixon, he was thwarted, throughout his period in office, by a nominally Democratic but markedly conservative Congress. His hopes for obtaining legislation that would increase medical aid for the aged, improve educational facilities for the young, produce more attractive towns for urban America, and ensure a more stable income for rural America, were repeatedly frustrated by adverse majorities on Capitol Hill. The few tangible legislative achievements – notably the Peace Corps and the Trade Expansion Act – were generally related to foreign rather than domestic policy. Kennedy's importance at home will probably prove to have been not so much what he did as what he made possible. By the time of the President's assassination in November 1963, his vigorous, progressive approach to domestic affairs was clearly far more acceptable to the nation than it had been when he had taken office. Not without reason, he assumed that the 1964 election would give him an eloquent mandate to carry on with his forward-looking policies.

When that election came, it was won – by one of the most overwhelming landslides in American history – by his successor. Lyndon Johnson projected a very different image from that of Kennedy. Kennedy was a Northern intellectual, Johnson a folksy Southwesterner; the former would read (and write) books and policy statements, the latter would look to the telephone as his chief source of information; the Kennedys would invite Nobel prize winners to dinner, the Johnsons would slap thighs, wear high hats, and lap up whisky with their cowboy cronies. But, despite these outward differences, there were two things that these men shared. Both were ruthlessly thorough politicians fascinated by power, and both irrevocably committed to the patient and progressive policies outlined in Kennedy's Inaugural Address.

At the time of writing, Johnson's annihilation of his Republican opponent, Senator Goldwater, is still hot news. Much of America and most of the world is relieved that the isolationist, xenophobe, white supremacist, anti-urban, anti-welfare, protagonist of states rights forces that projected Senator Goldwater into national prominence have been so resoundingly defeated. American liberals are delighted that their opponents have had their noses rubbed painfully in the mud that they spent much of the campaign slinging at President Johnson. American conservatism was almost totally discredited in the 1964 election; in the years since Little Rock and "Sputnik", to be sure, it had never accumulated much respectability to lose. In the years following the Presidency of John F. Kennedy and the candidature of Barry M. Goldwater, it will in all probability retire to lick its wounds.

In the two decades since the end of the Second World War, America came to accept with increasing enthusiasm the two great innovations of the Presidency of Franklin D. Roosevelt: progressive social policies strongly spiced with Keynesian economic measures, and the irrevocable commitment of American men, money and prestige to the international community of which the United States was a part. By the same token, she rejected the last-ditch efforts of conservatives to reject these policies. The only place where, throughout two decades, American conservatism continued to wield power was in the disproportionately rural Congress. The other two branches of government, the Presidency and the Federal Courts, tended, within the framework of the American political spectrum, to lean towards the left of centre. Consequently, the period 1945–64 saw not only a clash between liberalism and conservatism, but also one between the Presidency and the Courts on one hand and the Congress on the other. While these clashes may have prevented dangerous impulses from carrying all before them, they also had the result, all too frequently, of bringing the machinery of government almost to a standstill. It is possible that the relatively liberal Congress voted into power on President Johnson's 1964 coat-tails will prove more amenable to presidential leadership than its more stubborn predecessors. Even if it does not, a series of Supreme Court decisions ordering the reapportionment of Congressional seats on the basis of recent census figures will, in all probability, have the eventual effect of bringing Congress into line with the more liberal thinking that is shared by so many Americans in 1964.

On the walls of the National Archives building in Washington is the inscription, from Shakespeare: "What's past is prologue". Future historians may well view the years 1945–64 as the mere prelude to a period of inspired social reform, as a necessary preparatory step towards the eventual emergence of what President Johnson calls the "Great Society". Whether Johnson's rosy but hazy picture of America's future will prove to have been accurately prophetic or whether the "Great Society" was little more than a campaign slogan, only time can tell. But if the progressive elements in American politics are serious in their professed aims, they will not have to cast around far in their search for problems to solve. There are the identical, sprawling, slummy cities that need to be cleansed and beautified, there are the thousands of farmers who can produce surpluses but find it well-nigh impossible to earn a living, there is the dirt and squalor of the old mining town and the Indian pueblo, and there is a degree of racial injustice unparalleled in the modern world outside South Africa and her neighbours. Whether these problems will be solved, we can not predict. But the hindrances to their solution were, in the eloquent repudiation of Goldwaterism in the 1964 election, largely eroded away. If the creeky political machinery can be adjusted to meet the needs of the day, then the "Great Society" might yet become a reality.

CHAPTER 5

THE EMERGENCE OF MODERN CHINA

by Victor Purcell

"The image of China, which is likely to be on most people's minds, varies from time to time but is always related to current politics – especially those of the United States. Unless they are specialists in Far Eastern Affairs they are likely to receive most of their impressions from the press." So the current picture of China is of a huge totalitarian giant with a population approaching 700 million which is about to overflow its borders and to occupy huge areas of its surrounding territories in order to provide for its surplus population. China is furthermore pictured as being opposed to any pact with the West involving nuclear disarmament since it is confident that if the worst came to the worst it (and it alone perhaps) would survive an atomic war. Furthermore China is invariably pictured as subject to great internal stresses and strains on account of its economic planning, and its population is often reported to be on the verge of starvation.

How far is this a true picture? Personally I regard it as a distorted and highly misleading one, but in order to demonstrate why I think so I must give you a summary of modern Chinese history as a background for my reasons.

China's civilization first arose in an angle of the Yellow River and was extended by "civilizing" the surrounding more primitive peoples. China's history, according to the most up-to-date scientific opinions, goes back to about 1500 B.C., and the inscriptions on what are known as the "oracle bones" of Honan are in characters which are basically the same as the modern Chinese written language. China was first unified under the Ch'in dynasty (221–206 B.C.) and reached the dimensions of what used to be known as China Proper (the original eighteen provinces) in the Han dynasty (206 B.C.–A.D. 220) The extent of Chinese territory fluctuated with the rise and fall of dynasties but reached its maximum extent in the eighteenth century during the Ch'ien Lung reign (1735–96) when China filled up the vacuum in Central Asia created by the break-up of the nomads (the Mongols and other uncivilized tribes who had conquered China periodically over the centuries), at the same time that Russia was beginning to advance with like intent from the other side of Asia.

For many hundreds of years China was by far the most important country in the huge region beyond the Himalayas and for this reason regarded itself as the "Middle Kingdom" and as the only source of civilization. The surrounding countries were at one time the tributaries of the Chinese Emperor – except Japan which was able to keep its independence because of its isolation. But even Japan derived its literary culture from China, though it set its own individual stamp on what it borrowed.

Western intercourse with China was for the first two thousand years or so of their common history of a very tenuous nature. Although silk was imported into the Roman Empire in large quantities through third-parties, the two empires had scarcely any knowledge of one another's existence or location. When in the thirteenth and fourteenth centuries the Mongols conquered the greater part of Asia and even threatened Europe, there was a temporary lifting of what I may call the "Bamboo Curtain" and European merchants and missionaries made their way in considerable numbers into China. Then with the fall of the Mongol dynasty that was ruling China and the succession of a native one (the Ming 1368–1644) the Curtain came down again. It was not actually lifted at anytime, but was penetrated by the

Jesuit missionaries who arrived in China at the end of the six-teenth century. Just as Marco Polo had been three hundred years before, the Jesuits were impressed by the superiority of China to Europe in nearly every respect.

This brings me to a very important fact regarding China which is, in my opinion, at the bottom of its present difficulties. It is this. Up to, and into, the period of the Renaissance in Europe, China was in advance technologically of that Continent. A great number of inventions and discoveries had originated in China and had travelled to the West over periods ranging from one to ten centuries. Among these were the Chinese decimal-place values (decimals in their earliest form) and the basic knowledge of the magnetic phenomena (including the com-pass). Furthermore (as Joseph Needham, mentions in his great work, *Science and Civilisation in China*) many other inventions including efficient harness for draft-animals (avoiding the ob-struction of their wind-pipe as under the old method) which transformed European agriculture, the technology of iron and steel (including cast iron), deep-drilling for oil, gunpowder, paper (A.D. 105), printing by movable type, the mechanical clock, basic engineering devices such as the driving belt, the chain-drive, together with the segmental arch-bridge and naut-ical techniques such as the stern-post rudder all came from China. Moreover inoculation against small-pox and other dis-eases was in use in China from the early 1500's long before it was introduced into Europe, and China also contributed several ideas to astronomy that have now superseded earlier European conceptions. The only European techniques which travelled in the reverse direction to China during this long period were three in number – namely the crankshaft, the force-pump for liquids and the screw.

Yet in spite of being so far ahead of Europe in technology, China was now behind it in science having missed the great de-velopment which took place in Europe in the sixteenth and seventeenth centuries which we call the Scientific Revolution. This was due to the fact that Chinese society was more stable than European society and there was no stimulus for the kind of vast transformation in outlook that took place in Europe. But it meant that China failed to experience an industrial revolution which, from the eighteenth century onwards, had completely altered the nature of European society. So long as China remained isolated from the West behind her "Bamboo Curtain" she was almost completely unaware of what had been happening elsewhere – and in any case indifferent to it. But when in the Opium War with Britain of 1839-42 China's isolation was rudely shattered, it was obvious that China was inferior to the West in respect of technology, and in consequence, in military power.

China's history since then has been basically of her attempts to modernize herself to meet the Challenge of the World. For decades she failed to make any progress in this direction. The reasons for this were several. One was her huge extent and diversity; another was the presence on the throne of a decadent alien dynasty (the Ch'ing or Manchu) and the fact that the country was ruled through highly conservative Chinese Mandarins who were for long opposed to any innovations. Even when they did at last see the necessity of importing Western techniques, the Chinese went about it in a piece-meal and half-hearted fashion.

Now, in the meantime, China's smaller neighbour, Japan, was being subjected to a similar experience – and responding to it in a very different manner. Japan was first discovered by Europeans (the Portuguese) about 1540, and for the next seventy years or so was visited by Europeans – Spanish, Dutch and English – in increasing numbers. Alarmed by what they considered to be the aggressive intentions of the Europeans, especially the Spanish, using their missionaries as the spearhead of an intended conquest, the Japanese, in the 1630's, withdrew behind what I will, for convenience sake, again refer to as a "Bamboo Curtain". No Japanese were allowed to go abroad on pain of death if captured, and no sea-going ships were permitted to be built. For over two hundred years the Japanese remained behind their Curtain. But they retained one little peep-hole on the outer world, namely the small artificial island of Deshima in Nagasaki Bay where the Dutch were allowed to carry on trade and it was they who kept the Japanese informed as to developments in Europe and elsewhere. Then in 1853, the American Commodore Perry with a squadron of modern ships arrived off the coast of Japan and demanded in the name of the President of the United States that the Japanese should open their ports to foreign trade. There ensued a long period in which the Japanese were divided as to the course they should follow, but having, as they felt, no alternative, they decided in the end to bow to the greatly superior military force of the West. But in doing so they determined to adopt from the West the techniques which made it powerful but at the same time to retain their native institutions and national outlook. This, in what is known as the Meiji Restoration (1868–1912), they succeeded in doing with a surprising measure of success. They modernized their navy on the model of the British navy and their army on that of the Prussian army – the most powerful and efficient of the Western armies and navies of the time. But they also adopted some of the Western ideas of law and government and even introduced a new constitution, though they kept the real power in the hands of the Emperor. Before the end of the century, the Japanese had so reformed their legal system that the foreign Powers no longer had any excuse for retaining extraterritorial rights – in particular the right of foreign consuls in Japan to try law cases involving their own nationals. Japan also rid herself of unequal tariff agreements. By the 1890's Japan was definitely a "Power" on her own account. She had greatly developed her industries and in order to find new markets abroad she now embarked on a policy of expansion (i.e. "imperialism") to find markets for their products abroad. This brought her into collision with her old teacher, China, over Korea (which Japan wished to bring into her own sphere of influence) and in the war which took place in 1894–5 she utterly defeated the Chinese whose attempts at military and naval modernization turned out to be a sham.

What, you will ask, had China been doing all this time? For the reasons I have mentioned, China's response to the Western challenge was extremely slow. The reigning dynasty was further weakened by the great Taiping Rebellion (1848–62) and the Manchus, in order to save themselves, became increasingly subservient, first to the Western Powers and then to Japan. After the great defeat at the hands of Japan in 1895, a reform movement got under way and resulted in what is known as the "Hundred Days" in 1898 when the young Kuang Hsü Emperor issued a rapid series of edicts introducing widespread reforms. But these mostly remained on paper, for in September of that year the Empress Dowager, who felt her position threatened, staged a *coup d'état*, imprisoned the Emperor, and repealed most of his reform edicts.

China was now so weak that it looked as if she must split up into pieces at any moment, and the foreign powers were already dividing her territory into "spheres of influence". The foreigners had obtained concessions already for railways and mining in China which threatened the latter's sovereignty. Then in 1900, what is known as the Boxer Uprising took place. This was a spontaneous movement among the peasantry led by a branch of the old White Lotus Society which had started rebellions in the past. In the final stages the Manchus assumed the leadership for the Boxers had no real plans for governing China. Theirs was merely a negative anti-foreign movement whose resentment was directed in the first place against the foreign missionaries since they were the most evident and accessible expression of the foreign attempt to control China. The Boxers collapsed, an allied force occupied Peking, and a huge indemnity was imposed on China – already paying another indemnity to Japan for her defeat in 1894–5. But the foreign powers had learnt a lesson from the Boxer Movement, which is usually regarded as the birth of nationalism in China, namely the impractibility of partitioning China in face of popular opposition.

The Manchus now made a big show of reform, though still aiming at retaining the real power in their own hands. But they were decadent and discredited, and the dynasty only lingered on ineffectively until the 1911 Revolution occurred.

The 1911 Revolution was inspired by Sun Yat-Sen and other Chinese revolutionaries, but they lacked effective control over the armed forces. The result was that Sun Yat-Sen had to give way to Yuan Shih-K'ai, a mandarin who had built up modern forces under his personal control, and he now became President of the Republic. The Manchus abdicated as from 1st January 1912. Having defeated the forces loyal to the Kuomintang (Sun Yat-Sen's Nationalist party) in 1915–16, Yuan Shih-K'ai attempted to restore the empire in his own person. But although he accepted the iniquitous "Twenty-one Demands" which the Japanese sought to impose on China in 1915 (taking advantage of the fact that Britain, France and Russia were at war with Germany) he failed to secure Japanese support for his plans. He worshipped at the Temple of Heaven (which only the Emperor was allowed to do) and invented a reign-title for himself, but, frustrated at every point, he died a broken man on 6th June 1916.

From the death of Yuan Shih-K'ai dates the era of the "war lords", that is to say the splitting up of China under local generals or even bandit-chiefs who were working in cliques, each in collusion with one group or other of the foreign powers. In 1921 Sun Yat-Sen had established himself precariously in Canton, but when he died in March 1925, he had never been in effective control of the affairs of his country.

Sun Yat-Sen, however, had bequeathed to his party, the Kuomintang (KMT), what is known as the Three Principles of the People. These Principles were Nationalism, Democracy and "the People's Livelihood", or Economics. These principles, he held, were the ones that should direct China's future. Upon the basis of these Three Principles, Sun's successor, Chiang Kai-Shek, reorganized the party and started a great drive from Canton to the North in 1926, with the object of reuniting China. This move received a wide measure of popular support from the Chinese people who were tired of the rule of the "war lords" and of subservience to the foreigners.

But in the meantime a new element had come into being in Chinese politics. This was communism. The Chinese Communists date their revolution from what is known as the Fourth of May Movement of 1919 – a spontaneous student demonstration against Japan and the Twenty-one Demands, but this was a Nationalist and not a Communist demonstration, and it was not until 1921 that the Chinese Communist Party (the CCP) was founded. To begin with the CCP attracted comparatively few members, but in 1923 and 1924, when Sun Yat-Sen, disappointed in his hopes of support from the "democratic" Western Powers, turned to Russia for assistance, the Communists attained a new importance. The Russians sent advisers to Canton (Borodin and others) and the Communists obtained a foothold in the left wing of the KMT.

But Chiang Kai-Shek was no Communist; he belonged to the extreme right wing of the KMT, and he was resolved to counter the Communist bid to take over the party. In April 1927, when he was marching towards the north, he came to an agreement with the financiers of Shanghai (Chinese and foreign) whereby he undertook, in consideration of large financial subsidies, to liquidate the Communists, whether inside or outside the KMT. In the purge which followed, those Communists who escaped Chiang's vengeance took to the hills with their comrades and formed groups out of reach of Chiang's troops. In the meantime Chiang had formed a KMT Government of his own at Nanking which was able to overwhelm the left-wing government set up at Wuhan. Henceforth Chiang was master in China, completed his drive to the north, and gave China a greater unity than she had known since the Manchu dynasty.

The years 1927 to 1931 were the ones in which the new KMT Government at Nanking had an uninterrupted opportunity to put their Three Principles into practice. But, of the three, the first – nationalism – was the only one they made any attempt to implement. In doing this they claimed all persons of Chinese race, wherever they might live or whatever their other national status, as Chinese citizens, and this led to collision, not only with the Colonial Powers of South-east Asia, but also with Independent Thailand, and alienated the sentiment of the region generally which was afraid of China's new pretensions. The second principle, Democracy, was never brought into being and the KMT Government remained a "Party" dictatorship right down to the moment of the Communist Victory in 1949.

The Third Principle of Sun Yat-Sen was "Economics". But here Sun had been uncertain. He was Socialist in outlook but felt that capitalism still had a part to play in the modernization of China. Chiang and his associates (the Four Families – Chiang, Kung, Soong and Ch'en) were all capitalists and they controlled the greater part of China's finance and industry. What Chiang attempted to do was to modernize China within the framework of foreign capital investment, of which the most important was now that of Japan, centred in Manchuria, but America and Britain were the biggest investors elsewhere on the cultural front; Chiang was in close association with the United States. He himself was a Christian (converted by Americans to Methodism about 1931) and so was his wife (a "Soong Sister"). The American influence was therefore paramount.

But Chiang had Japan to compete with. Japan had defeated Russia (a European Power) in 1904–5 and had thus become the hope of many Asians who hoped to make themselves independent of the Western Powers. But Japan herself in becoming a Power had adopted the ambitions of imperialism. There was a conflict of opinion in Japan in the 1930's between the liberals who believed in peaceful expansion and the Army who pinned their faith on military conquest. In 1931 the military took over Manchuria, setting up the former "boy" Emperor of China (P'u Yi) as the puppet Emperor of "Manchukuo". The League of Nations' intervention was ineffectual. Then in 1937 the Japanese extended their operations by occupying the ports and economic centres of China, and Chiang and his government fled to Chungking. The Japanese were not foolish enough to attempt to "conquer" China (which would have entailed taking over all her problems – if they were successful in subduing her) but wished to reduce the KMT Government to complete subservience to Japanese interests. Chiang resisted – but whether he would have done so without Communist pressure is another question.

For many years Chiang tried to suppress the Communists. They had formed so-called "liberated areas" in remote places, and against these Chiang conducted a series of campaigns endeavouring to enclose the Communists in a steel trap. So nearly did he succeed that in 1934, the Communists, led by Mao Tse-Tung, carried out what is known in Chinese history as the "Long March". Their journey carried them first south and west, through the borders of Tibet and the Gobi Desert, and then eventually to the north-west where they were able to take refuge in comparative safety in the region of Sian, out of the immediate reach of Chiang's armies. In this region, as they had in their previous retreats, the Communists experimented with their theories, notably in land reform.

In 1936 Chiang Kai-Shek was kidnapped by Chang Hsüeh-

Liang, a northern warlord, while conducting his campaign against the Communists, and in captivity he was compelled to come to an agreement with the CCP to form a united front against Japan. This nominal alliance subsisted through the war with Japan (1941–6), but at times it was wearing very thin.

The outbreak of the Pacific War in 1941 meant that China was now one of the Allies against the Axis and Japan. But the KMT were much more concerned with their differences with the Chinese Communists, and stored up most of the arms and money they received from the United States for use in the coming civil war which both sides felt to be inevitable once the Japanese were defeated. All that Chiang Kai-Shek's armies did during the Pacific War (according to General Stilwell, the general representing America in the Far Eastern Zone) was to "contain" eight Japanese divisions.

When the Japanese surrendered there was a period of truce between the KMT and the Communists during which Mao Tse-Tung visited Chiang Kai-Shek, but when the Chinese Government moved back to Nanking from Chungking (after eight years of exile) it was to continue preparations for the struggle. The mission under General Marshall despatched to China by President Truman failed to bring about a compromise between the two sides and in 1946 the civil war was reopened in earnest. Chiang Kai-Shek took an uncompromising line in the belief that the United States had no alternative but to support the KMT whatever line it chose to follow. The U.S.A., however, stopped short of all-out support for Chiang which would have involved the employment of American ground troops – a course which American public opinion would not sanction.

The civil war in China continued for the next three years and was marked by the failure of the KMT on all fronts. Chiang Kai-Shek effected no internal reforms of importance and maintained his own autocracy. The end came in 1949 when the Communists armies poured down over the Yangtze and Chiang fled to Formosa. In 1951, during the Korean War, the United States Seventh Fleet stationed in the Formosa Channel, were ordered to prevent any invasion of Formosa from the mainland with the result that the Communists could not overrun it, and the Government of Formosa was recognized by the United States as being the legitimate government of China, and it continued as such to occupy China's seat in the United Nations. Britain, on the other hand, recognized the People's Republic of China at Peking.

When the Communists took over in 1949 many observers prophesied that when land reform had been carried out the revolution would be at an end. Agrarian trouble had been a recurring feature of Chinese history when the bulk of the land had once more got into the hands of a minority of landlords, but the KMT (being in alliance with the landlords) had failed in spite of promises to do anything effective towards a solution of the problem. The Communists, now in power, proceeded to put into operation the far-reaching plans for land reform which they had already tried out over the years in the "liberated" areas under their control. They dispossessed the "landlords" (i.e. those who took no direct part in farming their land but lived on its income in the cities) and the "rich peasants" (who took a share in farming their land but left most of the work to managers and hired labour), but left the "middle peasants" (those who owned a considerable piece of land but did most of the farming themselves) in possession of their property. The confiscated land was distributed to the "poor peasants" and to those who owned no land at all.

But far from being over, the Communist Revolution had only just begun. The Communist plans were ambitious and these were no less than to carry out the modernization and industrialization of China on a vast scale. The "bourgeois" revolution of 1911 onwards (as they called it) had failed to bring China into the modern world within the framework of capitalism, and the

Communists now proposed to attempt it under the Communist system, which being totalitarian, they regarded as more efficient than capitalism, besides being more just. The People's Government determined to dispense with foreign capital and to rely on increasing the agricultural output of China. With the money received from the export of their surplus agricultural production they intended to purchase the capital goods (machinery, etc.) necessary for exploiting China's vast natural resources (coal and other minerals, etc.). But the farming of small plots of land, even under a co-operative system, was quite inadequate for the purpose and the Communists therefore planned measures leading to complete collectivization.

In 1958, the measures hitherto taken had been so productive of results that the Communists planned what was known as the Great Leap Forward. The overall intention had been (in simplified language) to bridge the gulf caused by the fact that China had missed the Scientific Revolution within a single generation, if possible, reaching a stage which it had taken the Western industrialized nations some two hundred years to achieve, and now the intention was to go ahead even more speedily than before. China felt herself threatened by outside forces (notably America) and had no time to lose. The Great Leap Forward did succeed in some measure, but there were also miscalculations on a great scale, and a succession of bad harvests (1959–61) meant that the Communists had to reconsider the whole of their planning and recast it on a more modest scale. For the time being industrial production was given a second place to agricultural production – especially of foodstuffs.

The year 1958, which saw the "Great Leap Forward", also saw the birth of the Communes. The first Communes appear to have been the outcome of a spontaneous move on the part of the peasantry to greater, and more efficient, collectivization, and beginning in certain regions was extended to the others. In the Communes local government was merged into the collective organization of agriculture, and later (in the towns) into that of industry also.

The impression given in the Western press as a whole is that the Commune system has failed and that the Chinese people have been brought to the brink of starvation. This is by no means the case. It is true that the number of Communes has been increased from some 26,000 to some 78,000 (the smaller unit having proved the more manageable) but this is still a small number for a country the size of China, and they continue to function efficiently. Nor do they involve the reduction of the peasantry to the status of "ants" (as has been alleged in many Western newspapers). Nor has "the family" been destroyed by the segregation of the sexes in "dormitories". Progress continues and if at a slower tempo than before 1958, nevertheless it is real.

I now return to the image of China so very widely accepted in the West to which I referred originally – namely that of the "expanding giant". No one can prophesy for certain what will happen in another generation, but the present situation seems to be this. China's plans for the immediate future seem to be centred on her own territory. This amounts to some 3,800,000 square miles, a larger area that the United States. The population is nearing 700 million, but some two-thirds of this is located to the east of a line drawn from Burma to Manchuria and representing an area not more than a third of China. It is true that much of the region to the west is mountain, desert or marginal land, but nevertheless much of it is capable of being made to sustain a greatly increased population. This, by great irrigation and afforestation, is what the Communists are planning to do and already millions of people have been transferred with their consent from the overcrowded regions to the under-populated ones. The Chinese, moreover, claim to have reduced (by propaganda methods) their annual increase of population to about 10 million – a large figure but one which they say that they can absorb. In any case (the Chinese claim) the "Population Explosion" is a world problem, not one confined to China, and must be met on a global basis.

Leaving aside the plausibility of these claims (and there is nothing to disprove them in the face of things), if China *is* "expansionist" in intention at the present time one would expect to see signs of her impending overflow. Such signs are not apparent. Unlike the KMT who claimed all Chinese by race as Chinese nationals, the Communists have made a treaty with Indonesia whereby they disown any jurisdiction or influence over Chinese who are Indonesian nationals, and have offered to extend the same principle to other South-east Asian countries. China has also succeeded in signing treaties of "amity" and non-aggression with all her neighbours except India. The Sino-Indian border dispute, however, is the outcome of the ending of the British Empire in India, and not only has China an undoubted "case" (as has been shown by neutral experts) but has shown outstanding moderation to date in dealing with the question. Nor can the $11\frac{1}{2}$ million Overseas Chinese in South-east Asia be shown to be a "spearhead" of expansion and there is no evidence that they are being organized as a "fifth column". They are in too great a minority for this and besides are hopelessly divided politically. Their problem is how to come to terms with the indigenous peoples among whom they live.

China has recently exploded her first "A-bomb" and it is foretold that she will have the "H-bomb" in about two years' time. This is held widely in the West to prove her aggressive intentions. The Chinese Government's statement on the other hand, on 9th October (*Peking Review*, 16th October 1964) includes the following:

The Chinese Government hereby formally proposes to the governments of the world that a summit conference of all the countries of the world be convened to discuss the question of the complete prohibition and thorough destruction of nuclear weapons, and that as a first step, the summit conference should reach an agreement to the effect that the nuclear powers undertake not to use nuclear weapons, neither to use against non-nuclear countries and nuclear-free zones, nor against each other.

The great Nuclear Powers have no ground for declaring that this offer is insincere unless they put it to the test. China at least can only profit from universal nuclear disarmament.

I would say that Communist China considers herself threatened with encirclement, and certainly the disposition of foreign forces, especially those of the United States, gives colour to this claim. The long-drawn-out war in Indonesia, for example, is an obvious by-product of the American policy of attempting to "contain communism" (i.e. China). However, I, for one, am unwilling to prophesy that China will in no circumstances become aggressive and "expansionist". Japan only became expansionist when forced out of her isolation by the aggressive West. If she is sufficiently provoked by the policy of "containment" (i.e. encirclement) she may respond in a fashion which will be a threat to all of us.

My own approach is that of a non-Communist. I do however, as a historian, appreciate the reasons that have induced China to turn to communism. The attempts to modernize the country within the framework of foreign capitalism was a glaring failure, and China only turned to communism when other methods had failed after more than a century of Chinese weakness and exposure to foreign exploitation.

I have said nothing of certain important matters such as the Sino-Soviet dispute. All I need remark is that, in my opinion, nationalism is an even more important factor than communism in shaping the destinies of the world and that the gulf in interests imposed on China and the U.S.S.R. by geography and history is too great to be bridged by mere similarity of political or economic doctrine.

The picture I have given you of the emergence of modern China will, I fear, conflict with the image of the country which exists in many of your minds. That this is so is largely the fault of Western – especially American – domestic politics, in which certain influential forces have found it expedient to build up the notion of a "Yellow Peril". So successful has the "China Lobby" (financed in the first place from American funds diverted by the KMT) been in doing this that now the United States Government is compelled to reconsider American policy in the Far East, it is tremendously handicapped by the state of public opinion and public information regarding China.

Such is the power of propaganda!

[It is with profound regret that I have to record the death of Dr Purcell shortly after he had passed this contribution for publication. Ed.]

CHAPTER 6

THE PHENOMENON OF NATIONALISM IN ASIA

China, Japan, Indonesia, Pakistan and Ceylon

by Ian Thomson

The European dominance of Asia began in 1498 when a Portuguese navigator arrived at Calicot. It reached its zenith in the nineteenth century when Britain conquered the whole of India, Burma, Ceylon and Malaya; the French conquered all Indo-China; the Dutch extended their sway over the East Indies, and all the colonial powers combined to bring large slices of Chinese territory under their sphere of influence. Until the eve of the Second World War the whole of Asia except Japan, Thailand and Afghanistan lay under the control of Western colonial powers. Between them Britain, France, Holland, the U.S.A. and Portugal ruled the whole of South and South-eastern Asia. After 1945 came a swift, dramatic period of decolonization.

The reasons for this are to be found, partly in a quasi-voluntary withdrawal of European interest, but, far more substantially, in Asian nationalism, the embryonic, revolutionary success and therapeutic qualities of which, together with the shattering dangers that arise when nations find themselves against one another, form the substance of this chapter.

China

Taking up some of the threads already spun in the previous chapter, it could be said that in the nineteenth century China was like a huge dragon, half-asleep. In the early part of the century she had little enough contact with the outside world, disdained what contact she had, and tended to regard the non-Chinese world as well below the salt. The latter half of the century saw a very different picture. Western Powers had invaded the thickly populated coastline commercially, established extra-territorial rights, exercised any amount of diplomatic privilege, and in subtle ways had infiltrated deep into the life of China, partly if not largely to China's humiliation. Western influence through trade and education, with the help of outside protection and the work of missions, was getting a strangle-hold over the life of the nation. Some Chinese accepted the benefits, which were considerable, and saw the situation as a challenge, as did Dr Sun Yat-Sen, while others merely seethed with indignation against the day of reckoning. Thus was nationalism in China born of two parents, challenge and humiliation.

Dr Sun Yat-Sen himself typifies the struggle. As a young man he became the first doctor of modern medicine, studying in Canton and Hong Kong in the late 1870's and early 1880's. Stimulated by his own advance he longed to see his own country step forward into the modern age, letting slip the restricting forces of superstition and backwardness. At the age of twenty-seven he requested an interview with the Viceroy, only to be treated with such silent contempt as to turn him into a revolutionary on the spot. Years later, in the autumn of 1911, while he was crossing the United States by train, the revolutionary spirit he had fostered in China broke out in full spate, overthrew the decadent Manchu dynasty, and ushered in the Republic. Sun Yat-Sen, the man of ideas, lacked the organizing genius of a Lenin, and there followed many years of civil war and general unsettlement, and many changes of leadership. How many people in Britain realize that two of the young men who worked together as colleagues at the College that trained officers for the army were Chiang Kai-Shek and Chou En-Lai? Chiang Kai-Shek was commandant on the military side. Chou-En-Lai looked after the political side. Chiang looked to the West, especially the U.S.A. for support and supplies. Chou looked to the U.S.S.R. for direction and ideology. When China was invaded by Japan the two sides half-sank their differences in the national interest. In 1949 the tough, single-minded Communist forces drove Chiang Kai-Shek's government out of office, and nationalism in China found itself married to communism, whether the people wanted it that way or not.

Nationalism in China was born of humiliation, when pride was stung; worked itself out against "the West"; was further forged in self-defence against the Japanese; and eventually synchronized itself, or came to terms with, an ideology outside itself, which it proceeded to develop indigenously. At every stage the momentum is understandable.

China's vindication as one of the really great nations of the world once again was reached when Chou En-Lai took part at the Bandung Conference in April 1955. The Middle Kingdom once again became the focus of world attention, a key factor in the Afro-Asian alignment, the dread of certain small neighbours, a serious rival to Russia in the leadership of the international Communist world, and an anxiety to the United Nations because of her non-membership.

Japan

Japan's evolution from out-worn feudalistic isolationism to the makings of a high-powered modern state was quick, calculated and thorough. Some resistance was to be expected, but not enough to hold up the transformation. In the race to adopt new techniques in an industrial age Japan was determined not to be left behind. Nationalism showed itself as a passionate desire to learn everything possible from others and use the new knowledge and skill for Japan's advance into the twentieth century. Eventually the island kingdom proved too small even to hold its own population, and too small to provide for itself economically. Territorial expansion was acutely desirable, if not inevitable. Hence in part, the attack on Manchuria; hence the landing on the mainland of China. But Japan's constant successes inflated her aspirations, and tempted her to overreach herself. The vast areas she conquered and held in the two world wars were too much for her to subdue and absorb, and she collapsed from momentary greatness to the pit of ignominious defeat. If nationalism could be equated with strength of arms Japan would be still of no great account in all probability. But nationalism is concerned with spirit and sacrifice, discipline and purpose, and in these regards Japan ranks high among the nations. Her fantastic recovery of strength in half a generation and her place of respectability are a constant marvel. Her latest *pièce de résistance*, October 1964, has been the staging of the Olympic Games, which for organizational efficiency, imagination and smooth-running, has left everyone full of admiration. This in turn redounds to the strengthening of nationalism, and further induces pride in achievement and the satisfying of honour.

Whereas China's "nationalism" demands that she fulfil a doctrinaire programme, and prove its workability, Japan's "nationalism" depends more on the sum total of individual effort to fulfil a part in society which has less reference to any overall blue-print, but which is nevertheless intrinsically understood. Both have their merits.

Japan's nationalism infects the whole nation with a driving desire to increase productivity more rapidly than others, to export hard, to work her way into the markets of the world, and undercut others in trade. Her vastly increased investments in North America and elsewhere are a measure of her phenomenal recovery and resilience. Success merely confirms the reality of national vitality, over and above the incentive of profit.

Responsible Japanese look forward to the day when there will be an easement of the relations with China, with a confidence that they will judge how to come to terms with a giant and wary neighbour. Less confident is their attitude to Russia, which is regarded as more suspiciously expansionist. The acute political problems besetting the situation strengthen Japan's sense of nationalism, which is sensitive to any moves that hamper her trade or restrict her freedom. The touchiness of her reactions was evident when the United States sailed a nuclear submarine to her naval base on a courtesy call in 1964. Japan had not forgotten 1945.

Indonesia

We now turn to Indonesia, potentially one of the world's richest countries, and the story of Indonesia is largely the story of Sukarno.

President Sukarno is one of this century's successful revolutionaries. For sixteen years he dreamt of political independence and worked for it, from 1929 to 1945. For another four years it was much in the balance. For the last fifteen years he has led the nation which he helped to create. He has never failed to remind them of 350 years of subjection to foreign domination. In speech after speech with mesmeric impact he has talked about the early days of resistance; the nationalist movement that worked for independence from colonial (Dutch) rule, and which survived Japanese occupation; the enunciation of philosophical principles; the rejection of the old order; and the proclamation of the new State. All this has built up a dynamic nationalism. President Sukarno talks about the Indonesian Revolution within the context of the Revolution of Mankind, based upon "the awakened Conscience of Man" and the demand for social justice. He assumes the rôle of political theorist, not merely to give direction to his own people, but also to justify his aspirations in a wider context. Strangely enough the very language he sometimes uses ("the exploitation of man by man and nation by nation") provides the very seed-bed for doctrinaire communism which in other ways he tries not to encourage. The Communist Party in Indonesia has grown steadily in momentum, and is already poised ready to take advantage of every opportunity to press its claims for more and more consideration and exercise of power. "Guided democracy" was a subtle phrase, calculated to offset the worst fears of the West and the caution of the Communist powers. For years it was nicely balanced, but has run the continuing danger of being too much of a compromise. It is doubtful if the compromise can be any longer maintained in face of prevailing pressures. In the early days of Indonesian sovereignty Sukarno declared frequently that the Republic was founded on the Five Principles (*Pantja Sila*) of Belief in God; Sovereignty of the People; Nationalism; Internationalism; and Social Justice – principles wide enough to incorporate the most diverse interests, and bridge most inalienable rifts.

These principles seemed to have reached some fulfilment when Indonesia played host nation at the Bandung Conference in April 1955. This was the moment when twenty-nine countries, mostly Asian, with a few African, celebrated jubilantly their emancipation from foreign domination, and a wave of optimism swept the independent nations. But this optimism had to be kept alive by proofs of success, proofs of progress, and "shots in the arm" to bolster nationalism. Hence, the spirit of aggression that demanded territorial expansion; that promulgated the idea of Maphilindo (the union of Malaya, the Philippines and Indonesia); and that reacted violently when the Federation of Malaysia was formed in 1963. Where nationalism begins and ends, and where nationalism gives way to internationalism, is often not clear.

At the time of Bandung, Indonesia's stock ranked high among the Afro-Asian nations, and her respectability was something to trade upon. The United States was willing to give vast sums in foreign aid, and Indonesia was a beneficiary from many quarters. But her policy of beating the war-drum, and generating wars of nerves, created endless suspicion as to her further purposes, and she began to run the risk of losing friends, and losing the full confidence of some whose wish it was to help her develop.

Extremely sensitive to the rumblings from Djakarta was Australia, and several moves were made to come to some understanding, but little reassurance has come from these overtures. The very organizations which were set up to keep watch over the situation regionally are themselves put in the embarrassing position of seeming wholly partisan. The more SEATO interests herself militarily the more she appears to be the instrument of the Western Powers, with minimal concern for national rights. The more SEATO intervenes the more the Communist world can point the finger of rebuke, and the more her case is validated. Thrown on the defensive justice seems to be on the side of the aggressor. Out of this tension and turmoil the most strongly organized political party is likely to come out on top, in Indonesia as elsewhere. Effective organization is half the battle, so long as it is allied with what counts for nationalism.

Pakistan and Ceylon

We turn now to a pair of countries, as different as two nations can be in many respects, Pakistan and Ceylon, to see how nationalism has worked itself out in the years since independence.

Both countries have this in common that their nationalism is partly expressed in their religion. Pakistan is avowedly based on Islam. She set out to become "the Land of the Pure", tied to the tenets of the Prophet and the Koran.

Dr Jinnah, the Father of Pakistan, justified his determination to break with India on the grounds of racial and religious differences, after years of struggle to maintain unity.

It is true that Pakistan has often given the impression of sitting lightly on this initial impetus and vision, but at heart, among the common people even more than in the ranks of the élite, religion is the *raison d'être* of the nation, and this is written into the constitutional life of the country. The voice of Iqbal, poet, philosopher and visionary, who dreamt of the creation of "Pakistan", is still alive. There were even ambitious Muslims who fondly hoped that Pakistan might assume a place of leadership in the Mohammedan world, outpacing other contenders. Karachi could not compete with Mecca and Medina, and never intended to. But the pilgrimage centres carried little political authority, and this was what had been lacking ever since the demise of both the Sultanate and the Caliphate. Islam wanted a pivot of power and authority, and for a moment Pakistan – geographically midway between the Muslims of West Africa and the Muslims of Indonesia – hoped to put in a bid. It had no hope of succeeding. Economically the first decade nearly saw disaster, and Pakistan's very survival was a precarious issue. It was a miracle that Pakistan welded her peoples into a nation out of the ashes of partition with so little in the way of machinery of government with which to start. This itself is a tribute to the spirit of nationalism, without which Pakistan would have been still-born.

Meanwhile, in the latter months of 1955 something happened the significance of which has been overlooked and underrated. The leaders of Russia, on a visit of goodwill to the East, deliberately snubbed Pakistan by not paying a visit, and aggravated the situation by verbal attacks on the country from India. This put the Soviet Union right out of court, and Russia may have thought that little would come of the affront. This is proving to be a grave mistake. As the Communist world began to split into two camps China looked to Pakistan as a nation to be wooed, and Pakistan was prepared to trust China rather than another, if sides had to be taken. This served China excellently. Russia's fraternization with India and Afghanistan left Pakistan out in the cold, but created a point of weakness which could later serve other interests. The harder China willed to pressurize India on her northern borders the keener she was to befriend

India's uneasy neighbour Pakistan. Such are the techniques of diplomacy within the game of power politics, and such is the measure of the distance from the realization of internationalism.

Pakistan's effort to achieve stability was vitiated for years by four main factors: the delay in working out a satisfactory Constitution, which brought its own legacy of political uncertainty; the long-drawn-out argument with India over the division of the waters of the Indus; the festering sore of Kashmir, which both India and Pakistan equally claimed as of right; and consequently, the drain of a heavy Defence budget which the country could not afford.

Recovery of purpose followed the *coup d'état* on 8th October 1958 of General Mohammed Ayub Khan, Commander-in-Chief of the Army. Corruption in high places was quickly reduced. Government became more efficient. Confidence in the outside world as to Pakistan's future was restored. A revived nationalism took hold of the country again, and expressed itself in new hopes. A new capital was planned to replace Karachi, and it was to be named Islamabad, and in this name the true texture of Pakistan's nationalism was epitomized. The new capital is adjacent to Rawalpindi.

Ceylon by strong contrast is small in size, with a relatively small population, and an island, overwhelmingly Buddhist. These are the measure of her strength and weakness in the contemporary world. Her position is strategic. Holland and Britain had long known the value of her bases as a lifeline to the East. Russia and China are equally aware of this, and for years have vied for acceptance and favour. Ceylon could be an invaluable pawn in the game of world revolution, and a springboard for advance. There was a time when nationalism in Ceylon represented the first interests of the island in terms of trade, commerce and progress, with little ideology behind it. But this was called in question in 1956, and Buddhist pressure led to the fall of the Nationalist Party. Russia began to woo the Buddhist centres, not without success. China looked likely to be outpaced and outmanœuvred.

The problem is complicated by internal politics and the need to establish the right relations outside, and to keep the two sufficiently separate. Ceylon is too small a nation to do more than maintain her trade, hold as delicate a balance as possible between all the countries which keep an eye on her, and justify herself as a viable island-nation. The very Buddhism which is part of her nationalism cushions off certain apprehensions, but also opens her to ideological pressures which could capsize her into one of the great power blocks. Her position and her smallness render it hard for her to resist, and she has to play an uncomfortably difficult game on other nations' goodwill. How long this can last, and how good it will be for Ceylon in the long run, it is impossible to say.

India

by B. N. Pandey

Twenty years in the life of a country is too short a period to evolve patterns of political, economic or social change. For this reason any account of Indian or Asian progress since the Second World War is bound to be incoherent. Yet it can be clearly enough seen how India was the pivot of Asia in ancient times and still remains one of the two giant powers today. Before gaining independence India had already been a source of inspiration to the other emerging nations of Asia. The ideas and methods of the Indian nationalist movement were adopted and followed by a number of other Asian countries: she played an important rôle in the settlement of the Korean War, in supporting Indonesia's struggle for independence, and in bringing freedom and partial peace in Indo-China through a series of conferences at Geneva.

It is due to India's policy of "active neutrality" that a bloc of non-aligned nations has now grown up. Further, with a view to ease world tension India put forth the principle of peaceful coexistence. The powerful nations of the world have now accepted this principle as a basis of their mutual relationship.

Apart from these contributions which India has made in the last twenty years its importance lies in the fact that it is a nation of 400 millions, a third of the total population of all the economically underdeveloped nations. Further, it is the biggest democratic country in the world. Almost all the new nations of Asia in the early years of their nationhood adopted the Anglo-American type of democracy but by 1958 most of them gave this system up. India has so far maintained a most stable democratic government. In fact, democracy is on trial in India. If India fails to solve its problems by democratic means, if it fails to provide the minimum necessities of life to its citizens in their life-time, the cause of democracy will receive a severe setback.

India is the only country in the economically underdeveloped world which has got a most sophisticated leadership and a large intellectual élite. Its industrial and commercial community is of very long standing and it has got an extensive set of financial institutions. The Indian Civil Service has got a proud tradition of competence and integrity and the Indian Judiciary is the most independent in the world.

India's size, its rich traditions and its potentiality make it as important a study as do its great problems and limitations.

Problems Following Independence

a) *Economic and Social.* The distinguishing features of India's economy in 1947 were poverty, malnutrition, subsistence agriculture and relatively little industry. The situation had been worsened by the Second World War and the partition of the sub-continent into Pakistan and India. It had then a population of 360 millions, of whom nearly 65% were illiterate and 70% of whom depended on agriculture for their livelihood. The average income of an Indian was thirty-two times lower than an American and sixteen times lower than a Briton. Between 1947 and 1951 the life expectation of a newly-born Indian child was thirty-two years, less than one child in three of primary school age was in school, only one adult in seven could read or write. In the village areas there was one doctor to 25,000 people and one hospital to 50,000; only one city in four had a safe drinking-water supply; not half of even the larger towns had electricity; only a handful of India's 560,000 villages were served by all-weather roads.

Unlike European countries in a comparable state of backwardness in the eighteenth century, India was faced in the twentieth century with the problem of "high expectations": her people knew that with proper measures their lot could be improved.

Like other Asian countries, once colonial rule, which had to some extent created a unity of nationalist resistance to it, was withdrawn, India was faced with the emergence of communal, centrifugal or racial forces. Nor did Indian leaders believe in the "two nations theory", in the contention that Hindus and Muslims were two separate nations, and yet they had been compelled to accept partition.

b) Foreign Policy. Apart from economic and domestic problems, India was faced with the task of establishing a relationship with the Western and Communist blocs into which the world then seemed to be sharply divided. The obvious choice which lay open for the weak Asian nations was to join one or the other through military pacts or defence alliances. In formulating her policy towards the power blocs India had to reckon with two factors. The first was the anti-Western feeling among her people which had naturally grown out of a long struggle for freedom from Western dominance. The Soviet Union, on the other hand, had, so it seemed to the Asians, a clean history with no association whatsoever with a Western type of imperialism. The Soviet Union had further drawn their attention by its open denunciation of imperialism, colonialism and racialism. Of all the "isms" associated with the Western dominance of Asia, racialism was the most unpleasant one. The free nations of Asia had doubts about being accepted by the Western powers on equal terms. Their suspicion and distrust of erstwhile imperial powers might have caused them to seek friendship and protection from the Soviet Union. But the Soviet Union was in those days under Stalin's dictatorship. It was not possible to be a friend of Russia without being a Communist. Besides, Stalin's Russia had openly denounced the non-Communist Asian leaders of freedom movements as protégés of Western imperialism. In the case of India, the second factor to be taken into account was the gradual emergence of China as a Communist power. The emergence of communism in China was a potent factor which shaped India's policy towards the power blocs.

Thus, poverty, instability and the politics of power blocs were some of the main problems which faced the new governments of Asia generally and India particularly.

Indian Progress since 1947

In her plans, form of government and foreign policy India has been influenced by her age-old Hindu traditions. A certain degree of Hindu relativism can be discerned in her economic planning, her secular constitution, her neutralism, her policy of non-alignment and peaceful coexistence, in her relationship with Muslim, Christian and Communist states of the world.

a) Economic Planning. India had the choice of two methods of fighting poverty: the capitalist method as practised by the Western countries over two hundred years; the Communist method which was also evolved in the Western countries and was adapted by China, the first Communist country of Asia. For obvious reasons India could not adopt the pure capitalist method of progress by private enterprise. Even with the additional advantage of foreign aid, it would have taken centuries for India to evolve a welfare society through purely capitalist methods of production. On the other hand India was not in the least inclined to take to the Communist system of coercion and force, although she had before her the example of apparently highly successful planning by the Soviet Union. In a remarkably short space of time that country transformed itself from a virtually feudal economy to an industrialized and rapidly growing one. India's problem, however, was to do it democratically. To quote a member of the planning commission, V. T. Krishnamachan, "In our plans we try to find our own particular solution to the problems of democratic planning and strike our own national balance between liberty and progress, central control and private initiative, national planning and local authority." The Indian economy is called mixed because it is a mixture of capitalist and socialist economy.

The first Five Year Plan started in 1951 and ran until 1956, the second was from 1956 to 1961 and the third was started in 1960–1 and is to last until 1965–6.

The main targets of the plans are: (*a*) to double the national income by 1973–4, (*b*) to reduce the proportion of the dependents on agriculture from about 70% to 60%, and (*c*) to introduce free and compulsory education all over the country for boys and girls in the age group 6–11 by the end of 1966. Roughly speaking, India envisages establishing a welfare state through planning by the end of the year 1975. This sounds ambitious on the part of a country like India which with its 400 million people had to start virtually from scratch. But looking at the progress India has made since 1951, in spite of severe setbacks it has suffered during this period in the nature of substantial unexpected increase in population, bad harvests and border disputes with China and Pakistan, it can be safely said that India will attain its targets.

b) Stability of Government. The problem which most of the Asian countries faced after their independence was one of political stability. Most of the Asian states started with an Anglo-American type of democratic government but by 1958 it became clear that democracy in Pakistan, Burma, Indonesia, Laos, South Viet-Nam, and to some extent in Ceylon, had failed. Democracy in its pure Anglo-American model survives only in India, Japan, the Philippines and Malaya, though the latter achieved independence only in 1957 and it is too early to be certain about its future set-up.

In its first eleven years of nationhood Pakistan had four Governors-General and eight cabinets. The army took over the power in 1958, democracy was swept aside, political parties were banned and a military dictatorship was established, under the presidency of Ayub Khan. Western democracy was replaced in Pakistan by a "basic democracy" at village level. It is a system of local government with a mixture of elected and appointed representatives, and is calculated to be "simple to understand, easy to work and cheap to sustain". Basic democracy is supposed to ensure "the effective participation of all citizens in the affairs of the country up to the level of their mental horizon and intellectual calibre". In Indonesia democracy gave way to "guided democracy". President Sukarno of Indonesia found Western democracy alien to the Indonesian way of life. In Ceylon, Laos and South Viet-Nam civil strife caused more and more concentration of power at the top, and curtailment of civil liberties.

There are now three general types of political system in Asia – democracy in India, the Philippines, Malaya and Japan, Communist dictatorship in China, North Viet-Nam and North Korea, and non-Communist authoritarianism in Pakistan, South Viet-nam, South Korea, Thailand, Burma, Indonesia, Nepal, Afghanistan and Cambodia.

What then are the general causes of instability and failure of democracy? Is the Western type of democracy unsuited to Asian life?

Among the general causes may be first listed the widespread poverty on one hand and high expectations on the other. Other causes may include a tradition of antipathy to government, the absence of a loyal opposition, a long tradition of autocracy, a large gap between the Westernized élite and the uneducated ignorant masses, shortage of trained civil servants, small size of middle class, lack of leadership and the existence of large minorities in every country ready to undermine internal unity at the slightest opportunity.[1] The conditions which obtained in the Western world – a high level of literacy and a general level of prosperity do not obtain in Asia. But from this it does not follow that Western democracy is unsuited to Asia for there are countries in the West which are not democratic though they possess the classic conditions of democracy and there is India, which, though she does not possess those conditions, is still democratic and the most stable among the Asian governments.

The serious crisis which India faced immediately after its independence was the occurrence of Communal riots. This was due to the partition of the country on religious grounds. This together with the emergence of provincialism gravely threatened India's unity. The assassination of Mahatma Gandhi was a great shock but it turned the tide against the Communalists. Communal organizations and their leaders fell prey to mob fury and Communalism seemed to be wiped out of existence. The next factor which saved India during this crisis was the commanding position of the Indian National Congress and the foresight, courage and idealism of its leaders. Jawarhalal Nehru

[1] A good analysis of the political instability has been given by B. Brecher in *The New States of Asia*, 1963.

launched his crusade against Communalism and was successful in reviving Hindu tolerance towards the minorities. Neither the Congress leaders nor the Hindu masses believed in the principle on which the country had been divided. They had been taught to evolve a secular attitude and were reluctant to subscribe to the two-nation theory. On the other hand the very existence of Pakistan was based on the two-nation theory, hence the leaders of Pakistan could not afford to preach secularism to their followers. India maintained its hold on Kashmir. This gave additional impetus to the Hindus to practise as well as believe in secularism. Secularism became the creed of India in 1950 when the Indian Constitution came into force. India became a secular democratic republic. Pakistan, on the other hand, became a theocratic Muslim state. Under the present constitution of Pakistan nobody but a Muslim can become the head of the state. Thus partly due to their religious background – the tolerance of Hinduism and the intolerance of Islam – and partly due to the force of political circumstances, the Hindus of India adopted a secular constitution and the Muslims of Pakistan an Islamic constitution. India's stand may be summed up with the words of Nehru,

> . . . we have never accepted, even when partition came to India, the two-nation theory, that is that the Hindus are one nation and the Muslims are another. . . . I say we cannot accept that because once we accept that nationality goes by religion, we break up our whole conception of India. . . . 35 million Muslims remained in India [after Pakistan]. Today, there are more Muslims in India than there are in West Pakistan. . . . [1]

In the same interview Nehru said that if Kashmir went to

[1] Michael Brecher's interviews with Nehru, selections from which have been reproduced by the author in his book, *The New States of Asia*.

Pakistan it would have powerful effects on the Communal elements in India, both Hindu and Muslim.

The emergence of provincialism in general and of movements for the reorganization of provinces on linguistic bases was bound to arise in a big country like India, which is inhabited by people from all religions and races, who speak 845 languages and dialects of which fifteen are the major languages with highly developed grammar and literature. The provinces of India were reorganized on a linguistic basis in 1956. As far as provincialism, localism or sectionalism are concerned, these are gradually subsiding with a gradual increase of interest among the masses in national affairs.

Apart from these India, in the course of the last twenty years, had no other serious threats to her internal security. It is now the most stable of the new Asian states. The Congress Party has been in power since 1949. So far, three general elections have been held – free from violence and corruption. The question which used to be asked before May this year[1] – what will happen after Nehru – has now been answered. India is still stable and democratic and there is no fear of the Army or the Communists seizing power in the near future.

c) Foreign Affairs. When India achieved independence the world seemed to be sharply divided into two blocs, each claiming the totality of truth and each intriguing to destroy the other. The newly born nations of Asia seemed to have no choice left but to join one or the other power bloc.

To India which was fully alive to its Hindu legacy, neither of the blocs represented the totality of truth, justice and good in the world. Hers was a typically tolerant and undogmatic Hindu approach to the world problem. No system, no philosophy and no religion contains absolute truth. All religions, philosophies and systems of government represent only various means to a

[1] 1964.

common end. Therefore, let all coexist in harmony and peace, influence each other and evolve a better system which may synthesize the best of the existing opposite systems. Apart from the Hindu legacy there were some material influences on India's policy of non-alignment and active neutrality.

India realized that a sharp division of the world into two blocs could lead to a war which would be disastrous to the poor nations of Asia and Africa. The surplus energy of the powerful states must be diverted to the economic improvement of the developing countries. And then there was again the non-material Gandhian influence of non-violence and Satyagraha. India must stand by and fight a non-violent battle for the truth. Since none of the powers was absolutely right or absolutely wrong how could India stand for the truth by completely aligning herself to one or the other? India, therefore, decided not to align herself with any bloc, and to judge all policy issues "on their merit". Her policy was in the beginning misunderstood by some of the Western powers and India was criticized for "sitting on the fence". But to the Asian nations India gave a lead in a new direction. But for a few notable exceptions most of the nations of Asia and Africa and a few from Europe have now joined the group of non-aligned nations. By taking a firm stand on many issues of international importance India has made it clear that neutralism is not passivism.

The emergence of a non-aligned bloc has had a positive influence on the easing of world tension. The neutral nations have "provided an important channel for diverting the surplus energies of the super-powers from direct conflict to peaceful competition for the support of the neutralists". Their energies have now been diverted into a "very beneficial competition in the form of economic development and aid among the states of Asia and Africa". If the prospect of world peace seems brighter today than it was in 1945 it is partly due to the emergence of neutral states under India's lead.

If the Hindu legacy inspired India to develop the theory of non-alignment, practical considerations of national security against Communist interference from outside guided her in the formulation of the principle of coexistence. It had been the strategy of the Communist states to aid and organize subversive movements in non-Communist states. The emergence of China in 1949 as a Communist power implied a threat to South and South-east Asian states, to their internal security. India's policy in general was to make Communist China less dangerous by befriending her. Since India was non-aligned it was easier for her to earn Chinese friendship. Besides, the fact that the Chinese Communist movement was a mass movement against a corrupt and autocratic Chiang Kai-Shek administration had aroused some sympathy and respect among the Indians for China. With these considerations India extended her warm friendship towards China. India was the second non-Communist country after Burma to recognize Communist China and the first to plead for China's admission to the United Nations Organization. It was in an atmosphere of warm friendship that the Tibet agreement was signed between India and China. And it was on that occasion that India extended her Five Principles to China to which China agreed. The five principles are:

1) Mutual respect for each other's territorial integrity and sovereignty.
2) Mutual non-aggression.
3) Mutual non-interference in each other's internal affairs.
4) Equality and mutual benefit.
5) Peaceful coexistence.

The Indian name for the Five Principles is *Panch Sheel*.

China's acceptance of the Five Principles was a great relief to India and other Asian countries who had harboured the fear of Communist interference. Since then India has tried to extend the principle of coexistence to other countries and consequently to expand the "area of peace". It was, indeed, a great victory for the adherents of this principle when the Soviet Union under Khrushchev's leadership accepted it as a part of her policy towards the Western countries. Through the practice and advocacy of *Panch Sheel*, India has exerted great influence to lessen fear, bring about a climate of peace, and prevent the outbreak of war.

Indo-Chinese friendship lasted for only ten years. It showed signs of wearing thin at the time of the Tibet Revolt. Three years later both countries got involved in a border war. Why did China commit a war of aggression against India, who had been her best non-Communist friend? Were those disputed barren areas on the border so vitally important for China that she had to get them even at the cost of a war with India? The motives for Chinese aggression were not clear then but now we can enumerate them with some certainty.

First, China wanted to keep the international situation in turmoil in order to prevent the Soviet Union from coming to terms with the U.S.A. and other "imperialist enemies". Second, China wanted to cripple India's challenge for Asian leadership. A democratic, socialist India presented a great challenge to Communist China. India's success in solving her problems democratically would undermine the course of communism in poverty-stricken Asian and African countries. Indian resources must therefore be diverted from economic development to wasteful military activity. Thirdly, China wanted to undermine Indo-Russian friendship and to force Russia on the one hand to side with an ally against a friend, and India, on the other hand, to align herself completely with the Western world. This would demolish her concept of non-alignment and peaceful coexistence, which India had championed so far.

Another main reason seems to have been China's urge to reclaim "lost territory". The areas which China claimed from

India were the areas which she thought were lost to British imperialism when China was weak.

Behind all these lay China's basic motive to assert herself as the strongest power in Asia. Some of China's motives were partly realized. Chinese action created a world tension. The image of India as the strongest power in Asia was tarnished. To the new states of Asia and Africa India looked weak. Taking into account China's recent atomic test, she has come out with an image of strength, and the attention of the whole world has been drawn towards her. But Chinese aggression failed to force Russia to abandon India's friendship. The Soviet Union under Khrushchev's leadership maintained its neutrality during the course of the Indo-Chinese war. Perhaps for the first time the Soviet Union did not back a Communist country in her battle against a non-Communist country. It had a two-fold result. First, there was a marked rupture between China and the Soviet Union. Secondly, the Western countries, especially the U.S.A., came to trust Russia a little more and there was a marked improvement in East and West relationships. Further, the Chinese aggression did not succeed in forcing India to abandon completely her non-aligned policy. The Soviet Union and the Western world both stood by the side of neutral India. Thus the principles of coexistence, and non-alignment, have survived the Chinese challenge.

CHAPTER 7

THE PHENOMENON OF NATIONALISM IN AFRICA

The Emergence of Nationalism

by Colin Legum

In 1945 there were only four independent states in the whole of Africa – the ancient Kingdom of Ethiopia, the modern Kingdom of Egypt, the Republic of Liberia and the white supremacy state of South Africa. Their combined population was about 65 millions. Twenty years later there are 35 independent African states, with a total population of about 250 millions. The swiftness of this transformation of a continent from one almost wholly colonial to almost complete independence can be briefly explained in terms of three contemporary phenomena. First, the decline of imperialism which began after the First World War and reached its floodtide after the Second World War. Second, the rise of colour-consciousness throughout the world, prophesied by the American Negro leader, Dr W. E. B. Du Bois, in his memorable phrase: "The problem of the twentieth century is the colour line. . . ." When DuBois spoke these words at the first Pan-African conference in London in 1900, few took him seriously. European supremacy was accepted as a fact of life over the greater part of the world: it was confident, assertive, creative and strong. In international terms the challenge of the coloured peoples – whether of Asia or of Africa – was hardly to be taken seriously. But colour-consciousness grew as imperialism declined, and of course contributed to its decline. These two factors contributed to the growth of the third phenomenon – modern African nationalism. If I emphasize modern nationalism, it is because nationalism itself is of course not a contemporary phenomenon at all.

Africa's modern nationalism is significantly different from most of the older forms of nationalism which proliferated before the twentieth century. In its modern form African nationalism is characterized by three distinctive elements. It is a protest against alien rule and domination. It is an assertion on the part of black peoples to their right to be considered and treated as equals by white peoples. And it is a belief in the importance of bringing backward and underdeveloped societies fully into the twentieth century.

Thus described, African nationalism is not only a response to Western imperialism expressed as a desire to free Africans from dependence on the West; it is, more positively, an aspiration to reform and transform African societies into modern economic and political societies.

This modernizing aspect of nationalism is of great importance in understanding the dynamics of independent Africa. At one level it expresses itself continuously as a struggle against all forms of black inferiority; at another level it engages the modern world (especially the West) in a struggle to catch up with the modern world, but as a free and equal part of it, and on terms of the Africans' own choosing – not simply as "subjects" to be modernized, missionized, urbanized, detribalized, assimilated and exploited.

By no means all Africans share this enthusiasm for the modern world of technology and progress; there are strong forces pulling all the time in the opposite direction: back towards the traditionalism of the past. But these forces have, almost nowhere, been strong enough to deflect the thrust of modern nationalism. This explains how it became possible for African nationalism to be captured and controlled by the continent's educated élite, comprising those Africans trained in Western institutions and strongly exposed to Western ideas and culture. Although this educated élite rejects the inequalities of their old relationship with the West, they do not reject the West as such. On the contrary, because there is so much they admire in the modern world and so much they dislike in traditional African society, their highest aspiration is to build twentieth-century societies in Africa. These modern aspirations of the educated élite give them the character of a "modernizing élite". Thus nationalism in Africa is a powerful modernizing force.

All this goes to explain the astonishing paradox that Africa, the continent with the highest illiteracy rate (85–90%), should have invested its intellectuals with more power and status than anywhere else in the world. Somewhat less than 0·075% (75 in 100,000) of Africans have received higher education, and most of these are confined to a few countries – especially in North and West Africa. A country like Tchad, with a population of almost 3 millions, has only 140 people with a higher education. Nor is there much hope that this situation might change rapidly – even if the present ambitious plans succeed in increasing the number of university students to 250,000 by 1980, it will still mean that only 1·5% of Africans will have access to higher education. These figures give some idea of the colossal challenge facing the "thin black line" of intellectuals who now dominate the governments of all the independent states in Africa. Their success or failure will determine how Africa's modern nationalism turns out in the end.

So far I have been talking about nationalism without having defined what it is. For those who have grown up in a European milieu of liberal democracy, nationalism is a dirty word. The spontaneous reaction is to think of it as something outdated and anachronistic in a world which should be thinking more in terms of supra-nationalism and world government or, at least, of a United Europe. There is a natural tendency to associate nationalism with the bitter conflicts which have more than once brought Europe to her knees. Small wonder, then, that Europeans think of nationalism as reactionary, selfish, inward-looking, negative and destructive. These reactions are undoubtedly the right ones in the context of Europe's modern experience: this makes it all the harder to undertake the intellectual exercise needed to understand why nationalism should be unhealthy and negative in the Western world, but healthy and positive in the present stage of Africa's development.

The first step towards a proper understanding of Africa's modern nationalism is to overcome the natural temptation to interpret African nationalism in the light of Europe's experiences. This fixedly ethnocentric approach makes for serious distortion because it tries to make African nationalism comprehensible in European terms instead of in African terms. There can be no proper understanding of African nationalism unless one first discards the notion that Africa exists simply as an extension of Europe. This has never been true. What *is* true is that for five hundred years Europe extended *herself* into Africa, producing a deep involvement between the two continents. Europe is now being extruded – mostly peacefully, sometimes violently. And Africa is now engaged in trying to establish a new and different kind of relationship with Europe; how it turns out in the end depends partly on developments inside Africa and partly on Europe's attitude to, and understanding of, these developments. What is certain is that there can be no escape from this involvement.

But before we can assess African nationalism we need to clear our minds of what we mean by nationalism. A useful starting point is to consider the extent to which African nationalism conforms, or fails to conform, to classical definitions of nationalism which derive largely from the European experience. Much of the difficulty one has in discussing modern African nationalism is that the nation, as conceived in Europe, exists hardly anywhere in Africa south of the Sahara. In its African context, therefore, there is little or no meaning in defining a nation as a "materially and morally integrated society; with a stable and enduring authority at the centre, with fixed frontiers, and with a relative moral and spiritual and cultural unity shared by those who consciously belong to the state and accept its laws".[1]

There is, however, some relevance in the definition produced by a Chatham House group of experts who defined nationalism as "a membership in a nation, or of a desire to forward the strength, liberty or prosperity of a nation . . .".[2] But its vagueness carries us little further. By giving a different definition to "nation" Professor E. H. Carr opens up a more useful approach: "The modern nation is a historical group. It has its place and function in a wider society, and its claims cannot be denied or ignored. But they can in no circumstances be absolute, being governed by historical conditions of time and place. . . ."[3]

By defining the nation as a "historical group" Professor Carr helpfully removes much of the confusion caused by the usual importance attributed to such considerations as linguistic and ethnic affinities, established frontiers, etc. What is helpful, too, is the introduction of a dynamic quality into his definition by setting the modern nation in the context of "a wider society", and by introducing the important factor of power – the nation's claims that "cannot be denied or ignored".

But while "time and place" is obviously important, the crucial point needs to be made "that the nation is a product not merely of the past, as historians tend to assume, nor solely of the present situation, but of the future – what people *aspire* to be, to have and to do".[4] One might think of these aspirations as "presuppositions" which Thomas Hodgkin adopts in investigat-

---

[1] *Spearhead*, Dar-es-Salaam, February 1962.
[2] Chatham House report on *Nationalism*, London 1939.
[3] E. H. Carr, *Nationalism and After*, London 1945.
[4] Carr, op. cit.

ing African nationalism. He uses "presuppositions" in a Collingwoodian sense as "equal to statements expressing basic beliefs – particularly, in this context, beliefs about the kind of social, political and moral order which (in the view of those holding these beliefs) it is desirable to realize".[1]

But these "presuppositions" or "aspirations" become significantly important only if they can be made politically viable. At this point one welcomes Professor Karl W. Deutsch's use of the concept of "social mobilization". He says "a nation is the result of the transformation of people, or of several ethnic elements, in the process of social mobilization".[2] He offers the further useful hypothesis that the prospects of success may be judged "by the completeness of that transformation and the intensity of social mobilization around the symbols of the new national community".

With these clarifications in mind it is perhaps useful to accept Professor Coleman's brief definition of African nationalism:

> Broadly, a consciousness of belonging to a nation (existent or in the realm of aspiration) or a nationality, and a desire, as manifest in sentiment and activity, to secure or maintain its welfare, prosperity, and to maximize its political autonomy. The reference group for "nationalism" can be a *de facto* nation or nationality, or a territorially defined group in which certain members believe and advocate that it ought, or is destined, to become a nation.[3]

These few ideas should help to shift our minds away from thinking of nationalism along certain fixed grooves.

---

[1] Thomas Hodgkin in an unpublised paper read to a conference of the "Past and Present Society", London 1962.

[2] Karl W. Deutsch, *Nationalism and Social Communication*, New York 1953.

[3] James S. Coleman, *Background to Nationalism – Nigeria*, University of California 1958.

Modern African nationalism developed largely as a reaction to European nationalism which was rooted in its own ideas of European supremacy and of a world revolving around Western Europe. Its reaction, therefore, is not only against alien rule (anti-colonialism) but equally against race supremacy. For the African nationalists the ending of colonialism is the beginning not the end of a struggle – a point not sufficiently understood.

How often does one hear the complaint: "Now that colonialism is finished, what more do the Africans want?" They want to abolish the status of inferiority – social, cultural, economic and political – cast upon Africa as a continent, and upon Africans as a people. African nationalism is a forceful assertion of the dignity of the individual African; and it is a force struggling to establish real equality between Africa and the rest of the world, especially with its former alien rulers with whom it remains deeply entangled – not altogether unwillingly.

These "aspirations" give it two distinctive qualities. Externally, it operates as a force working for the total abolition of the old relationships as between superior and inferior – Europe and Africa – and as between European and African. Internally, it is a regenerating force seeking to destroy Africa's "colonial mentality" and to uplift the African – economically, culturally and socially. It seeks to bring about a cultural *renaissance* in Africa as well as an economic revolution.

An important aspect of African nationalism is its ambivalence towards Europe: the very nationalist leaders working actively to extrude Europe are at the same time willing to continue working with the former colonial powers and their allies. African nationalism does not reject Europe altogether; it seeks to create a new relationship based on independence. There is a surprising absence of hatred and even of bitterness. There is, of course, bitterness; but it is not sick. It has not produced the kind of neurotic nationalism one has encountered so often in

Europe where hatred between nations, between the conquered and their victims, had made rational intercourse between them impossible for generations, produced deep-seated symptoms of national paranoia, and fed on feelings of vengeance and retribution. African nationalism is, in its present stage, on the whole, astonishingly free from these neurotic symptoms of European nationalism. This is one of its most remarkable qualities, and one that clearly distinguished it from the European experience.

In international affairs, African nationalism has a desire – not to establish the policy or image of a single state – but of a collective African attitude, if not yet a collective policy. It has a fierce determination to impress an African presence, or personality, on world affairs. For centuries Africa has been history's victim; there has been no time when it controlled, or to any great extent even influenced, world affairs: always it has been the victim of those affairs. Now Africa has mounted the world stage. Its ideas are largely those of non-alignment, not to be confused with neutralism. Unlike the neutrals, the non-aligned are not isolationist: they insist on having their say in world affairs. While making the deliberate choice of staying out of the East–West struggle, they never profess disinterest in the progress of this struggle; they are too deeply concerned with the implications for their own future to be unconcerned, for example, about nuclear warfare. The emergence of Africa on the world scene at the height of the Cold War has given them an importance and an influence which in other times they could never have hoped to achieve in terms of their real power. But although Africa's combined military strength amounts to very little, Africa could help decisively to tilt the balance in the Cold War.

Achieving sovereign independence is, psychologically at least, an assertion of equality: an African state enjoying an equal vote at the U.N. with the great nations of the world has its morale greatly lifted. Independence makes it at least possible to establish respect between states. But African nationalists never for a moment allow themselves to forget that there can be no equality worth having so long as they are weak and the European nations are strong; so long as they are miserably poor and the great industrial nations are growing increasingly more affluent. They know that so long as they are educationally, technologically and industrially "backward" that they are, in fact, "inferior" – no longer as between individuals or as between races – but as between nations, and as between Africa and the industrialized nations. Norway, Sweden and Switzerland may be smaller, weaker and militarily insignificant in comparison with the big Powers, but the quality of their relationship and of their attitude to each other is as between equals. And this is not yet true of the relations with African states. Recognition of this disparity infuses African nationalism with one of its strongest impulses – the passionate aspiration to "make up for the centuries that have been lost under colonialism"; and to "catch up" with the developed countries. Hence the concentration on modernization, technological advancement, higher education, industrialization and (to a lesser extent) on agrarian revolution.

It is this enthusiasm to "leap across centuries" that gives to the mainstream of African nationalism its revolutionary fervour. Because it is essentially a modernizing force (as it became in Japan) it is impatient with traditionalists, tribalists and peasant conservatism.

An important presupposition of African nationalism is that there is an essential community of interest between all African states in co-operating to achieve rapid economic development for the continent as a whole. This aspiration towards Pan-Africanism expresses itself practically in efforts to create continent-wide institutions to cover every aspect of economic, education and technical development. These are set out in the Charter of the Organization of African Unity.

Another contrast between African and European nationalism

is that the struggle in Africa was never primarily to establish nation-states. The foundations of the modern centralized state in Africa were created not by the nationalists but by the alien rulers. And the supra-tribal concept of the modern nation grew largely out of the experience of the anti-colonial struggle. While therefore, it was convenient and more effective for the liberation movements to fight within certain recognized territorial limits and in the name of the nation, the effort to create a nation-state was secondary to the main tasks of African nationalism. The aim was "liberation" and "freedom"; the enemy was the alien ruler; the chosen weapon was the "national liberation" struggle; the immediate field of contest was the territorial unit fixed by the alien ruler. But although the nationalist struggle was segmented for reasons of convenience and effectiveness, its aims were shared by all Africans. Victory for one was victory for all. "Ghana's independence is meaningless without the independence of the whole of Africa," Dr Nkrumah proclaimed in his moment of triumph. Others have said the same. Tunisia and Morocco risked their independence to help Algeria, and so on.

As each victory was recorded, African nationalism developed new thrusts against "the remnants of colonialism". Thus the decision taken at the Addis Ababa summit conference of Heads of African states in May 1963 to throw their weight behind the "liberation movements" in the Portuguese territories, in Southern Rhodesia, in South-west Africa and in South Africa should be seen as flowing naturally from this sense of African unity in the face of "European supremacy". Even those nationalist leaders reluctant to become too involved in these struggles were not sufficiently convinced of their practical interests to withstand the collective voice of African nationalism at the Addis Ababa conference.

What, it will be asked, will unite and reactivate the fervour of African nationalism once there are no more "outposts of colonialism" in Africa? Will not African nationalism then do what

European nationalism did before: become divisive and turn inwards against itself? This cannot of course be ruled out. However, it is important to recall that there was no time when European nationalism operated as an European unifying force against external or internal enemies. European nationalism in the nineteenth and twentieth centuries set out to divide European nations; African nationalism sets out to unite them. Their basic motivation is different, even if there are similarities in their power drives. If, therefore, African nationalism should one day become divisive, it will be in a different situation from that known in Europe. It is certainly premature to conclude that because nationalists behaved in one way in Europe they must necessarily behave the same way in Africa.

Meanwhile, however, there is no sign of African nationalism being in any great danger of running out of enemies in the near future, thus depriving it of one of the forces that unifies it. Ahead lie the struggles against Portuguese colonialism. Beyond that the even deadlier struggle against *apartheid* in South Africa – a struggle that might easily transform the present relationships between Europe and Africa; possibly even alter the nature of African nationalism from its essential tolerance of Europeans to a bitter intolerance.

Some Problems of Independence
by Robin Hallett

On the map Africa presents the simplest shape of any of the continents. In recent history most of the countries of Africa seem to fit into the same pattern of experience. This simplicity and these similiarities disguise the vast differences that exist between the various states of the continent. Take size: the Congo or the Sudan are each as large as Western Europe, Togo or Burundi smaller than Scotland. Or population: Nigeria, "Africa's giant", contains over 55 million people, Gambia, Gabon and Mauritania each have a population considerably smaller than Birmingham or Glasgow. Or wealth: the average income per head in Ghana is more than £70, in Ethiopia or the Voltaic Republic less than £20. Or historical experience: Morocco possesses a monarchy and a highly developed culture reaching back more than a thousand years, Kenya, by contrast, is made up of a variety of tribal groups, most of which only three generations ago had hardly been touched by the outside world. To these differences must be added the glaring contrast between the handful of white-dominated states in southern Africa and their newly-independent neighbours to the north, a contrast made sharper by the fact that South Africa, with its solid industrial base, is the only African country to have reached the stage of economic "take-off". Here then is a diversity greater than Europe affords. And yet, leaving aside the white-minority states of southern Africa, one may say that all the governments of all the nations of Africa find themselves facing broadly similar tasks – the creation and maintenance of national unity, the improvement of the life of their people by the development of new sources of wealth, the establishment of a harmonious relationship with the outside world.

Most of the newly independent states of Africa are in a literal sense "new nations". Never before has there been a sovereign Nigeria or Kenya or Cameroun. Yet these are new nations set in old countries, countries with a complex political history. That part of West Africa, for example, transformed by the British between 1861 and 1914 into the colony of Nigeria, contained a century ago a multitude of political societies ranging in size from tiny independent village communities to the powerful Fulani Empire of Sokoto. Every other country in Africa presented in the last century the same phenomenon, an extraordinary range of independent units whose people frequently

187

differed sharply from one another in physical appearance, in religion, in language, in customs and in political institutions. At the end of the last century the European powers spread their rule over most of Africa; in doing so they established definite frontiers for their colonies most of which were far larger than even the largest African kingdoms of the past. Thus peoples who had often fought one another – the Masai and the Kikuyu in Kenya, for example – found themselves forced to live peacefully together under the framework of law and order established by the new colonial administration. The colonial order lasted little more than half a century. As the colonial powers prepared to withdraw, it became clear that in every colony after independence some new political machinery would be needed to hold the territory together and to prevent it from being torn asunder by a recrudescence of the old tribal tensions. This new political machinery, this new unifying force was provided in most African countries by the emergence of political parties capable of acquiring a mass following.

Kwame Nkrumah's Convention People's Party, founded in the Gold Coast (now Ghana) in 1949, provided the model that many other African parties were to copy. With an efficient chain of command reaching from the leader in the capital to the local secretary in the village in the bush the new parties gathered a country-wide following. At the same time they used modern techniques – slogans, rallies, party newspapers, youth leagues and so on – to encourage a sense of purpose and develop a spirit of national unity. But if one can detect a basic similarity in the new African parties, their development varied from country to country. In Tanganyika only one significant party was ever established; in the Belgian Congo more than a score of parties contested the elections held just before independence; in Ghana and in Kenya the major party was confronted by a number of smaller groups representing local tribal interests.

The presence of more than one party in most newly-independent countries suggested to some outside observers that African states would follow the democratic pattern of free elections and a vigorous opposition. In fact in most newly-independent states the opposition parties soon came to be regarded by the party in power as seditious forces. This view was not entirely unreasonable: in many African countries politicians in opposition, despairing of achieving power by legitimate means, were prepared to use violence to overthrow the existing government. The threat of violence was met by the suppression of political liberties. To hold a country together in the difficult years after independence it was essential, many Africans argued, to create "a one-party state".

Is the "one-party state" merely an euphemism for dictatorship? No, advocates of the system have pointed out, because within the single party there may still be complete freedom of discussion. Yet in fact in African one-party states they include not only Ghana, Kenya and Tanzania but most of the former French territories; the men at the top have tended to become quickly resentful of criticism from the rank and file. It is here that the theory of the "one-party state" is at its weakest. Opponents of the single party find that the only effective way in which they can express their criticism of the government is by violent means, by attempted assassination or by *coup d'état*. However well-established they may appear, few African governments can now discount the possibility of revolution.

In order to strengthen their position, all African governments have to pay particular attention to the civil service, the army and the police. Without an efficient civil service there can be no hope of orderly development; without an efficient police force backed by the power of the army it becomes impossible to maintain law and order. Yet most African countries have seen a serious decline in the efficiency of these services since independence. Such a decline was not unexpected. At the time of independence in nearly every African country most of the senior posts in the civil service, the army and the police were still in European hands; after independence many Europeans resigned of their own accord or were forced to retire to make room for African successors. Some of the new African civil servants and army officers have shown themselves men of remarkable ability; others have not been able to cope with the new responsibilities thrust so suddenly upon them. The situation is seen at its worst in the former Belgian Congo: the mutiny of the armed forces against their European officers a few days after independence marked the start of a period of anarchy which still continues. All African politicians have now to face the fact that the army must be regarded as a political force, a force that may be used – as happened in the Sudan in 1958 – to remove them from power. Dictatorship and revolution – in Latin America, in the Middle East and in South-east Asia the pattern is a familiar one; it seems now to be imposing itself on Africa.

Political difficulties cannot be divorced from social and economic problems. All African leaders have been borne to power on "the revolution of rising expectations"; all are pledged to bring to their people – in the slogan adopted by a Nigerian party – "Life More Abundant". In some parts of the continent one child in ten goes to school, while four children in ten die before the age of five – these may be extreme figures but even the wealthiest countries in Africa can produce depressing statistics of poverty, ignorance and disease. Against these immemorial enemies remarkable progress has been made in the last twenty years. Yet one cannot assume that progress will continue indefinitely.

In many parts of Africa the natural obstacles – poor soil, too little rain, too much disease – are exceedingly formidable. The human problems are little less intractable. How does one persuade a poverty-stricken, illiterate and intensely conservative peasant farmer to use chemical fertilizers regularly on his crops and so increase their yield? The task is an essential one, for agriculture provides the basic wealth of every African country.

If a peasant farmer can be taught to produce more, he will earn more money for himself, be able to provide his family with a better diet, contribute more to the cost of the schools and hospitals that he needs, enlarge through his own purchases the size of the internal market without which local industries have no chance of becoming established. To teach an African farmer to use fertilizers – the task seems absurdly simple; in fact it is exceptionally arduous, for it means changing the ingrained habits and the thought-processes of communities whose traditional way of life has altered very little whatever revolutions may have occurred in the distant cities of their land.

Education clearly provides part of the answer; and in no other field of development have such spectacular advances been recorded. Yet the great increase in the number of children attending school has brought unforeseen problems. A boy leaves his village in the bush to attend a school in the town. When he finishes his years at school, he may well prefer to stay on in the town rather than return to his home. In the town, after all, life seems more rewarding and more exciting: a junior clerk may earn a cash salary of £100 a year, a farmer in the bush no more than £20. Yet the economy has not developed fast enough to provide a greatly increased number of new jobs. So the labour market is flooded with school-leavers and the towns with unemployed young men. Unemployment breeds bitterness and discontent.

The unemployed – and they are to be found in every great city, the real "angry young men" of Africa – cannot help contrasting their lot with that of their more fortunate fellows – the small élite of politicians and civil servants with large salaries and generous allowances. In some West African countries a member of parliament receives £800 a year for attending a session that lasts two months; to earn the same amount in cash it would take many African farmers forty years. Thus one of the consequences of independence has been the emergence of social divisions based on wealth of a kind which hardly existed before. To some extent the tensions are muted by the fact that every successful man in Africa finds himself called upon to support a horde of relations, the members of his extended family. Yet when a man feels that his primary obligation is towards his own family, he can make corruption and nepotism, the disposal of the assets of the community for his own benefit, appear at least in his own eyes the most venial of offences. Corruption and nepotism are rampant abuses in many African countries. Unchecked they produce among honest men a sense of impotence, cynicism and despair.

Unemployment can be reduced by creating new industries in the towns; the isolation of rural communities, one of the basic causes of peasant conservatism, can be broken down by the building of new roads. Roads and industries feature prominently in the development plans which all African countries have drawn up. But in financing these plans most African countries face one particularly grave difficulty. Much of their revenue comes from the taxes imposed on export crops. Yet the price of these crops is subject to constant fluctuations in the world market. If the prices of raw materials fall as they have done in recent years, African countries are bound to find that they can no longer finance their plans. One way out of their dilemma is to diversify their exports: Nigeria and Libya, for example, are profiting from the discovery of rich deposits of mineral oil. Another way is to work towards an international agreement that will guarantee stable prices. Yet, even with stable prices and diversified exports, African countries will find themselves dependent for the forseeable future on foreign aid – whether it takes the form of money to pay for essential equipment or technicians to establish new industries, or teachers to pass on new skills.

So grave are the internal difficulties facing every African state that some African leaders may well regret that they must devote so much of their time to foreign affairs. Yet no African state, no matter how small or remote, can isolate itself from the outside world. Every new nation is a member of UNO and of the Organization of African Unity. Every African government must look abroad for aid. Ten years ago the continent was still largely a colonial preserve. Today America and Russia, China and India, West Germany and Israel, indeed most of the states of Asia, Europe and America, seem anxious to extend their contacts with the new nations of Africa. In this situation there exist the possibility of developments that some may find disquieting.

For African states, however passionately they proclaim their belief in "non-alignment", may find it hard to avoid being drawn into the dreary conflicts of the Cold War. Already indeed one can detect an ideological divide between the "progressives" – Ghana, Tanzania and Algeria among them – who find a large measure of inspiration in the East and the "conservatives" – they include Nigeria, Senegal and Liberia – who are more at ease in the West. Already too, in early 1965, there is evidence of many foreign powers, African and non-African, Communist and anti-Communist, fishing discreetly in the troubled waters of the Congo.

The Congo will remain a political quagmire for years to come. Even graver, however, is the crisis that looms over southern Africa. The members of the Organization of African Unity have proclaimed their determination to remove the last remnants of colonialism, as represented by the present governments of the Portuguese territories, of Rhodesia and of South Africa. Yet the new nations of Africa are too weak militarily to seriously threaten the well-armed states of southern Africa. The only way in which they can achieve their ends is by persuading the great powers of the world – Britain and the U.S.A., Russia and China – to intervene in southern African affairs. Southern Africa threatens then to become the scene of a crisis of enormous complexity and frightening proportions. Such a crisis could hardly develop without having a profound effect on the internal politics of many African states.

In the history of most revolutions the first careless rapture of success has been followed by long hard years of gloom and strain. Africa seems likely to be following this pattern. Yet looking back the leaders of African nationalism can claim one profoundly creative and beneficial achievement; they have restored the dignity and self-respect of their peoples and won for their nations an assured place in the councils of the world. From the outside world the peoples of Africa need neither pity for their difficulties nor condescension for their failures, but only a humane, realistic and sympathetic understanding of the tasks that will be with them for many generations.

CHAPTER 8

THE PHENOMENON OF NATIONALISM IN THE MIDDLE EAST SINCE 1945

by Professor E. Kedourie

The area known to contemporary writers as the Middle East lies in South-west Asia and North Africa. For over thirteen centuries now, this region has been at the centre of the Muslim domain. In the last century and a half it has come under the domination of Europe and its cultural influence. Today, the political and military domination has largely vanished, but European cultural influence has gradually penetrated all spheres of life with profound and sometimes disconcerting consequences.

One consequence of the contact with Europe has been the prodigious spread of a European idea, the idea of nationalism. Nationalism as an ideology was prevalent in Europe early in the last century. It asserts that humanity is naturally divided into "nations", that these "nations" must each preserve their own original and peculiar character, that to do so they must be organized into independent and sovereign states. According to this doctrine it is wrong and immoral for one "nation" to rule another, and nationalism must by definition be, as the term goes, anti-colonialist and anti-imperialist. Nationalism has many unmistakable characteristic manifestations in the political life of a society, but owing to the very tenets of the doctrine, the political activity nationalism most emphasizes is the struggle against alien rule.

If we look at the Middle East in 1945, we find that of the various groups inhabiting it, it is the Arabic-speaking group which is still in many ways subject to European rule and influence, and we might therefore expect Arab nationalism to be the most active in the years following the Second World War. It is true that during the war, Iran was jointly occupied by British and Russian troops, but soon after the war discord between the Western Powers and the Soviet Union resulted in a situation such that both the British and the Russian armies had to evacuate the country. Again, in 1950–1 there was a brief episode in which the Anglo-Iranian Oil Company was accused of practising "economic imperialism"[1] and expropriated. But internal and external opposition brought about the speedy downfall of the Musaddiq government, which had carried out the expropriation.

The Arabic-speaking areas of the Middle East were, in 1945, bound in one way or another to two European Powers, Great Britain and France, of whom the first was unmistakably the paramount power in the Eastern Mediterranean, and the second in North Africa. These two powers had taken a prominent part in the two World Wars and, in 1945, found themselves greatly weakened, their dominance and that of Europe seemingly at an end. That dominance had been both short in duration and extraordinary in character. It had lasted for somewhat less than a century and a half, during which Europe was the political and military centre of the world, its intellectual and moral prestige incomparable, its standards and way of life the object of universal emulation. The Europe which reached such a pinnacle was, as the poet Valéry described it, a mere peninsula of Asia and, compared to the world it dominated, a dwarf in point of

---

[1] The idea of "economic imperialism", in which the doctrine of nationalism and Marxism–Leninism meet, has many variants: one variant (favoured by Lenin and Hobson) considers that military conquest is caused by the desire for economic exploitation, another holds that alien rule must lead to exploitation, yet a third – the one most prevalent today – has it that "capitalist exploitation" is tantamount to actual imperial rule, that it is "neo-colonialism".

territory, population and resources; and yet the world acquiesced in its domination, which was destroyed not by a revolt of subject populations, but by a ferocious and ruthless struggle between the Great Powers of Europe. Nothing perhaps better exemplifies the extraordinary manner in which Europe dominated the rest of the world than the very small number of Englishmen who until 1947 ruled India with the ready acquiescence of its millions.

In 1945 this dominance was gone, and Europe was overshadowed by two new Great Powers, the U.S.A. and the U.S.S.R., confronting each other across the world, the rulers of which were by doctrine, and by inclination, "anti-imperialist" and "anti-colonialist". The views, wishes and policies of these two Powers would have a decisive effect on the behaviour of those European states whose paramountcy had disappeared, but the past rewards and trappings of which still in some measure subsisted in the years immediately following the Second World War.

Be it noted that in spite of their diminished position, Great Britain and France were still at the end of the Second World War easily and overwhelmingly superior, in point of industrial and military capacity, of administrative organization and political stability, to the Middle Eastern countries where their authority and influence was to be successfully challenged. It was their inferiority *vis-à-vis* the U.S.A. and the U.S.S.R. which led to the loss of their position. Time and again these European Powers found themselves obliged to defer to the wishes and views of these two Powers and quite unable to checkmate them. Now both the U.S.A. and the U.S.S.R. were "anti-colonialist". Their respective traditions and official doctrines, the temper and habits of their public men, their immediate interests and their very rivalry in all parts of the world made the two countries adopt – from different motives, to be sure – a line of policy hostile to the maintenance of European rule and influence in the Middle East. This was the case when the

U.S.S.R., no doubt in the hope of ousting the British from Palestine, supported partition in 1947; this was again the case when the U.S.A. – as appears from the first volume of Sir Anthony Eden's memoirs – between 1952 and 1954 constantly exhorted, cajoled and pressed the British government to give up the Suez base; it was supremely the case in 1956 when the U.S.A. and the U.S.S.R. adopted policies which concurred in frustrating France and Great Britain from prosecuting their quarrel with Egypt.

To the anti-colonialism of the two dominant Powers may be added that of the intellectual classes in Western Europe. Great Britain and France enjoy constitutional and representative régimes in which the franchise is universal and the voters literate. Publicists and journalists therefore can reach and influence this electorate, the opinions of which governments have at one time or another to take more or less into account. Large sections of the intellectual classes of Great Britain and France have for some time now laboured under strong feelings of guilt for past domination. These feelings, their revulsion from the autocracy of colonial régimes, their fervent desire to make amends they have constantly expressed eloquently and persuasively. Their views have found some resonance in the public, and have created a climate of opinion in which "dominion over palm and pine" has become utterly discredited, and its feeble and hesitant apologists held up to ridicule.

Such, then, was the favourable climate in which Middle Eastern nationalism found itself operating in the two decades since 1945. As has been seen, the most active nationalist movements in this period were those of the Arabic-speaking countries. It remains now to discuss the character and aim of these movements, and the extent and nature of their success. It is convenient to begin with Egypt. The recent history of this country is different from that of its Arabic-speaking neighbours. The ambition and the extraordinary ability of Muhammad Ali endowed Egypt in the first half of the nineteenth century with a solid state structure effectively independent from that of the Ottoman Empire of which Egypt was nominally a province. His dynasty, and notably the Khedive Isma'il, built on the foundations he had laid. The British, after their occupation of the country in 1882, were anxious to minimize Ottoman claims and interference in a country so important strategically; they continued and improved Muhammad Ali's work. So that when, at the end of the First World War, the British position in Egypt was first seriously challenged, the country was endowed with a tough administrative structure, and its official, political and intellectual class had, for some time, been accustomed to think of Egypt as a political entity on its own. Egyptian nationalism, which became a powerful political force after 1919, aimed at the total evacuation of British forces and at the creation of an absolutely independent Egypt. Egyptian nationalists did not look beyond such a goal which came to be sensibly within their reach with the signature of the Anglo-Egyptian Treaty of 1936, which limited the number of British troops in Egypt and confined them to certain bases, and clearly envisaged their eventual total withdrawal. But developments in the Middle East after 1918 introduced a new factor in Egyptian political calculations which have had far-reaching and as yet unexhausted consequences. In 1924, the Turkish Grand National Assembly abolished the Ottoman Caliphate, and Fuad, the descendant of Muhammad Ali and now King of Egypt, aspired to this, the highest political office in Islam. Such an ambition meant that Fuad considered Egypt's stature now to be such that it could replace the defunct Ottoman Empire as the leading state in Islam. But to aspire to a Caliphate after 1918 was to indulge in antiquarian fancy, for the political conditions of Muslim countries, the disruption of traditional Islamic society, the rapid and irresistible spread of secularism among the Muslim literate and intellectual classes, left no scope for an office which was as much religious as it was political. It is therefore not surprising that the attempts to establish an Egyptian Caliphate between the wars should have been utterly fruitless, and that the Egyptian ambition to play a leading rôle in the Middle East in the end took a different channel. After the outbreak of the Second World War Egypt wished to be not so much the leading Muslim state as the foremost Arab state, and it thus became the active proponent of Arab nationalism after 1945. This Arab orientation was – like so much else – adopted and greatly emphasized by the officers who carried out a *coup d'état* in 1952, substituting a Republic for the Monarchy and confirming the adage that the president of a republic is only a king writ large. Arab nationalism had this in common with specifically Egyptian nationalism, that both after 1918 were directed against European Powers, and particularly against Great Britain. But this is not to say that after 1945 Egyptian nationalism becomes completely submerged in Arab nationalism; it remains a distinct strand which might become more powerful should Egypt's Arab policy continue to be unsuccessful. How distinctive Egyptian nationalism was and how it might come into conflict with the objects of Arab nationalism may be illustrated by a small but significant incident. In 1949 Egypt was at war with the state of Israel, a war in which she had become engaged in pursuance of her Arab policy; she was at the same time engaged in acrimonious debate with Great Britain over the evacuation of British troops from Egypt. It happened that Israeli troops fighting on their southern front came to encroach on Egyptian territory. The British Foreign Secretary at the time, Mr Bevin, was distinctly friendly to the Arab cause in Palestine and hostile to the Zionists; by the terms of the Anglo-Egyptian Treaty of 1936 Egypt could call on her British ally for help in defending her territory; British troops were near the scene of the operations. And yet the Egyptian government would not invoke British help in a matter which Arab nationalism claimed to be one of life and death: British help against the Zionists was for Egypt less acceptable than Israeli invasion of its territory.

What then was this Arab nationalism of which Egypt has become the leader and advocate? We may, for a start, say that it is Pan-Arabism. It is, in other words, a doctrine to the effect that the Arabs form one nation and must come together in one state. The doctrine was first mooted by some obscure writers at the beginning of the twentieth century when Arabic-speaking lands in Asia generally formed part of the Ottoman Empire; it was taken up by some young Arabic-speaking officers in the Ottoman Army in the last years before the First World War. With the destruction of the Ottoman Empire in 1918, some of these officers, who had deserted from the Ottoman Army and joined the rebellion of the Sharif of Mecca, which the British government had sponsored in 1916, came to be the principal men in the new state of Iraq which Great Britain set up and which was formed out of the three Ottoman vilayets of Mosul, Baghdad and Basra. These officers, with their Pan-Arab ideals, were in control of the Iraqi state machine. They could, and did, spread Pan-Arab doctrine in the state schools and strove so far as they could to advance Pan-Arabism in the neighbouring Arabic-speaking countries. In the period between the wars Pan-Arab ideology made great strides among the younger generation, and it was then that the doctrine became fully developed, was endowed with a respectable body of literature, and equipped with a wide range of arguments. The reasons for this rapid and extensive spread are interesting. In the first place, there was increasing central control by capital cities over the provinces, a control made possible by the overwhelming military superiority of the Western Powers who had inherited the Ottoman position in these lands, and by the efficient administrative machinery which their agents created and in some cases themselves operated. This efficient central control broke down the isolation of provinces, made for increasing ease of communication, and worked towards the spread of literacy which for the first time exposed whole populations to the seductions of the written word, and thus created an ever-widening audience for publicists and ideologues. In the second place, the disappearance of the Ottoman Empire and therefore of Muslim supremacy in these immemorially Islamic lands created a sense of shock, a disorientation, and a resentment which was all the greater in that the Muslim Ottoman power was now replaced by a Christian European power. But this shock and resentment could no longer be expressed in Islamic terms. Turkey, the centre of the Caliphate, had itself abolished the Caliphate in 1924 and adopted secularism as a rule of public life. As the kings of Egypt found when they wanted to acquire the Caliphate for themselves, Islam as such and by itself was no longer a focus of political loyalty. In these conditions, the shock and the resentment found their expression in the new doctrine of Pan-Arabism, which provided a justification and a goal for the struggle against Great Britain, France and Zionism.

So that by 1945 a new generation was coming into positions of power and influence which, as no generation before it had been, was committed to the doctrines of Pan-Arabism. What was the scene which confronted them? It was a complex and confusing scene for which the simple certainties of their faith provided little guidance. Their goal, they had been taught, should be the formation of a single Arab state. If they looked round them, they saw a multiplicity of states all indeed proclaiming their great desire for unity, and yet making not the slightest effort to bring about this unity. Egypt had been endowed during the nineteenth century with a stout administrative structure; the British Mandatory in Iraq and the French Mandatory in Syria had worked to create independent structures of the same kind and all these structures were now controlled not by foreign officials but by indigenous ministers, bureaucrats and officers who were loath to give up power and influence in favour of some larger structure, the ultimate nature of which was absolutely unknown. If the men actually in control in 1945 proclaimed the slogans of Arab unity, it must have seemed to the younger generation pressing behind them that this was mere insincerity, that these men repeated such slogans either because they were committed by past pronouncements which they dared not disavow, or else because these slogans were useful in the struggle for power in which they were continually engaged. To the younger men there was no better proof of this than the Palestine fiasco. Here was an issue on which there was absolute unanimity. The Zionists were a grave danger to Arab unity, and had to be resisted at all costs: such had been the universal verdict. And yet how different the actions of the Arab leaders were, compared to their words. What they showed was indecision, improvization and a mistrust of one another perhaps even deeper than their common hostility to the Zionists. If they finally went to war, this was a last-minute decision unconsidered, unprepared for, taken more in order to forestall their ostensible allies than to prevent the partition of Palestine. What better proof of this than the incredible and ignominious defeat at the hands of the hitherto despised Zionists?

After 1945, and particularly after 1948, the rulers of the Arabic-speaking countries had then to contend with the profound disaffection of an appreciable segment of the intellectual and official classes. This disaffection they themselves had in a large measure created by systematically inculcating in the younger generation a political ideology by which they came to be judged and found wanting. To give a single but most significant example. Nuri al-Sa'id (1889–1958) began his career as an officer in the Ottoman Army, from which he deserted in 1914 as a result of his involvement in Arab nationalist conspiracies. After the First World War he became a leading politician in Iraq, and in the 1940's and 1950's the most important political figure in the country. He was all through his life a leading advocate of Arab unity, and his efforts during the Second World War led to the formation of the Arab League which embodied the utmost in the way of co-operation and agreement which the Arabic-speaking countries have hitherto been able to attain. In July 1958 in the course of a *coup d'état* he was murdered and his body dragged through the streets of Baghdad, this being proclaimed the just reward of a traitor to Arabism and a servant of British imperialism. The leader of the *coup d'état* was Abd al-Karim Qasim who, born in 1914, was the exclusive product of the educational and military system shaped and controlled by Nuri and his colleagues who, like him, were mercilessly swept away in 1958.

In the 1940's and 1950's then, Arab nationalism proved to be a force directed primarily against existing régimes within Arabic-speaking countries of the Eastern Mediterranean. As for the foreign European Powers whose presence and control had evoked and often fostered this nationalism, for the reasons set out above, their position in the world was much too weak, their counsels too divided, for them to set up much resistance to an assault on their remaining positions in the area. French dominance in Syria and the Lebanon had with British assistance been destroyed with little effort before the end of the war, whilst Great Britain herself voluntarily gave up her bases in Egypt and Iraq in 1954 and 1955 respectively. If it was a war the European Powers were engaged in, it was a phantom war which was fought – and decisively lost – in London, Paris and Washington. In the Middle East, it is true, they were denounced and constantly held up to hatred, contempt and ridicule, but they rather served as convenient sticks with which some Pan-Arabs beat other Pan-Arabs. The one struggle against a non-Arab interest in which Arab nationalists found themselves engaged in the Eastern Mediterranean was the Palestine War of 1948. Of the long-standing and uncompromising hostility to Zionism among the Palestinians and their correligionists in the neighbouring countries there can be no shadow of doubt. But we still do not know in any detail the stages by which the members of the Arab League decided to intervene militarily in Palestine in May 1948. The evidence now available indicates that this was an improvized and belated decision, the consequence as much of inter-Arab rivalry as of the desire to prevent the establishment of a Zionist state. The war ended in immediate defeat for the Arabs, the establishment of the state of Israel and a military deadlock which is still unresolved.

The one other war in which Arab nationalists were involved after 1945 took place in the Western Mediterranean, in what used to be French North Africa. In this area Algeria had been occupied by France in 1830, and intensively colonized by European settlers since that date. Algeria was divided into three *départements* which – whatever the actual facts – were supposed to be indistinguishable from the *départements* into which metropolitan France was divided. Tunisia, on the other hand, was a protectorate under French control since 1881. Morocco too was a protectorate, but its territory was divided between two Powers: Spain, which had a small zone in the north-west of the country, and France, which controlled the rest since 1912. In both Tunisia and Morocco European settlers had established themselves, but they never became as numerous or as powerful as in Algeria; and, what is equally important, the régime of the protectorate endowed these two countries with an efficient administrative structure which served to unify the country and facilitated by its very orderliness the creation and organization of anti-French nationalist movements. So long as France was a great power these movements made little headway, but in the decade after 1945, France, humiliated by German defeats, beset by troubles at home and abroad, was in no mood to resist a challenge by Tunisian and Moroccan nationalists. In fact there was very little French resistance to such a challenge in the first half of the 1950's, and by 1956 the French protectorate was terminated in both countries. Had France in the 1950's been able and willing to emulate Soviet methods as they were seen in Hungary in 1956, the outcome might have been quite otherwise. But as in the Eastern Mediterranean, here too the disappearance of European dominance was, to use an expression of the historian Marc Bloch, an *étrange défaite*.

But this was not the case in Algeria. Here a long and cruel war from the end of 1954 to 1961 ended by a defeat for France, the expropriation and departure of the settlers, and the creation of an Algerian republic ruled by the successful leaders of the rebellion. The anti-French movement began in 1954 in a distant part of Algeria, organized and supported by a handful of rebels; the conditions they confronted seemed unpropitious and their prospects desperate. It is true that the anti-colonialist climate in the world favoured them, that after the withdrawl of French control over Tunisia and Morocco they had in these two countries privileged sanctuaries immediately to the east and west of Algeria, and that substantial help was reaching them from friendly countries. But their own achievement remains undeniable. It is to have managed, in the face of formidable and determined resistance, to break decisively the cake of custom which made the Algerian population acquiesce in French rule for a century and more; it is to have rendered Algeria ungovernable by the French. Algeria remains the only war which was fought and decisively won by Arab nationalists. Palestine was a defeat, and the rest shadow-boxing.

Thus, two decades after the end of the Second World War European dominance over the Middle East has almost completely receded, and if a principal object of nationalism is to do away with foreign control, then Arab nationalism has attained its object. But if Arab nationalism be taken to mean Pan-Arabism – and this has been its meaning in the past and so it remains today – then we must conclude that Arab nationalists have had remarkably little success. The rulers of 1945, Nuri al-Sa'id,

King Faruq, Shukri al-Quwatli, were accused of using the slogans of Arab unity for their own ends, and no doubt the accusation was justified; no doubt Arab unity meant for Egypt her own supremacy over the Middle East, and for Iraq Arab unity likewise meant Iraqi predominance. The critics bitterly denounced these intrigues and claimed that if they had been in power they would have spurned such manœuvres, that it was only because Nuri and the others were reactionaries in league with the imperialists that the aspiration of the people to unity has been thwarted. The critics are now in power and find themselves on the same treadmill as their predecessors whom they had so confidently denounced. They find themselves, in fact, loath to trust their fellow-Arab rulers with power, mistrustful of one another, playing the same desperate game of power which no one, so far, has been decisively able to win, with Arab unity still an unattainable goal, and the prospect before them that of

> a darkling plain,
> Swept with confused alarms of struggle and flight,
> Where ignorant armies clash by night.

Editor's Note on Israel

With the consent of Professor Kedourie, whose treatment of nationalism in the Middle East deliberately excluded Zionism which he considers to be a European rather than a Middle Eastern movement, I have added a brief statement for the convenience of readers wishing to take this factor also into account.

It can be said to contain four ingredients:

1) The historical influences, viz. the ancient Jewish kingdom of Old Testament times, annihilated by the Romans – the Diaspora or long period of the dispersal of the Jews throughout the world – the birth of Zionism in 1897 – the 1917 Balfour Declaration guaranteeing the creation of a Jewish National Home – the British Mandate from 1920 to 1948.

2) When on 14 May 1948 Britain ended the Mandate partition of Palestine between Jew and Arab took forcible effect, and the State of Israel was declared; armies from Egypt, Jordan, Iraq, Syria and Lebanon crossed the border to support the Palestine Arabs. The Jews defeated them, and in 1949, after the failure of a United Nations' Conciliation Committee, a temporary Armistice Agreement was made, which did not however establish a permanent frontier of Israel.

"Ever since then Egypt and to a lesser extent the other Arab states have claimed that a state of war still exists. They have refused to recognize the government, have imposed an economic blockade and have denied Israel the right to use her national lifeline to the East – the Suez Canal" (p. 27, *Middle East Issues*. David Ennals and Ian Campbell, Research Series 220, Fabian International Bureau).

3) A continuing series of border incidents resulted in the Sinai Campaign of October 1956 and the Suez Crisis in which so many Great Powers' interests were at stake that a regional dispute became an international incident, marked by U.N. intervention. Since then UNEF (the Emergency Force), UNTSO (the Truce Supervisory Organization) and UNRWA (the Relief and Works Agency) have uneasily stood watch over Arab-Israeli relations, always threatening to explode into open hostilities, and UNRWA continues to succour the million or more Arabs, who became refugees from Palestine after 1948.

4) The city of Jerusalem, divided between Jew and Arab, may properly be regarded as symbolic of a twofold predicament:

a) Unresolved conflict between Arab nationalism with a strong Islamic religious element in its bloodstream and Israeli nationalism with a strong Judaic religious element in its bloodstream – both claiming possession of a narrow strip of Eastern Mediterranean seaboard, which cries out economically for joint treatment by them.

b) Jealousy between the U.S.A., the U.S.S.R. and other

states regarding control of oil and strategic centres in the Middle East, this makes an already complex situation of passionately opposed nationalisms still more complex by reason of their connection with Great Power rivalry.

CHAPTER 9

REVOLUTION AND REFORM IN LATIN AMERICA

by Harold Blakemore

The dictum of Alexander Dumas that "all generalizations are suspect – including that one" is useful to remember when discussing Latin America. For here is a region which embraces twenty different states but one which, all too often, that mythical but useful creature, the average Englishman, assumes to have a unity and common character. One imagines that the assumption derives partly from the fact that the term Latin America is not merely geographical but cultural as well, referring, of course, to the twenty states of the Western Hemisphere which were formerly the colonial possessions of three Latin powers of Europe – Spain, Portugal and France – and of which no less than eighteen were parts of a single empire. The long colonial experience of the region, some three hundred years, imprinted firm European features of which language and religion are the most obvious. Thus, eighteen states have Spanish as the common tongue, Brazil has Portuguese, and Haiti, French, and all twenty are, nominally at least, Roman Catholic in religion.

Other common traits certainly create affinities among Latin Americans, but their significance can be exaggerated, and it is more often the differences between states rather than the similarities which strike the student of Latin America. These, too, go back a long way. The Spanish empire itself was never a unity: its sheer size and geographical diversity, coupled with a scattered pattern of settlement, predisposed its parts to think in local rather than imperial terms, and foreshadowed the later national pattern. Moreover, in the century and a half since independence, the states have gone their own ways, not least in developing nationalisms which are as strong as anywhere else in the world and which accentuate those other factors – size, population, racial composition, degree of political and economic maturity – which differentiate one state from another.

Yet we can still take comfort from the second part of our opening aphorism, and reasons of space demand that we do. For, in looking at Latin America today, we can say that, for many states, the big issues are similar in kind, however different in detail. Politically, the major problems concern stability in government, the orderly transfer of power, and the translation into practice of democratic principles enshrined in many constitutions. Economically, the common aim is to secure growth, and to diversify economies still critically dependent upon the production and export of too few commodities. Socially, almost all the states face acute difficulties in transforming traditional societies into modern ones, though not all the ruling classes are yet convinced that this is either necessary or desirable. Moreover, these broad issues are played out against a background of population explosion in which Latin America leads the world, with an annual rate of increase of around 3%. Finally, for a continent long accustomed to being somewhat on the periphery of world affairs, the emergence of a Communist régime in Cuba since 1959 not only brought the front line of the Cold War nearer; it also projected into sharper focus the interrelated issues of political stability, economic development and social justice which concern nearly all the states.

The challenges, then, are common, but the responses vary, depending upon the particular historical factors which have given each republic its unique character.

To many people, Latin America is synonymous with instability, with revolution and dictatorship as customary features of political life. The reasons for this are many and involved, but a few deserve mention. First, the long colonial era was dominated by absolutist precepts which cared nothing for notions of self-government, denying the local population opportunities to acquire experience in public affairs, a situation which offers a striking contrast both to the British colonies of North America which formed the United States, and also to the states of Asia and Africa which have emerged more recently from British tutelage. The Latin American states, therefore, were ill-equipped to govern themselves after independence.

Secondly, in much of Spanish America, though not in Brazil, independence came only at the cost of long and violent wars with the metropolitan power which exalted men in uniform to positions of authority. In addition, the revolutions were followed in many places by long periods of civil strife as local leaders competed for power, and this further underlined the rôle of the military. When anarchy was the alternative, even dictatorship had its merits, and the tradition of the *caudillo*, the autocratic military leader, was thus strongly established. It is far from dead today.

But civilian strong men have been equally prominent, and the reasons for this are also not hard to seek. The revolutions for independence were basically political, without much economic and social content, their main effect being the replacement of Spaniards from Spain by Spaniards born in America in the seats of power. Many states were huge, their communications poor, and with the masses both illiterate and indifferent to wider events. Thus, a minority class, dominated often by landowners, took politics as its own preserve; the numerically larger groups of Indians or *mestizos* (the mixed race of Indian and Spanish blood) were excluded from government, and an oligarchical system resulted. These ruling classes were socially homogeneous, and the lines which divided them politically were generally ideological – the form of constitutional organization, for example, or the position of the church in society. Since, in addition, political parties usually arose around dominant personalities, the latter often exercised great influence and power, and the importance of this personal element in politics has remained a characteristic of Latin American public life. Again, the narrow class basis of politics, the prominence of the military, and the attraction of the strong man explains, to some extent, the factor of "revolution" in Latin America, for the word is often a misnomer: more often than not, "revolutions" have been engineered by small groups, have taken the form of quick *coups d'état* or barrack revolts, have been comparatively bloodless, and have had little content but the replacement of those in office by those outside. The masses have rarely participated.

While these are features of much of Latin American history in the nineteenth century, the spectrum is naturally broad. Both Brazil, a monarchy from 1822 to 1889, and Chile, ruled by a remarkable, close-knit, landed aristocracy, avoided turbulence for much of the period, and so did Argentina after mid-century. At the other extreme, to give three examples, Central America, Bolivia and Uruguay reeled from dictatorship to anarchy which promised nothing for the future.

The new states began their independent existence with economic disabilities no less formidable than their political ones. As colonies they had been reservoirs of raw materials – not least, precious metals – for the home countries, but they were prohibited from activities inimical to home manufacturers. Thus, with land-holding as the dominant factor – social, no less than economic – and with large-scale manufacture and trade prevented, there was little local capital available, and entrepreneurship was underdeveloped. Consequently, the foreign banker, merchant and man of enterprise filled the breach for the new states. It was the hey-day of free trade doctrines, to which the ruling oligarchies subscribed: they imported their consumer goods from abroad, and allowed foreign capital to enter to develop resources, the export of which they taxed for revenue. Thus, the "export" nature of the economy was perpetuated since foreigners were mainly interested in resources their home markets and industries required, though it is also true that foreign money went into public utilities, thus laying a foundation for future growth. And, although this is necessarily a highly simplified picture, Latin America fell broadly into a pattern of dependence on a limited range of exports, with little development of home industry, thus making them particularly vulnerable to changes in world trade outside their control. They also relied heavily on foreign imports for essential manufactures. Hence, Chile's economy was governed first by copper, then by nitrates, and then, as now, by copper again; Argentina developed a pastoral and agricultural economy on meat and grain, but very little else. Almost every state of Latin America would furnish a similar example.

These, then, were the broad political and economic patterns of the past. Reduced to its essentials, the history of modern Latin America is the story of the attempt to break these moulds, and of the resistances which that attempt evoked. It is far from being a completed story but the pace has undoubtedly quickened in the post-war world, as outside influences have made a greater impact on Latin America, and as that great solvent of the static society, the revolution in communications, has made it clear to Latin Americans that democracy and development for the common good are not unattainable.

The roots of change lie in the late nineteenth and early twentieth centuries, when Latin America was integrated into the world economy. Foreign immigration, foreign capital and foreign enterprise represented a challenge to the old order of semi-feudal societies, governed by élite classes and traditional ideas. Consider Argentina: between 1857 and 1930, over 6 million immigrants entered the country; already, the combined operation of the railway, barbed wire, better breeds of cattle, and refrigeration had propelled Argentina from a backwater to the mainstream of international trade, as the world's leading exporter of meat and a principal producer of grain. The change was accompanied by the rapid growth of towns and cities, facilities for commerce and banking, the development of ports and docks, and it created new classes outside the traditional nexus of master and man. A new middle class – lawyers, bankers, doctors, teachers and merchants – and a new, urban, working-class arose, many of their members of immigrant stock, unencumbered by old ideas, and fiercely nationalist, as naturalized citizens tend to be. The old political structure was inadequate to represent their interests, and new political parties emerged to do so, as well as other European forms of organization such as trade unions. These new parties, Radical and Socialist – more in name than in nature – challenged the older Conservative and Liberal groupings, and politics became more aligned on social and economic issues. For example, the new forces favoured protection not free trade, they sought wider representation in opposition to élite politics, and they expressed a stronger nationalism than the ruling classes whose ties with the foreigner, not least in economic matters, they sometimes regarded as a betrayal of the national interest.

Argentina is the classic example but the same forces were at work elsewhere – in Brazil, notably the south, in Chile, in Uruguay, and in other states, also, though in varying degrees. They had their successes, but space forbids a catalogue, and the old governing classes showed, and still show in places, a remarkable ability to counter attack.

These growing pressures for more genuine democracies and for radical changes in economic structure, accompanied by strong nationalist under-currents, were stimulated further by three events of the twentieth century: the two World Wars, and the Great Depression, 1929–31. Each was a catalyst for political and economic discontent. Thus, the First World War dramatically revealed the fundamental weakness of the Latin American economies, cutting them off from traditional markets for their exports, and from traditional suppliers of manufactures. Indeed, it stimulated Latin America – or parts of it – to begin serious industrialization, boosting further the growth of urban working classes. The war also had an ideological impact, since Allied propaganda, arguing that the world was being made safe for democracy, encouraged Latin American intellectuals and progressives to question dictatorships at home, and the Russian Revolution of 1917 similarly stimulated the parties of the left. The Depression shattered the Latin American economies even more, and it precipitated political convulsion in almost every state. The Second World War had a similar, though more profound, effect to the First, economically and ideologically. It gave a massive stimulus to both industrialization and agricultural diversification, and, politically, the paradox that Latin American dictators could declare war on the Axis totalitarian powers exposed them to a challenge to practice at home what they professed abroad. The result in the mid-1940's was a number of civil triumphs over military dictatorships, and generally a wind of change for freer political discussion and organization in countries still ruled by strong men.

But it would be tedious and confusing to detail the post-war changes and chances of the fleeting Latin American political world. Already, in sketching hastily and sweepingly the background to contemporary events, we have ignored two countries – Uruguay and Mexico – which earlier escaped from the round of revolution and dictatorship, characteristic of a number of their neighbours even to today. Uruguay did it in the early twentieth century under the guidance of a most remarkable statesman, José Batlle y Ordoñez, who erected a democratic structure through constitutional reform, effective suffrage and press freedom, and who created a "welfare state" by a series of social measures such as pensions, educational reform and similar acts. Uruguay has since remained something of a model republic in the continent. Mexico's development was far different. After the long and repressive dictatorship of Porfirio Diaz, 1877–1911, a dictatorship which promoted much economic growth but basically at the expense of the masses, a violent revolution and civil war swept away much of the old order. From the chaos there emerged eventually a one-party state which has pursued large programmes of social reform and welfare, and, particularly since 1940, impressive schemes of economic development, though possibly at the expense of the social aspects. The governing party has the curious name of the Revolutionary Institutional Party, for Mexico's remarkable transformation has, in fact, flowed along institutional channels, and revolution, militarism and dictatorship as norms of political action seem to have been completely exorcized.

Uruguay and Mexico are exceptional cases, and they have little affinity with the broad background sketched above. Elsewhere in Latin America, however, we can point more confidently to other examples of the challenge of change in the light of that, somewhat theoretical, explanation. And, as Goethe observed, "all theory is grey", so it may give colour to the contemporary Latin American scene if we devote the rest of this essay to a consideration of individual cases which have been significant for one reason or another. For, however much they differ in detail, each represents our general theme of the battle between the old and the new forces in Latin American society and politics.

Our first case-study is Argentina under Juan Domingo Perón, 1946–55, superficially a typical Latin American military dictatorship, but, in fact, a régime which represented currents of change in its character and programme, and which gave a fundamental shift of direction to Argentine politics. Since the nineteenth century, the latter had been dominated by the small class of great landowners whose fortunes had risen with Argentina's rural transformation, though the twentieth century had seen some liberalization of politics, and even Radical administrations in power. In 1930, however, the economic chaos caused by the Depression, and the ineptitude of the Radical president then in power, led to a strong Conservative reaction and army intervention in politics. From then to 1943 the old classes ruled by fraud and corruption.

Meanwhile, a silent revolution had been in progress in Argentina. Between the two World Wars, the cities, and notably Buenos Aires, had grown enormously at the expense of the countryside; at the same time industrialization proceeded to the point that by 1942 the net value of industrial production equalled the combined value of the pastoral and agricultural sectors. But, by then, this remarkable change reached deadlock: with the masses having only low purchasing power, the internal market was small, and, more fundamental, Argentina's destinies were in the hands of men who no longer represented the economic needs of the nation. Politics had failed to reflect the changing social and economic picture. During the 1930's certain groups, notably some officers of the army, espoused the ideology of a strong, nationalist Argentina, freed from dependence on foreign markets and foreign manufactures, becoming the great power of South America, and many were attracted by the European dictatorships of that period. In 1943, these military groups moved: in a coup they took over the government, intent on a purified political system and determined on a kind of national reformation. After a military dictatorship, in which trade unions were suppressed, colonels took over from provincial governors and even university deans, and the government showed its strong anti-foreign flavour, a series of palace revolts brought to the fore Colonel Perón as Secretary of Labour and Social Security.

It was from this base that Perón built up a position to strike at supreme office. He converted the police force into virtually a private army, secured the support of labour by social benefits – policies he continued later – and, for prestige reasons, urged free elections. After further intrigues at the top, too complicated to detail, Perón emerged triumphant, and carried the polls as President in 1946. For nearly ten years Perón ruled Argentina as a dictator, suppressing all opposition, stifling the press, purging the universities, while, at the same time, preserving the forms of constitutional government. But, despite its totalitarian features, the Perón régime rested on a basis of considerable popular support, particularly from the *descamisados*, "the shirtless ones", the urban working-classes. Part of Perón's appeal lay in his own personality and good looks but he had a powerful ally in his wife, Eva, a striking blonde who came to be regarded almost with reverence by the masses, partly because she sprang from them herself but also because of her drive and initiative in matters concerning the underprivileged. With great publicity, she plunged into questions of health, working conditions and philanthropy, urged on by fierce ambitions for power and prestige, as well as by a desire to revenge herself on the privileged classes in Argentine society.

But programmes as well as personality ensured the Peróns a mass backing for change. The economic programme was strongly nationalistic and it aimed to make Argentina the strongest, self-sufficient power in South America. It was also anti-foreign, and foreign-owned utilities such as the British railways were nationalized. Perón sought to accelerate Argentina's industrialization, and organizations were set up to promote this, as well as to control the country's foreign trade. In fact, throughout the Perón period, there was excessive government interference in economic activities on many fronts, and this eventually created considerable difficulties for the government. Socially, a great deal was done for the masses: higher minimum wages, shorter working-hours, holidays with pay, and other benefits were legislated into existence, and there is no doubt that such measures were long overdue. Those who benefited, chiefly the urban workers, now organized into massive trade unions with Peronist leaders, were the government's strongest allies, but the middle and upper classes suffered, the former particularly by the impact of inflation which Perón's policies encouraged. Moreover, Perón neglected the countryside. Cereal-growing and stock-raising were still vital to the country's health since they earned Argentina's income, yet, despite election promises, Perón did virtually nothing to stimulate production or to alter the tradi-tional structure of rural economy and society. One result of the heavy emphasis on industrialization was a rural migration to the towns, which exacerbated the problem of the country's eco-nomic balance, and, indeed, it was this disequilibrium between the various sectors of the economy which brought a severe economic crisis to Argentina in the 1950's.

Argentina had acquired large foreign-exchange reserves during the Second World War, but these were expended after the war on expropriating the foreign-owned utilities. With industrialization encouraged and agriculture neglected, the volume of exports declined, and a foreign-exchange crisis de-veloped. Moreover, drought and bad harvests in 1952 made matters worse, and, from that date, Perón was obliged to modify many of his basic principles. Other factors intervened: the death of Eva Perón, at the age of thirty-three, in 1952, was a bitter blow, depriving the dictator of his best ally and, indeed, perhaps of the driving-force of his régime. Finally, Perón quarrelled with both the army and the Church.

Faced by a combination of adverse factors, of which the economic was the most serious, Perón changed his policies from 1952. He began to encourage foreign investment in some enterprises but this failed largely since his earlier nationalistic utterances and actions had frightened off foreign capital. Indus-trialization was slowed down, and credits were extended to farmers, and, for almost the first time since he came to power,

Perón began to show a solicitude for employers and white-collar workers as against the manual workers in industry. In fact, this apparent *volte-face* on so many lines of policy disillusioned some of his supporters as circumstances obliged Perón to become more orthodox economically and much less nationalist in his utterances. One example of this change of attitude which had serious consequences was Perón's apparent willingness to allow foreign capital to develop oil-fields in Patagonia, perhaps necessary from the point of view of Argentina's economic position since the cost of oil imports was a major factor in the adverse balance of payments. But this move antagonized many nationalists in the army, and they were later prepared to assist in Perón's downfall. Again, coupled with the undoubtedly repressive nature of the régime with regard to freedoms of speech and organization, was its atmosphere of graft and corruption, particularly in administration and the vastly-expanded government bureaucracy. Finally, Perón's quarrel with the Church, not sufficient in itself to bring him down, was yet a catalyst for many discontents which proved too strong for the dictator and his government.

Events came to a head in the summer of 1955, though the internal story of complicated manœuvres between the various interested parties – the forces, the Church, the trade unions, and so on – cannot concern us here. Suffice to say that when, in September, with discontent rising, the rumour developed that Perón intended arming his trade unions, the army and navy decided that the time had come to act. The navy blockaded the River Plate while provincial army forces moved to take over Buenos Aires; Perón was permitted to go into exile, and officers of the army took over the government, expelling Peronists from all offices. After three years of military rule, elections for Congress were held in 1958, though the Peronists, who represented one-third of the electorate, were not allowed to put up candidates, and the later Presidential election saw Arturo Frondizi, the Radical leader, win with the help of Peronist votes. Yet, he too was deposed by the military in 1962, after allowing Peronist candidates to stand in elections in March. He was deposed because, in those elections, the Peronists won overwhelming successes. Civilian government again returned to Argentina in 1963, after another military interregnum, but the country is still faced with severe economic problems, and the question of political stability is far from solved. Peronism is still a powerful force, though the recent (December 1964) attempt by the ageing Perón himself to return to Argentina was a complete fiasco, and it is likely that, however the movement develops, he himself will not play a prominent rôle.

The future political and economic development of Argentina is obviously a matter of pure conjecture, and Latin American politics have a habit of confounding the best-informed of observers. Nevertheless, it is clear that the Perón régime represents a watershed in Argentine history. For the first time the working classes were able to challenge the old order, and the very duration of the dictatorship for nearly ten years made it inevitable that these new forces must be taken into account in all subsequent political arrangements. The army and the Peronists are still antagonistic interest groups, though each runs the spectrum from extreme left to extreme right. Certainly, the dominant power of the rural-based oligarchy in Argentine affairs has been broken, and politics have become much more the reflection of social and economic interests than they were. The middle class, 40% of the population, is the largest in Latin America, the upper and working classes constituting 10% and 50% respectively. Government, industrial and service enterprises have grown enormously in the last twenty years, and nearly three-quarters of the people now live in cities. Argentina possesses also the highest literacy level in Latin America, one of the highest levels of *per capita* income and one of the most equitably distributed, a relatively low rate of population increase, and, not least, a racial homogeneity which saves her from the complications of some of her neighbours who also seek political stability and economic growth.

But the problems are still formidable. Since 1950 economic growth has failed to keep pace with population expansion; political life has been complicated by the antagonism between conservatives and the military on the one hand and the Peronist working-class forces on the other, and not by any means have all the former recognized that Peronism stands for something more than an extremist working-class movement. Moreover, fluctuations in economic activity and rapid inflation, affecting the workers and the middle class, remain unsolved issues. The answers to the political, economic and social questions of Argentina's future have not yet been found, but the Perón era certainly gave them sharper focus, and no future government can afford to ignore that fact.

To move from Argentina to Guatemala, our second case-study, is to enlarge our argument, for in the Guatemalan revolutionary situation in the post-war period, Latin America had its first example of Communist government. In addition, Guatemala was a world away from Argentina in other respects. It was a "banana" republic, one of those Central American states which are the delight of romantic novelists and Hollywood producers who believe that Latin America is covered by jungle, inhabited by picturesque Indians, and ruled by moustachioed militarists. The real truth is much more interesting.

Half of Guatemala's 3 million inhabitants are Mayan Indians, the other half are *ladinos*, the local term for the mixed race of Spanish and Indian descent. The differences between Indians are basically regional; socially and economically, many live in their own communities on a basis of subsistence farming, though some also grow cash crops for the market. But the *ladinos*, apart from regional differentiation, range in type from the illiterate countryman to the aristocratic landowner, from the city boot-black to the businessman. Yet, the dividing line between Indian and *ladino* is not racial so much as cultural, and the former can transfer from one race to the other largely by adopting the clothing, the speech, and the way of life of his *ladino* neighbour and abandoning his own. This is a gross oversimplification of the cultural complex of Guatemalan society but it will suffice for our purposes.

In 1944 Guatemala had been ruled for fourteen years by Jorge Úbico, a typical *caudillo* who governed by strong-arm methods, and who had encouraged an older trend in his country's economic life by alliance with foreign business at his people's expense. Ninety per cent of Guatemala's exports of coffee and bananas, her staple products, came from foreign-owned plantations, and wages on the latter were incredibly low. Discontent was suppressed and forced labour of Indians was employed: in short, no effort was made to bring to the people as a whole economic and social progress, and politics were closed to all but Úbico's followers.

The war, however, fundamentally altered things in Guatemala, as elsewhere. Thus, the stationing in Guatemala, one of the Allies, of several thousand American troops, contributed to stimulating intellectual *ladino* interest in such matters as electoral freedom, and something of an economic decline which stimulated discontent also created the conditions of revolt. In 1944, therefore, a popular, civilian rising drove Úbico out of office, and put into power a three-man directorate to prepare for free elections. From these, Juan José Arévalo emerged as President in 1945, with a mandate for a strong programme of social and economic reform.

A former school-teacher, Arévalo launched an impressive programme of educational improvement, low cost housing for workers, and other plans of a similar kind. His support came essentially from younger *ladinos* who had been convinced that only revolutionary change could destroy the power of the élite class, representing landowning and business interests, which had dominated Guatemalan life for so long, but which was now an anachronism in the mid-twentieth century. Such reformers wished to integrate the Indians into the national life, give the state greater power in the economy, and set up a democratic system. Arévalo himself talked of "spiritual socialism", whatever that meant, but, in fact, it was the adherents of a ready-made political creed, Marxist communism, which began to infiltrate the unions, politics and government in Guatemala.

These elements of the extreme left achieved greater power under Arévalo's successor, Jacobo Arbenz, who became President in December 1950. He carried further and faster the social revolution initiated by his predecessor, but although the régime rested on the support of the army and organized labour, the Communist Party provided the organization. It took over the direction of the labour organizations which were united into a mass movement, and it provided the personnel for implementation of other policies. Foreign interests were plagued by strikes for higher wages and better conditions – frequently amply justified – and the Government supported these moves. In 1952 Arbenz put through legislation to expropriate some large estates, and land was distributed to the peasants, but, it should be noted, as tenants of the state, not as freeholders. In the same year the Communist Party was legalized, and it became increasingly clear that the faster pace of social reform, much of which was necessary in Guatemala, was only likely to be achieved by the curtailment of political freedom.

A variegated opposition developed in answer to these events, ranging from those who wanted reform but under a liberal, democratic umbrella to those whose privileged interests had suffered in the past few years and who wanted a pure counter-revolution. Moreover, the United States, with John Foster Dulles as Secretary of State, had become alarmed at the progress of communism in Guatemala, and it gave support and encouragement to Guatemalan exiles in Honduras. Finally, in 1954, Guatemala was invaded by these exiles under Colonel Carlos Castillo Armas, and the Arbenz régime was overthrown, not least because the army deserted the President at the crucial moment, since it feared that he intended to arm the peasants.

The Guatemalan revolution was arrested but it is still in dispute as to how far the social clock was put back after 1954. Certainly, communism had suffered a severe setback, and the Castillo Armas régime purged the country of left-wing elements. But the new leader paid more than lip-service to the cause of reform; he continued agrarian reform, though on a reduced scale, permitted labour unions to function while discouraging mass confederations, and his educational programme outshone those of both his left-wing predecessors. But Guatemala was again subjected to a one-party state, and, despite attempts between 1958 and 1963 to achieve some liberalization here, the military take-over of the latter year has effectively arrested all progress in that direction. The period between 1944 and 1954 broke the former élite's monopoly of power, as Perón had done in Argentina, and the reformist urge of those years, though much slower in pace after 1954, may yet be far from spent. Hope lies in the non-revolutionary left-wing forces, in a more sympathetic approach by the United States towards Guatemala's complicated social and economic problems, and in the growing realization that, as in other Latin American states, if reform does not come by evolution, revolution will point the way.

It pointed the way in Bolivia in dramatic and comprehensive fashion, and if Guatemala is an example of an arrested social revolution, Bolivia in the post-war period represents the most sweeping changes to come over a Latin American society since the Mexican Revolution much earlier in the century, and the Cuban Revolution a few years later.

Of almost all the states of Latin America at the end of the

Second World War, Bolivia had the most turbulent political history. Over four hundred changes of government had occurred since independence, many as short but bloody revolutions, and the country also had perhaps the most acute social divisions. Its 3 million people were divided into Indians, totalling over 50%, whites, and *mestizos*, and, although in Bolivia, as in Guatemala, the dividing lines could be crossed by cultural change, in Bolivia there was much less social mobility than in Guatemala. The economy was basically divided into two sectors: a mineral economy based on the privately-owned tin mines, and geared to the world market, and an agricultural economy, based on both small subsistence farming and on large estates, but affected only by internal factors. The agricultural workers, by and large, knew only local horizons; their lot was miserable, since many were bound to the estates in virtual serfdom, and the condition of the workers in the mines was no better. Their employers, absentee millionaires, lived in luxury on profits from tin, but the workers, their average expectation of life no more than thirty years, supported their families on exiguous wages and worked in conditions that would have seemed appalling in early Victorian England. These economic divisions were reflected in politics: control rested in the hands of a small upper class and the army, with the Indian masses, illiterate and voteless, outside the mainstream of national life.

It was the long and pointless Chaco War with Paraguay, 1932–5, which laid the seeds of change. The war, fought over disputed territory, ended in Paraguay's victory, and the prestige of the Bolivian army suffered. Many whites and *mestizos* found themselves in the front line with the Indian troops, and for some young officers and intellectuals it was a shattering experience. Similarly, for the Indians, uprooted as many had been for the first time in their lives, the war began a process of persuasion that they were part of the nation, and not a race apart. Moreover, in the Bolivian universities currents of Marxist and

Socialist ideas were fermenting in the same period, as were also ideas more in keeping with the philosophies of the European totalitarian governments of the time.

From this time of intellectual change, there emerged in 1940 a new party, the National Revolutionary Party, headed by Victor Paz Estenssoro, a former Professor of Economics. This party favoured the nationalization of tin mines and, from 1943 to 1946, it shared power briefly with the military and carried out a few reforms, but the military was still largely committed to support of the old élite and little of fundamental importance was done. In 1946, however, a violent revolution produced a new government and Paz Estensoro went into exile for six years, leaving Bolivia in the hands of a succession of right-wing governments which were faced by periodic outbreaks of violence from miners and other supporters of the National Revolutionary Party, known usually as the M.N.R. (Movimiento Nacionalista Revolucionario). In free elections in 1951, Paz Estenssoro, still in exile, was voted into the Presidential chair, but the result was negatived by army intervention. At this juncture, the miners, the students and the organized peasants revolted, and for three days La Paz was the scene of a violent battle which culminated in the victory of the revolution and the recall to the Presidency of Paz Estenssoro.

The M.N.R. had a programme to incorporate the Indians into the national life and to destroy forever the privileges of minority groups of mine owners and landowners. The mines were nationalized; educational and social reform plans were promulgated, and, his hand forced faster than he had intended by local peasant groups, Paz Estenssoro also implemented a radical programme of land reform, expropriating the landlords of big estates and redistributing the land to the peasants. The M.N.R. grew into a mass party, reaching down into every level of administration, and Juan Lechín, a radical left-wing leader of the miners, and Minister of Mines, declared that Bolivia's social revolution had been more complete than those of Guatemala or Communist China.

Lechín was right. But the social revolution was nearly accompanied by economic collapse. The agrarian reform, in fact, put Bolivian agriculture on a purely subsistence basis, with individual peasant farmers owning individual tiny plots of land. In place of the *latifundia*, the huge estates, there were now the *munifundia*, the very small farms which were incapable of producing enough to support the population. Moreover, the revolution coincided with the end of the Korean war-boom in commodity prices on world markets, and Bolivia's low-grade high-cost tin – the country's basic export – fell disastrously in price. At the same time, the miners, under Lechín's direction, had vastly increased in numbers, out of all proportion to the needs of the industry. The M.N.R. leadership was also split between moderates, led by Paz Estenssoro and his presidential successor Hernán Siles, and extremists under the demagogic control of Lechín.

What saved Bolivia was a remarkable exhibition of realism by the United States. Having recognized the régime, the United States embarked on a programme of economic existence to Bolivia, encouragement of American investment there, and technical assistance to assist in education, and other programmes of social reform. The moderates of the M.N.R. compromised with reality in the acceptance of this aid from a power they had previously stigmatized as an "economic imperialist", but they did so at the expense of the unity of the M.N.R. To detail the events of the Presidencies of Paz Estenssoro, 1952–6, Siles, 1956–60, and Paz Estenssoro again, 1960–4, would be tedious, and suffice to say that they have been marked by frequent struggles between the left and the moderates in the M.N.R., fluctuating fortunes but no sustained recovery in the economy, personal battles between Paz and Siles on the one hand and Lechín on the other, and a steadily deteriorating political and economic situation. The extremists of the left have gained ground at the expense of the moderates, and, in 1964, Paz's unwise move in getting through Congress a bill to enable a retiring President to succeed himself precipitated a military coup which cost Paz the Presidency and, again, forced him into exile. The military government of General Rene Barrientos has held power and shown its apolitical nature by exiling the left-wing leader, Juan Lechín, and attempting to make the mines economic, despite the protests from the formerly-privileged miners. The outcome – political and economic – remains uncertain.

But the Bolivian revolution, whatever its future course, has ended once for all the exclusion of the Indian from the national life; it has destroyed élite politics and an aristocratically dominated society; it has shown the masses their power, and it has provided for all of Latin America an illustration of the problems – and the penalties – of radical social revolution achieved at the expense of economic growth. How far the masses have benefited in Bolivia from the changes since 1952 is a matter of dispute, and the continuing economic crisis, which has certainly lowered the standard of living of many sections of society, may prove insurmountable. In that unhappy event, the Bolivian revolution may well prove to be not the triumph of change but its tragedy.

Similar doubts may be held about our last example, the Cuba of Fidel Castro, not on social grounds where the revolution was necessary, nor, despite recent hardships, for economic reasons where the old system stood condemned, but in political matters, where a potentially liberal-democratic revolutionary movement was transformed into a one-party Communist dictatorship.

From 1933 to 1958, apart from a respite between 1944 and 1952, Cuba was under the dictatorship of Fulgencio Batista, a military figure whose régime was characterized by no fundamental reform, though its earlier years were not without benefit to the masses. But it was a corrupt and personal régime, and, in its later years, it relied on terror and brutality. It was also under Batista that the American grip on Cuba's economy was tightened, so that by 1958, American interests not only controlled the economic prop of Cuba, the sugar industry, but also half the railways, nine-tenths of electric and telephone services, and much of tourism and mining. Sugar accounted for no less than four-fifths of Cuba's exports, and it was tied to American quotas, with foreign land-holdings in Cuba comprising some 60% of the total land area. Moreover, the seasonal nature of the sugar industry meant that rural life was dominated by part-time employment, and rural poverty, illiteracy and bad health were concomitants of the system.

Yet Cuba was not poor as other Latin American states were poor: its *per capita* income was higher than that of Italy or Japan, and industry had proceeded to the point, by the mid-1950's, of accounting for nearly half the national income. Over half the rapidly rising population lived in cities, and its dominant class was the middle class. And, despite Castro's propaganda on the question of illiteracy, Cuba had a high rate of literacy compared with many other states. But it was less the overall picture of Cuban development than the extreme gulf between rich and poor, between upper-class comfort and peasant poverty, that gave the Cuban revolution its social content.

The demand for political and other reforms came from intellectuals, and Fidel Castro, a law student at Havana University in the late 1940's, soon made a name after his disastrous attack on a barracks on 26th July 1953. At his trial he made a five-hour speech in his defence, attacking Batista and all he stood for, and outlining a programme of political and economic reform. Sentenced to fifteen years' imprisonment, Castro was released after two, as the result of a general amnesty for political prisoners. From Mexico, he organized an expedition which returned to Cuba in November 1956, only to be reduced to a handful in a fight with Batista's troops. The revolutionaries retreated into the mountains. Over the next few years they grew in strength, and established contact with other opposition elements in the cities, yet the band never totalled more than three hundred men until the very end of Batista's régime. What, more than anything, caused Batista's collapse was not the support of the peasant masses, nor the spontaneous rising of the urban workers (who, in fact, believed they had nothing to gain from Batista's fall) but the system of terror which Castro's guerrillas provoked Batista into creating. From this indiscriminate policy all sections of the nation recoiled, except the army which carried it out, and Batista was not so much overthrown by superior force as undermined by internal disintegration.

The revolutionaries came into power on 1st January 1959. Castro had promised democratic government and free elections, liberty of the press, and of organization; economically, he had promised land reform, with indemnities to existing owners who might be expropriated, he had not been too specific on nationalization and foreign interests, and, at times, had expressly disowned such ideas, and foreign observers might be forgiven for assuming that Cuba had inherited a movement believing in political democracy and evolutionary economic and social improvement. Indeed, the first President and Cabinet of 1959 were moderates, though mass trials of Batista's supporters were conducted in an atmosphere of hate which disturbed many foreigners. Programmes of rent reduction, wage increases, the building of houses and schools and hospitals were given great impetus, and, throughout, the revolutionaries gave an impression of personal integrity which contrasted refreshingly with the previous régime.

But it was not to last. An Agrarian Reform Law in May 1959 provided for expropriation of many properties, including foreign-owned ones, with compensation in the form of long-term state bonds, and American protests confirmed the Cuban view that Cuba would never be free so long as American interests remained in Cuba. Politically, 1959 and 1960 were years which saw the resignation of moderates from office or their dismissal, sometimes imprisonment on trumped-up charges for those who had looked to the revolution as Cuba's hope of democratic progressive government. Gradually, the Communist Party – Cuba's oldest political party and the only one with a developed organization – took over, though Castro's own charismatic personality, allied with his brother, Raul, and the Argentine, Ernesto Guevara, remained the dominant factor in government. Other events followed thick and fast, and we need not detail them all, but, as Cuba put out feelers to Russia early in 1960, American apprehension grew, and its government suspended the Cuban sugar quota. Castro's reply was summary expropriation of all American interests in July 1960, and there followed the long succession of bitter disputes and events from Cuban importation of Russian weapons, the abortive invasion by Cuban exiles of Cuba itself, half-heartedly backed by the United States, to the final "missile" crisis of October 1962, when the world was brought to the verge of war by the Cuban issue.

There are some commentators who believe that Cuba was "pushed" into communism by the ineptitude of American policies. But this hardly bears examination. It is true that Castro moved from an apparently liberal position to an apparently extreme left-wing one coincidently with the worsening of relations with the United States. But, as early as October 1959, a prominent leader of the revolution, General Hubert Matos, resigned in protest at Communist influence in the rebel army, for which he received twenty years' imprisonment for "counter-revolutionary activities". This was five months before Mr Mikoyan visited Cuba and signed the first Soviet-Cuba Trade Agreement, and, perhaps, indicates that the Cuban revolution was already committed to communism. Whatever the intimate history of the Cuban revolution, however, it is clear that Castro's broken promises about political freedoms for

Cubans litter its path, and that, whatever social benefits have come to the mass of Cubans since 1959 – and there are many – politically, the revolution was betrayed.

The economic balance-sheet of the revolution cannot yet be drawn. The state has taken over virtually all Cuba's resources; the old, parasitic classes have been destroyed; the status of the rural peasantry has been raised. But Cuba's economy has been pursuing a zig-zag course and many serious mistakes, creating food rationing and other controls, were made. It is likely that Cuba will weather this economic storm, supported by the Soviet bloc and China, but how far the ebullient Cuban people will continue to support a régime that cannot permit criticism is a question only future events will reveal.

The Cuban revolution has been perhaps the most dramatic confrontation in post-war Latin America between the forces of change and reform and those of inertia and the *status quo*. Like the other examples we have considered, it is unique in its form and character, but it raises related issues which have application to the whole continent. Externally for Latin America, the dominant political fact of the twentieth century has been the rôle of the United States of America, that Colossus of the North, in whose powerful shadow the states of the Western Hemisphere lie. Economically, the United States has come to occupy in Latin America that position held in the nineteenth century predominantly, but not exclusively, by Great Britain: the supplier of capital, the major trading partner, and, in many ways, the political big brother. Relations between the twenty republics of Latin America and the United States have been historically compounded of admiration and dislike: the attraction of American dynamism, the respect for American democracy, and the regard for the best in American leadership exemplified by such men as Franklin Roosevelt and John F. Kennedy have always been tempered in Latin American eyes by the ruthlessness of American capitalism, the lack of refinement in American relations, and the natural fear of smaller states for the powerful neighbour. In the Organization of American States, that regional organization of Latin America and the United States which has grown out of earlier Pan-Americanism, these feelings often express themselves as a love–hate relationship. For the Latin Americans are conscious of their older cultural traditions; they may be poor but they are proud, and they seek, at all costs, to preserve their independence.

Thus, in the post-war period, liberal Latin Americans have been more perturbed by apparent American indifference to military dictatorships in Latin America than to the possibilities of extreme left-wing take-overs of government. Castro's revolution may have moved left but, until the Cuban missile crisis, it enjoyed considerable repute in the continent as a movement which had challenged Uncle Sam on his own doorstep and got away with it. It would be a mistake to assume that anti-Americanism is the prerogative of the extreme left in Latin America; indeed, it is often shared by other segments of the societies, and it stems from America's dominant position in the Latin American economy, coupled with historical memories of how, in the past, America has often seemed to regard Latin America as its special concern, even to interfering in the republics' domestic affairs. Two examples of such attitudes must suffice: shortly before the Argentine elections of 1946 which put Perón in power, the United States Department of State published a book showing the considerable links which existed between certain right-wing leaders in Argentina and the Fascist powers of Europe during the war. It did so in the expectation that the Argentine people would dissociate themselves from men like Perón. The result, to which this ill-timed and ignorant gesture contributed, was his victory in the Presidential contest. Again, in 1964, at the initiative of the United States in the Organization of American States, a decision was made that all members should break off relations with Cuba, and this was binding on all members. Most did so, in order not to break the convention, but Mexico refused to do so altogether, and Uruguay and one or two other states only did so after considerable delay, and at the cost of popular demonstrations against the move.

In the case of Castro, happily the fact that he was prepared to involve Latin America in the Cold War has led in recent years to a revulsion against his régime in Latin America, and other factors in this have been his attempt to promote revolution in Venezuela, and his betrayal of the Cuban revolution to communism. But it was in answer to the movement of change that Castro represents in Cuba that a new initiative in Pan-American relations was undertaken in 1961 by the Alliance for Progress, whereby American economic aid would be forthcoming to Latin American states which showed some interest in basic internal reforms. After a hesitant start, and considerable criticism of the plan, the Alliance for Progress today offers a promise to Latin America which, if redeemed, could do much for these developing states.

Other factors in the post-war Latin American scene are encouraging: the development of institutions designed to serve the economic growth of the republics such as the Inter-American Development Bank and the United Nations' sponsored Economic Commission for Latin America; the establishment of the Latin American Free Trade Area and the Central American Common Market; the reviving European interest in a continent too long neglected, signally demonstrated by the visits in 1963 and 1964 by General de Gaulle, the President of Germany and other leaders, as well as by growing European desire to aid Latin America economically, financially and by technical assistance – all these reflect a recognition of a continent in transition. Most states face immense problems still in the achievement of political stability and economic growth: some, such as Mexico and Venezuela, have achieved much; others, such as Haiti, have achieved little or nothing. The spectrum is broad, the picture baffling in its complexity. But Latin America, with a rapidly-growing population likely to reach over 700 million by the end of the century, is still very much a potential power in world affairs, and can no longer be regarded as a passive rather than an active agent in a world of revolutionary change.

CHAPTER 10

THE GROWTH OF EUROPEAN UNITY

by Russell Lewis

There was such a precipitous rush of events in the extra-European world of 1964 that it is scarcely surprising that British public opinion has had little time to consider the Common Market. Indeed, ever since the breakdown of negotiations there has been the tendency in this country to regard the Common Market as something that was there all of a sudden – a club for us to join if we would deign to do so, and then, by heaven, one of the senior committee members of the club blackballed us – surely the supreme insult for any Englishman! Ever since there has been a sort of silent resolve among people in this country, excepting of course a few enthusiasts, that the Common Market which had suddenly come up, had gone away again: that was the Common Market, that was! Yet the Common Market is still there, and what is more, it has something highly relevant to contribute to some of the world's most pressing problems.

The plethora of European organizations which has grown up since the war can only be made sense of in relation to their history, and that history is short. Historical explanation does not require that we should find the origins of the European movement in the era of Charlemagne; we find it rather in the era of Charles de Gaulle. The question we have to ask then is what new factors prompted this drive for European unity which has been a constant factor in European politics since the Second World War. The surprising thing in a way is that this change did not take place sooner. The striking outward feature of Western civilization is its technology, the surprising thing is that the forms of political organization have responded so slowly to technological changes. An obvious example is improvement in communications.

A century ago the most highly-developed form of transport was by sea. In these circumstances, the most powerful sea power, Great Britain, was the most powerful country in the world. The greatest power in the world was a sovereign national state, and the only other powers in the world that rivalled it were other European powers, and international affairs were mainly the affairs of a few European states. Now with the development of wireless and telecommunications, it became possible to organize politically on a much larger scale. An historian once described Russia as a "colossus stuffed with clouts". Russia had to be a great power but it was difficult to bring that power to bear. The emergence of the super-states into world politics should have been already obvious by the end of the First World War, but it was delayed partly because of the Americans' preoccupation with their own internal problems especially after the slump, and also the gospel of isolationism which was very widespread and difficult for even Roosevelt to overcome. The Russians, for their part, deliberately opted out of an adventurous foreign policy and opted rather for socialism in one country. However, once the Second World War was over, it quickly became apparent that the dominating factors in world affairs were the super-states of Russia and America. This was the world to which a war-torn and shattered Europe had to accommodate itself. The change that has taken place in the twentieth century has not been so much the waning of nationalism, on the contrary, it has been the period when nationalism which was developed in Europe has been exported all over the world. Rather, it has been the period when it became apparent that the national sovereign state was no longer the dominant form of political organization, the continental size super-state had finally come into its own. I do not suppose, however, that the states of Western Europe so used by tradition to warring with one another would have given up their old practices, had there not been pressure from the outside, and the first reason why European states with such long-established enmities as Germany and France were able to sink their differences was that they feared each other less than they feared the Soviet Union. Yet if the nations of Western Europe had one external preoccupation, namely the danger from Russia, they also had what one might call an internal problem, this was how to accommodate Germany into the family of Western European Nations after the terrible things that had happened in the war. If Germany had emerged from the war intact this would not have been too difficult, but Germany was divided. The Iron Curtain ran down the middle and who was to say whether the Germans might not be tempted at some time to pursue their old drive towards the East, in order to unify their nation again, or, instead attempt reconciliation with the East – Rapallo style – which might be just as bad because without Germany, Western Europe is, so the military strategists say, "indefensible". The common problem of virtually all the Western European organizations, and indeed of a wider Western organization down the years has been that of fitting Germany in and not leaving the Germans in a state of psychological isolation, a state of mind in which they might be tempted to do something drastic and against the interest of their allies. Every one of the six nations forming the European Community, both the small ones, the Netherlands, Belgium, Luxembourg, and the big ones, Germany, Italy and France, have one thing in common about their war-time experience – that they all suffered the humiliation of defeat and occupation. We in this country have managed to keep clear of this experience ever since 1066. Our whole history seems to conspire to make us go on thinking we are invincible and the national state is the last word of wisdom in human political affairs. For us the war was only a confirmation of a glorious national story, 1940 was no humiliation but our finest hour. So it was that out of the war came the six nations tending to question the virtues of the national state, while we were confirmed in our loyalty to it, and this is really the psychological gulf that runs between us and the Continental nations. It is far more important than the geographical barrier of the Channel, and it helps to explain some of our differing attitudes towards European integration.

Now let us look at the history of post-war Europe bearing these factors in mind. I mean the technological change which has made the sovereign national state somewhat out of date, the fear of Russia, the problem of accommodating Western Germany in the family of Western nations, and the psychological scar which the war had left on the body politic of Continental Europe, but which had left Britain unmarked. The fact of most immediate importance in post-war Europe was the threat of aggression from Stalinist Russia. The feeling at the time was aptly summed up in that rather horrific book by George Orwell *1984*. It is as well to remember that 1984 is 1948 but inverted, that airstrip 10 in 1984 is a thinly veiled satirical portrait of contemporary Russia. But in 1948 things had started to move in the West and there were two experiences which had stimulated action. There was the first Berlin air-lift. The threat to Berlin was met then as later because of Allied firmness in spite of various military blandishments by the Soviet Union, but many people were awakened by this experience who had regarded Soviet Russia as a particularly friendly country during the war and not really in the rôle of an aggressor. The second, much more dangerous development, was the rape of Czechoslovakia. We must try to project ourselves back into the immediate post-war period, and try to imagine what it meant to people in the West when Czechoslovakia became Communist: of all the countries which we have come to regard as the satellites of Russia in Eastern Europe, Czechoslovakia seemed to be the best qualified for becoming a democratic state on the conventional Western pattern. Although it was a state with a short history, at least it had a generation of experienced leaders – a number of whom were well-known internationally. It was a highly industrialized country with a large and prosperous middle class, and the institutions of democratic life seemed to be well established there – it had as it were the right sociological foundation for a democratic state. Yet in this classic takeover the Communists allied themselves with the governing party, took over the Ministry of the Interior and without any help from the Red Army took over the government completely. Any observer was bound to be struck by the thought that what could happen in Czechoslovakia could happen elsewhere, notably in Italy and France, for there were to be found two of the largest Communist parties in the world.

How did the West react to this situation? It reacted on the military, the economic, the political levels: as for the first, the military, all that need be said about NATO is to remind ourselves that the working theory of NATO at its inception was the theory of George Kennan, then of the State Department. George Kennan believed that the object of the Western military alliance should be to contain the Soviet Union within its existing borders. In terms of the initial objective NATO has been an undoubted success; since its establishment the Soviet Union has not moved over its frontiers in Western Europe. But the West needed to fortify itself economically as well as militarily. It was this great need and also the generosity of outlook of the American people – probably the only people in the world capable of conceiving of giving away aid on such a scale – which made possible the Marshall Plan, a plan for reviving Western Europe from the ruins of the war. It was a plan to rebuild the factories, roads, bridges, railways which had been destroyed during the conflict. But it was a condition of this aid that the plans using it should be dovetailed into one another. Another condition was that the various obstacles to trade and particularly quotas, that is quantitative limitations on imports, which had been put up in such profusion by dollar hungry countries after the war (restrictions they had put up against not only America but also against each other) should be removed from their mutual trade. The organization which was set up to supervise the planning of the use of aid and also liberalization of these countries' trade was the Organization for European Economic Co-operation or the OEEC. There is no doubt that the Marshall Plan was a vast success; the revival of Western Europe has been the most important economic fact of the post-war world. The programme for abolition of quota trade barriers was so successful that by the end of the fifties they had virtually disappeared from industrial trade and the OEEC disappeared to give way to another organization, the OECD, which was concerned with aid and development mainly for African and Asian countries.

At the political level the attempt to create a new Europe however was much less successful. The political instrument concerned was the Council of Europe: this was a two-tier body, a committee of ministers, and a parliament which met for the first time in Strasbourg in 1949. That parliamentary chamber echoed some of the finest European oratory that ever has been or will ever be heard: Churchill, Spaak, De Gasperi, Adenauer, Schumann all spoke eloquently on the theme of "Europe Unite". But whenever concrete proposals came forward which meant the transferring of certain sovereign rights to some supra-national body they were always rejected. Perhaps the trouble was that the conceptions at the time were those of lawyers. The legal approach to politics is to make a constitution, and then everybody follows the constitution. This does not often happen in practice. In the case of Europe, the major move forward was made in response to a concrete problem. The problem was that of Germany and the origin of the problem was the spectacular success of the Marshall Plan. At the end of the war the widely accepted view of what was to be done about Germany, was that the country should be turned into a pastoral state, the industry which had made its war machine so formidable should be destroyed so that the German capacity for making war should be eliminated. These extreme views of the so-called Morgenthau Plan were quickly abandoned after the war. Germany was included like the other nations in the Marshall Plan. But as Germany bounded forward after the currency reform of 1948 the political problem presented itself. What was to happen if Germany's Ruhr should develop again, if its armament kings should come to the fore, if its coal and steel barons should re-enter German politics and show the sort of misjudgment that – to put it mildly – they had shown in the past? It was Thyssen after all who had financed Hitler. Was there any sign that Krupps and his kindred were repentant for the past? Yet it would have been no good to go and take over the Ruhr in the way that the French Army had in between the wars; this would only have fostered the kind of nationalist hatred which had bedevilled relations in the past. So a novel idea was put forward by Monsieur Schumann, Foreign Minister of France, but who as an old Alsatian, had known what it was like to be both a German and a French citizen. Monsieur Schumann proposed nothing less than the setting up of a supra-national authority to run the Coal and Steel Industries of Western Europe.

The reason behind this experiment was, therefore, not really economic so much as political, but there were good economic reasons too why this particular sector should be picked on for a supra-national experiment, coal seams being no respecters of frontiers. In both these industries the best location policy was one which ignored frontiers. There are examples of steelworks which are actually situated either side of the frontier since the Coal and Steel Community came into being. In these cases, heavy-bulk goods transport charges, which were made at the frontier, often had their origins in a very remote period such as when the widths of the railway lines in the different territories were different so that it was necessary to transfer goods from one lot of wagons to another at the frontier. Yet when the widths had been made the same, transfer charges remained. Monsieur Schumann proposed to brush such nationalist absurdities aside. There was to be free trade in coal and steel but, more important, there was to be an economic government for coal and steel and the supra-national character of this organization was emphasized by the name given to the administration, namely, the High Authority. This body with its attendant bureaucracy, or body of "Eurocrats" as they came to be called, governed the coal and steel industries from day to day, but many other crucial decisions had to be decided by the representatives of the nations concerned and these were assembled in the Council of Ministers. There was also a Parliamentary body – not very big, seventy-eight members – and a Court of Justice which determined conflicts which arose under the Treaty of Paris which set up the ECSC.

The importance of the European Coal and Steel Community is not to be measured by the many statistics, which it is possible to quote about the growth of production and trade between members. For just as it arose out of a political problem, so the importance of this Community was political. It had succeeded where other attempts had failed in forming a supra-national organization which was capable of attracting the loyalty of the people in the member states. It had a definite task, and most people considered that this task was accomplished effectively, namely the task of getting rid of the economic barriers which stood at the frontiers for these industries and also of supervising their growth and development from a European and not from a national point of view. A measure of the ECSC's success was the number of schemes which were put forward to duplicate the Community in other sectors, to suggest for instance that there should be a green pool for agriculture, a white pool for hydro-electricity. One ambitious attempt at a Community solution for a pressing problem in these years, however, was one which went down in disaster. This was the European Defence Community.

The object of the European Defence Community was to include German forces in a European Defence Force, and this would by-pass the difficulties of including Germany as an equal partner in NATO. This French initiative collapsed where it began in the French Chamber of Deputies, though there is every reason to believe that, had it not collapsed because of lack of French support, it would have probably collapsed for lack of Italian support, and it is significant that this was the time, 1954, when there was a new régime in Russia which appeared to be offering a new face towards the West; fortunately, the collapse of the EDC did not take the European Coal and Steel Community with it. A little band of influential European enthusiasts set to work on the most ambitious project of all. This was not the creation of a series of pools in different economic sectors, but a pool for all economic sectors. It was a proposal for the Economic Government of the Europe of the Six, and many of them hoped that the Europe of many more than the Six eventually should be pushed into the Community supra-national form. This was the Common Market. The Treaty of Rome which ultimately incorporated this scheme was drawn up with a remarkable swiftness in the year 1956 by a group of experts who went down to Messina to do it. Britain was eventually going to join in these talks but early on withdrew its representatives. The Six treated the project as one of the utmost urgency; it was realized that here lay an opportunity which might not recur. The top people in the main states were all pro-European, these included Dr Adenauer, Christian Democrat, Chancellor of the Federal German Republic, Senor De Gasperi, Christian Democrat, Prime Minister of Italy, Monsieur Guy Mollet, Socialist Premier of France, and of course Paul Henri Spaak, Socialist Premier of Belgium. I mention the party political affiliations to show that this was not, as is suggested in some quarters, a sort of conspiracy of the Right Europe, just a manifestation of Latin Catholic Democracy. This European pressure group at the very top level of politics was determined to press on with their own treaty with all possible speed, and it was for this reason and not in order to spite Britain's Free Trade area proposals, that they signed the Treaty in March 1957. The object of it was political. The only purely political statement in the Treaty is in the preamble where it states that the objective of the Treaty, is "the ever closer union of European peoples". We ought nevertheless to remember that the working theory of the architects of this document was that they intended to use an economic means to a political end. The parallel which was in their minds was that of the development of the German state in the course of the nineteenth century. Only a superficial reading of German history would say its creation was simply the result of Bismarck's Blood and Iron policy; those who look deeper would see the ground-work of German unity being solidly prepared by the slow but sure development of the Zollverein, or customs union, as the century progressed.

Now those who made the Treaty of Rome thought that the same thing would happen to Western Europe. If economic union were achieved, political union would irrevocably follow upon its heels. Let us now have a look at this programme of economic union and see if there are indeed any political effects yet emerging. It is a convenient way to look at the Treaty of Rome and to say that one half of it is Free Trade Adam Smith liberalism; the other half is planning, remembering of course that the word "planning" on the continent tends to be used over a much wider range than it does here and tends to include not only purposeful or detailed direction of economic policy, but economic policy in general. The Adam Smith half of the Treaty is that concerned with the removal of barriers, national economic barriers, barriers in the first place to the movement of goods, and in the main this means tariffs, so there is a programme of tariff reductions which is to be achieved over a twelve-year period like most of the rest of the Treaty. As originally conceived there would by 1970 be no tariffs between the member states in industrial goods, and on the outer frontier of the Common Market there would be one tariff. There are still quite a few, even among the so-called experts on the Common Market, who think this is as far as the Common Market goes, that it is a purely trading organization, a Free Trade area or a Customs Union. Some rather pretentious calculations have been made by economists about the effects of the Common Market on world trade, which are based on this curious assumption that the Common Market only deals in trade. In fact trade is only the tip of the iceberg. In the long run the economic union is much more important; the economic freedom aspect of this is the removal of the barriers to the free movement of the factors of production. The factors of production concerned are not quite the same as those to which the economist refers – capital, labour and land. Land, except perhaps in Holland, has the characteristic of being immobile, so the Rome Treaty talks about labour, capital and services. To achieve free movement of labour really means removing nationalist restrictions usually owing their origin to the period of heavy unemployment in the thirties when the object of national legislation was to protect jobs and reserve them for each state's own nationals. Free movement of workers involves getting rid of these restrictions and also making proper welfare provisions, by means of which seasonal and frontier workers, as well as the long-term migrant workers are just as well off in terms of social benefit as the nationals in the country where they have gone to work. Free movement of capital sounds rather technical and, of course, in many ways it is. It involves things like free movement of stocks and shares, but also homelier things very important to the freedom of the individual, such as freedom to take one's money out of one's country and use it to buy a house in another.

Lastly, there is free movement of services, which include things like free movement of films and freedom to establish businesses, that is the removal of nationalist barriers to stop foreigners from other community territories setting up in trade or business in any one of the countries. It also includes freedom of movement of the professions; this is potentially a *very* thorny problem indeed, partly because the definition of a doctor, or a lawyer, or an architect, or a surveyor, or an auctioneer, or a chartered accountant, or a chartered surveyor, varies from country to country. Professional associations often do not correspond to one another. The diplomas and qualifications which they recognize in each of these countries are consequently often very different, and of course standards vary. Thus to achieve generally acceptable qualifications in the professions in all these countries, is a very difficult task indeed, but it is intended to be done and one of the first things that the Commission did was to make a book of definitions of these different professions.

The Adam Smith aspect of the Treaty, the abolishing of national legislation, has a certain fascination for anybody with a radical turn of mind. But let us now turn to the common policy aspect. There is the common policy for agriculture. What this amounts to is, one system of protection for agriculture instead of six. Within the Community there will be one price structure and free trade in agricultural products. There will also be a common system for modernizing agriculture and at the same time encouraging a certain proportion of the farming population, which at the moment is rather underemployed, to move off the land and go into industry. For it is only by this method that it will be possible to reconcile the rising standard of living for a farmer, reasonable prices for the consumer, and a liberal policy in overseas trade.

There is also to be a common policy in transport, the economic importance of this is enormous for if the Common Market succeeds, it will mean there will be a greater concentration of industry, and as American experience shows, a larger distance between the consumer and the producer; so it is logical to believe that the transport system will in fact grow faster than industry before very long and it will become a very urgent matter to avoid economic distortion occurring, due to different standards and policies being pursued in transport in member countries.

Here is a homely example: in some countries it is a legal requirement that a driver has a mate, in other countries it is not, but the observance or non-observance of this rule makes a great deal of difference to competitiveness in road haulage. It is this sort of practical pressure which will require the whole field of commercial law to be brought into line in all the six countries.

We hope to have before long a common patent law for Western Europe, perhaps embracing more countries than just the Common Market, to have common legislation on such things as trade marks and the Common Market may well stand or fall according to its success in dealing with monopolies and restrictive practices. The European Commission, under recent Common Market legislation, already has the power to fine companies which offend against its control regulations to the extent of a million dollars. Nobody has had to pay up that kind of sum as yet, but the extent of this power shows how important the Common Market countries consider this competition legislation to be. There is rather a quaint phrase in the Rome Treaty about the harmonization of social conditions in an upward direction. This form of words is intended as a defence against those critics who suggest that any harmonization is likely to be the result in the reduction of social standards in those countries which have high standards already. Certainly the object of the Treaty is not uniformity – but compatibility; the differing emphases of the different systems of social benefits are likely to remain; by this I mean the French emphasis on large family allowances, the large German provision for pensions, the pre-eminence of the Dutch in mental health, these differences of emphasis in national social policies are likely to remain. The only specific uniformity is the acceptance of the principle of equal pay, which is supposed to be established at least legally by the end of this year, and the undertaking that member states should endeavour to maintain the existing equivalence of paid holiday schemes. The importance of the latter, I think, might have been immense if Britain had joined the Community as we are well behind the Continent in the number of our public holidays. Even the equal pay principle was really inserted at the behest of the French who already applied it at the time of the setting up of the Treaty and feared the competition of those who did not. This is how the Common Market works or is intended to work internally. But what about the Market's relations with the external world? This has two aspects; first it must pursue a common commercial policy, which is more than just having a common external tariff. In addition no Common Market country can now sign a trade treaty which does not contain a saving clause covering the Community's position. It had to be pointed out recently to the Russians (who were complaining that they were being discriminated against on account of the lowering of tariffs within the Community) that if they want to negotiate on trade, they would have to deal with the Commission and not with the member states. The Community now appears as a separate entity at international conferences; it is truly the main negotiator with America in the Kennedy Round, for the reduction of tariffs under the General Agreement on Tariffs and Trade. It plays a prominent part in the proceedings at the Geneva conference of the underdeveloped nations; the bargaining power of this bloc which is the world's biggest importer and exporter is obviously vast.

The other aspect of external affairs is the Common Market's

relations with what are mainly the African territories but also includes other underdeveloped associated countries such as Surinam. Originally it was not intended by the creators of the Rome Treaty to include anything to do with overseas territories, but the French insisted that they should. The French were very much attached, and still are, to their mission in Africa and they spend twice as large a proportion of their national income on aid, which largely goes to these territories, as we do in this country. The French see no reason why they should allow privileged access to these territories which they have been sustaining down the years by massive aid, without some corresponding contribution from the other member nations of the Six. So it was decided that the Treaty should include an association with the overseas territories of a member state, and a separate Treaty was signed for five years. This Treaty association was with mainly French associates, and because at that time they were not independent, France signed on their behalf. Last year this agreement was renewed after the first five years and this time these eighteen African territories signed the agreement themselves – there was no question of France signing for them because by this time they had all become independent. The main characteristics of this agreement are that they, the African territories, have certain advantages in the European market, they get the benefit from the reduction of tariffs between the European countries towards one another, while it is possible for them to go on protecting their own infant industries. Also they will get a programme of aid over the five years of 730 million dollars, to help them build roads, bridges, railways, schools and hospitals and other less spectacular but no less useful things like wells within their villages.

All this amounts to what President Hallstein called "a political union for economic and social purposes", and that is the first aspect to look at when one is considering the question how far it is true that economic union is leading to political union. For in modern times, much of politics is economic and social policy. Indeed the contemporary era is unique in that governments stand or fall largely according to the level of social benefits, the standard of living or the rate of growth, the rate if you like at which the national income increases. All countries are bitten by this materialist bug, the rate alone is what seems to vary. Lord Butler has talked rather modestly about doubling our standard of living here in twenty-five years; in Japan an election was won recently on a slogan "double in ten years". That is the materialist world we live in where economics bulks large in government policy. This also has certain indirect effects. The creation of common policies means nothing less than the gathering together gradually of a European ruling class. The identification of the ruling class is the key feature in the analysis of political systems and what we are seeing in Europe at the moment is the gradual achievement of a coherent European élite in government and this happens naturally in the Common Market institutions. In the European Parliament the M.P.s do not divide on national lines, they divide into three party groups: Socialists, Christian Democrats and Liberals. In Brussels, its Commission contains representatives of the civil services of many member nations discussing with the bureaucrats the achievement of common policies, many pressure groups from industry, commerce and from the trade unions who have headquarters of their group association located in Brussels with their representatives ready to lobby the Commission on some aspects of common policies. The Council of Ministers has a regular meeting place for Ministers, not the same Ministers each time, but varying with the subject discussed. At one time they are Ministers of Transport or Ministers of Agriculture; at another Ministers of Social Affairs or Ministers of Finance. For a great part of this year, the Ministers of Agriculture of the Six have met once a fortnight in Brussels, they have been seeing more of each other almost than their Cabinet colleagues in their governments at home. It will be strange indeed if this constant meeting within the institutions does not produce sooner of later a remarkable cohesive feeling among the people who count in making the policies of European states, a coherent European outlook.

This is what has been happening on the Continent in recent years of the development of the Common Market; things are not standing still, but it may still be asked if this Common Market is simply a result of certain conditions on the Continent, which no longer apply, such as the great importance I have attached in the early part of the story to the hostility of Russia. Is it quite the same now? Is there altogether too defensive a posture in the Common Market and its dependent organizations? The answer is on the contrary that the justification for proceeding with the Common Market is precisely that it meets the needs of the European countries. In the first place, it offers a better solution to national problems than the national state can provide. Almost every modern national state undertakes to guarantee in some measure full employment for its citizens. That the limiting factor on national policies in this respect is simply the balance of payments is one of which we have recently become pretty fully aware.

More and more of the European countries of the Six are pooling their resources in relation to this balance of payment problem. Had Britain joined, naturally one of the great benefits of the Common Market to her would have been precisely this sharing of a common currency pool, at least that is what it would have become in the end. There is no doubt in short that it is much more feasible to run a full employment policy on a European level than on a national level, and one of the most important features of the otherwise rather disappointing year 1964, was that the decision last April set up quite elaborate machinery for the co-ordination on medium term of economic policies and the strengthening of financial and monetary co-operation among the Six. Another difficulty of the national state is that of firmly entrenched interests in the nation which are so strong especially from the point of view of lobbying national governments that they are able to exert economic claims far out of proportion to their real importance and in effect hold the rest of the society to ransom. This is obviously true in the case of monopolists and cartel members, and yet the mere effect of creating a Common Market, of throwing down the national tariff barriers brings in international competition which weakens both monopolies and cartels, at least for the time being. This effect will, of course, not last forever but there is at least a chance to organize an anti-cartel and anti-monopoly policy on a Community level which gives, as it were, a second opportunity after the failure on the national level. The same thing goes for farmers. To some extent, the conflict of interest between certain groups of farmers of the Common Market seems to cancel out some of their effectiveness as a lobbying group. So here again, there is the opportunity to create liberal and coherent policies and not policies which are simply the result of undue pressure, by over-privileged groups. Again in the case of planning for growth the interesting thing from the point of view of English people who visit the Community is to find that the officials over there believe both in planning and competition. Of course the argument goes on as to just how much overall guidance there should be. There is agreement that there should be a *measure* of overall guidance by the government, and that this should be based upon a census of opinions of the decision taken, all of which amounts in a sense to a giant market research programme for the whole economy. This conception, this modern conception of planning which was invented by Monsieur Monnet was taken into the Community by him because he was the High Authority's first President. It needs little demonstration to show that this kind of planning on a Community scale is far more effective than it is on a national scale simply because the size of the unknown, that is the overseas market, is smaller in relation to the Community than to any one individual state. Now if the Community offers a more effective solution for certain problems which have defeated the national state, of which the national state has at least found rather inadequate solutions, it also provides an approach to certain world problems which ideally should be solved on a world level, but which the amount of world co-operation available at the present will not sustain. One example is the lowering of trade barriers. The organization appropriate to this task is the General Agreement on Tariffs and Trade. The very fact that the Common Market countries have got together as one negotiating person, so to speak, has already simplified the Kennedy Round negotiations. Indeed the Kennedy Round was only conceivable because of the existence of the Community.

The last of the great problems of the world is that of north and south. It now appears that the prediction of Marx that the increasing poverty of the poor and increasing riches of the rich which failed to work out nationally, at least not in Western Europe, seems to be working in a sort of international way between the northern industrialized countries of the world and the southern and, in rough terms, the less developed countries of the world. The gap between them tends to widen, some sort of aid is clearly necessary from the richer half of the world to the poorer half, at least this is the commonly accepted ethic. One question one must ask is can this aid be carried out without putting the less developed countries in a new kind of thraldom? Many of these countries are after all very suspicious of aid from the West because they think that it is a kind of covert imperialism. Here the Community has something to offer, for the Association Agreement is one of participation; the Council of Association which is a supreme body from the point of view of taking decisions about policy affecting aid is composed equally of representatives of the associated countries in Africa and representatives of the Commission and the presidency rotates between representatives of Africans and the representatives of Europeans. This is a happy working arrangement which the receiving countries have voluntarily accepted. Though the volume of aid which passes through the Community's fund is very much smaller than that which comes from national resources, it nevertheless may in the future become a model of how things ought to be organized.

Let us now turn to the future and enter for a moment into the great debate which is occupying the statesmen of Western Europe about what kind of Europe we want, both from the point of view of its internal organizations and also what kind of rôle united Europe, however it is united, will play in the world. The opposing views are those of two great Frenchmen of our time, de Gaulle on the one hand, and Jean Monnet on the other. De Gaulle has summed up his conceptions in a great phrase about Europe from the Atlantic to the Urals, but the reference to the Urals is, of course, a bit alarming. It indicates in a crisp way his idea of Europe as a third force in the world, not the abandonment of the Western Alliance, but nevertheless a Europe acting in a much more independent way than in the past, a united Europe under French leadership, which is a mediator between the ideological extremes of East and West and which brings about the termination of the Cold War. And though we in this country find it difficult to take anything but a rather jaundiced view of de Gaulle, his conception is undeniably a noble one. The strength of de Gaulle's position emanates to a great extent from the fact that he knows where he is going. He knows not only what rôle he wants a Europe organized under him to play in the world, he has also thought out pretty well the constitutional form of that unity. De Gaulle's formula is summed up in the so-called Fouchet Plan of political union. This has been revised more than once but the essential form of it in its various versions remains the same. There is to be a secretariat of tame civil servants from the national ministries, there is to be a powerless parliament, and one real decision-lacking body, a Council of Ministers which meets at very regular intervals. In other words, this is to be an autocratic union, one run by cabinet ministers. On the face of it, this looks like suffering from the troubles of so many international organizations in that its decisions have to be unanimous. This surely is what de Gaulle means by the "Europe des patries" where the sovereign power remains with the national states. However, according to certain semi-official versions of Gaullist thinking, notably one expounded by Monsieur Payrefitte, the eventual idea is to have a majority voting and voting powers will depend upon population. If this is the Gaullist plan, then it is easy to see the significance of the Franco-German Treaty, because France and Germany have more than half the population of the Common Market. In terms of this plan too, it is understandable that Britain, whose work would upset this dominance of France and Germany, must be kept out, especially as Britain is looked on by de Gaulle as altogether too much mixed up with American policy. The opposing view, that of Monsieur Jean Monnet, is essentially a federalist one; it sees the future of Europe as that of an equal partner with the United States within the Atlantic Alliance, and the Cold War issue is to be settled between the Alliance and the Soviet Union without any defection or attempt to play the honest or any other kind of broker by Europe. The constitutional emphasis of Monnet's idea is parliamentary control; an enlarged European parliament is to have an extensive control over the administrators and ministers, and this Community, federal style (as a matter of fact the old terms of reference in constitutional politics are not altogether appropriate for this new type of political organization, so you can call it a Community style of Government) is regarded as a model for world government in the future. The issue is far from settled; on the face of it, the federalist views have far more support on the Continent than the Gaullist one. But appearances are to some extent deceptive and moreover de Gaulle is in a very powerful position within the Six to influence future policy. He knows what he wants and is obstinate in the pursuit of his aims. Where does Britain stand as far as this conflict of views is concerned?

CHAPTER 11

GREAT BRITAIN: RETROSPECT AND PROSPECT

by James L. Henderson

Introduction: The Aftermath of Victory

It is hard for an Englishman to procure a correct perspective in which to survey the history of Great Britain in world affairs since 1945. For if one thing is certain, it is that her position as a Great Power among nations has vastly decreased during the last twenty years. For one who has shared that descent it is as easy to indulge in a lament for lost greatness as it is to underestimate the values of what may have taken its place. An attempt must therefore be made to eschew both errors by keeping steadily in view the three levels on which our society functions – political, economic and spiritual – and to understand something of their connection with the world outside Britain, perhaps even to gesture in the possible direction of her further evolution.

Two quotations from a special number of *Encounter* (July 1963, No. 118, "Suicide of a Nation?") may help to establish some essential ingredients of a correct record: on pages 5 and 6, Arthur Koestler compared the United Kingdom with a lion and an ostrich:

> The leonine qualities we take for granted; perhaps too much so; mere mention of them is considered in embarrassingly bad taste. Yet it needs to be brutally said that without the lion, France, Germany and the rest, would either still be ruled by Gauleiter, or they would have been "liberated" by the Red Army and shared the fate of Hungary. In either case

Europe would have lost its historical identity. Its élites liqui-
dated in series of purges, its active resisters crushed, its passive masses cowed, it could only hope and pray, as the early
Christians did in their catacombs, for a miraculous redemp-
tion, in the distant future. All this is difficult to imagine. The
hypothetical state of Europe in the 1960's, after a total victory
of either Hitler or Stalin in the 1940's, is hardly ever discussed. Yet there can be no doubt that if, after Dunkirk,
Britain had lost its moral fibre, the Americans could not have
landed on the continent, and the fate of Europe would have
been decided between two paranoiac Caesars.

On pages 65 and 66, Hugh Seton-Watson wrote:

In 1945 Great Britain was both a world power and a great
power. Huge forces under arms, on land, at sea and in the
air, held not only the whole British Empire but also large
territories of enemy powers. An important additional factor
in Britain's real struggle at that time was the prestige derived
from its war record. Britain was the only nation that remained
at war from September 1939 to August 1945. British refusal
to surrender, between the fall of Europe and the American
landing in North Africa, deprived Hitler of victory. . . .

Morally and materially Britain in 1945 was a great power;
in 1963 she is neither. Soon after 1945 British military
strength was demobilized. In the nuclear and missile age
which has followed, it has become clear that only powers with
gigantic resources can remain in the top class, and there are
only two of these in the world today. It is true that Britain
and France can have some nuclear weapons today, and it may
be that Egypt or Ecuador can have some tomorrow. But to
maintain all the expenses of weapons research and development, to explore all the avenues of the missile age and to meet
all the new types of threat which arise is more than any but
the two monster powers can face. It will be a long time before

China can enter this class. An integrated Western Europe of 300,000,000 skilled persons could compete, and Britain might have competed if she had kept her empire. But there is no integrated Western Europe, and the British Empire has disappeared.

Two years after this passage was written it is interesting to note how strained are the relations between the quasi-federal states of Europe and how long is the list of those countries, formerly belonging to the British Empire and now achieving independence: India (1947), Pakistan (1947), Burma (1948), Ceylon (1948), Ghana (1957), Nigeria (1960), Cyprus (1961), Sierra Leone (1961), Malaysia (1957-63), Tanzania (1961-4), Western Samoa (1962), Jamaica (1962), Trinidad and Tobago (1962), Uganda (1962), Kenya (1963), Malawi (1963), Zambia (1964), Malta (1964), Gambia (1965).

Skimming the Political Surface

This subtitle is used in no derogatory sense: it is merely meant to indicate that political actions are the resultants very much more than the determinants of economic and spiritual forces.

In July 1945, a Labour Government took office; in 1950 it returned to power with a reduced majority; in 1951 the Conservatives took over, increased their majority in 1955 and continued to rule the country until October 1964 when Harold Wilson became Prime Minister with a Labour parliamentary majority of four. During the first six years of this period (1945–51) the main domestic events were the nationalization of the Bank of England in 1946 and the introduction of conscription in peace-time for the first time in the nation's history, in 1948; this was to last until 1960. Within the Labour Party itself there were deep divisions about nationalization and about armaments; for a while it looked as if the left wing would assert its sway, (Aneurin Bevan and the Campaign for Nuclear Disarmament) but Bevan swung back from his extreme position, in the end

Hugh Gaitskell won the battle for moderation. He was to die before reaping the fruits either of office or restored party unity; this legacy was to be Harold Wilson's.

In foreign affairs there was the granting of independence to India and Pakistan but at the tragic price of a split continent, the granting of independence to Burma in 1948 and the British withdrawal from Palestine in the same year – an almost open admission in the case of the latter of the evil of our original ill-fated and contradictory pledges to Jews and Arabs at the end of the First World War. In 1949 Britain became a vital part of NATO, and in the following year the outbreak of the Korean War emphasized further her weak position relative to the United States of America in confronting the supposed ideological menace of communism.

The main features of the next thirteen years of Tory rule were first, the accession of Queen Elizabeth II to the throne in 1952, the same year in which Britain successfully exploded her first atomic bomb. This was followed by the creation of SEATO in 1954, to which the United Kingdom also belonged, then in 1956 occurred the so-called Suez crisis. Arraigned and halted by the United Nations Organization and with her own people deeply divided, shocked and bewildered by Prime Minister Eden's precipitate action, Great Britain suffered at this date a real moral as well as political reverse. The policy her government then attempted was a throwback to the anachronism of nineteenth-century gun-boat diplomacy and could perhaps be fairly interpreted as an expression of the frustration and exasperation of certain sections of all classes at the diminution of Britain's influence as a world power. A result of the crisis was an interesting one, namely, that the Queen had to decide, after seeking advice in various quarters, whether to choose Mr Macmillan or Mr Butler to succeed the sick and discredited Eden. That in fact it was Macmillan may have had something to do with the subsequent tone of the last six years of Conservative government.

This was a curious mixture of domestic affluence ("You've never had it so good") and domestic hardship (the North-east area) together with one or two abortive attempts of the Premier to take the initiative in international affairs (his visit to Moscow and his "winds of change" speech in South Africa), Britains' impotent observation of the Cuba crisis and her acceptance of Polaris weapons, and lastly of course the notorious Profumo scandal. The unedifying spectacle of the grab for Tory leadership during Mr Macmillan's illness and the strange elevation of the previous Lord Home to be leader of the Tory Party as Sir Alec Douglas-Home, led to the expectation of a big Labour victory when at last a General Election was fought in the autumn of 1964. Actually the verdict of the polls revealed a three-million Liberal vote and an almost equal division between the Conservative and Labour parties.

It is worth pondering why this was so: possibly because the electorate, while feeling that a change of government would be healthy, was too unenthusiastic about the alternative to do more than give it a grudging mandate. Allied to this may also have been the mounting suspicion among voters generally that the real political decisions were being taken more and more outside Parliament, which seemed to be becoming a constitutional organ unfit to discharge its traditional functions of debate and questions when the issues involved were too complex and speculative for the legislative to pass judgment on.

Identifying the Economic Determinants

There is an air of paradox about this level of our recent national history, for, while Britain is nothing like so rich relatively as she was before 1945, the great majority of her inhabitants enjoy a higher standard of living than ever before. Britain's share in world trade has been steadily declining: between 1953 and 1963 the volume of British exports increased by less than 40% while that of the Common Market countries increased by more than

140%; British industrial production shows a similar unflattering comparison. Mr Shanks has suggested that the two main reasons for these phenomena are, firstly, that a good deal of Britain's post-war investment was misdirected (e.g. Railway modernization) and, secondly, she has not gone in nearly enough for labour-saving equipment and newer, more sophisticated, types of industry. (See "The Comforts of Stagnation": *Encounter*, July 1963). Two topics can be discussed as illuminating something of the paradox: these are the Welfare State and Britain's unsuccessful attempt to join the Common Market.

The achievement of a Welfare State was undoubtedly the result, firstly, of the people's bitter memories of unemployment in the 1930's and their stern determination that this must never be repeated, and, secondly, of the experiences of the Second World War, especially evacuation from town to country, which revealed class to class with their differences at home and their solidarity, at any rate temporarily, in the face of a common enemy. The landmarks of the process were the Beveridge Report (1942), the creation of the National Coal Board and the National Health Service (1946), the raising of the school-leaving age to 15 (1947), the National Assistance Act (1948) – all this carried through with rationing of food still continued from the war, and only made possible by the toleration of austerities connected rightly and honourably with the then Chancellor of the Exchequer, Sir Stafford Cripps. Two dangers threatened the whole enterprise: one was the Dollar shortage (1949–50), shared with much of Europe, and overcome by the imaginative and mass support supplied through "Marshall Aid", the other which began to develop insidiously in the 1950's, namely the practice in business of "expense accounts" and all that this could and sometimes did stand for in terms of lax morality and inefficiency in the management of public affairs. When the Conservatives took office in 1953 most of the Welfare legislation remained on the Statute Book; steel was denationalized, and in 1954

R*

Britain tried to re-establish herself as a first-class power by the passing of the United Kingdom Atomic Energy Authority Act. Attempts were made to invigorate the economy by the Government's exhortation to management and labour alike to modernize their methods, step up production – especially for exports – and so catch up with the national product rate of other countries.

However, as Goronwy Rees so deftly and sadly pointed out (*Encounter*, July 1963),

We are at this moment in the middle of "National Productivity Year" – the British Committee of Management's grand campaign to revivify British industry, establish new standards of efficiency, and inaugurate Britain's entry into the twentieth century. There are times when the National Productivity Year reminds one of nothing so much as the great "Collateral Campaign" in Robert Musil's novel *The Man Without Qualities* . . . like the National Productivity Year (only in the Vienna of 1914) the Collateral Campaign was under the most august patronage and had the support of all classes in society, though even its originator, Count Leinsdorf, did not know exactly what it was meant to achieve; its vagueness, says Musil, "stirred him as he himself felt, more intensely than anything definite could have". Again, like the National Productivity Year, the Collateral Campaign had that quality of "whistling in the dark" which is so appropriate to people who do not know what they fear. To quote Count Leinsdorf, "As Cromwell said: 'A man never rises so high as when he does not know where he is going. . . .' ". How much Count Leinsdorf would have enjoyed National Productivity Year: how much he would have admired that television programme which was inaugurated by Prince Philip with the startling news that the time-and-motion merchants were to be introduced into Buckingham Palace.

Part of that "whistling in the dark" was Britain's belated attempt to join the European Community. Our whole approach had been unfortunate.

As the leading nation in this unique family [Commonwealth] Britain remained, it was felt by Right and Left alike, a great power of a unique type. As such, they argued, she remained only a short distance behind the two monster powers. As a nation with world-wide interests, she remained far above any European nation, and so her leaders – not always politely – rebuffed the appeal from Europeans that they should play a leading part in the creation of a new Western Europe. Many British politicians felt that West European politicians had a parochial view of the world as a whole, and failed to notice that they themselves had a parochial view of the continent of Europe (*Encounter*, July 1963, p. 67).

With both the main political parties divided on the issue, Mr Macmillan's Government formally applied for membership of the Treaty of Rome in July 1962 – the chief economic arguments being that the European Common Market could offer British manufacturers a better and more challenging market than the Commonwealth now did, and that in any case European and Commonwealth interests were complementary and not antagonistic to one another. General de Gaulle imposed his veto with a devastating "Non" in January 1963 on the grounds that the United Kingdom was not really genuine in her desire to join the European Community as a wholehearted member of it. It is hard to deny that he was correct, although his own motivation was obviously a mixed one, an element of it being the fear that if Britain were a member French influence would be weakened.

Since October 1964 a Labour Government has taken strong measures to bring health to Britain's stagnant economy: their success must clearly depend on the degree to which the public as a whole begins to appreciate the nature of the economic paradox in which it is involved. This means agreeing on how the national income is best raised, most efficiently administered, most justly apportioned, and also on the proper order of priorities of expenditure as between social services, defence and space travel projects. Such an agreement can only come from a commonly shared set of values, and that is why we need now to reflect on the value judgments in Britain since 1945.

Heeding the Spiritual Groundswell

We hold [wrote Arthur Koestler, to quote once again that most significant social document of our times, "Suicide of a Nation"] that psychological factors and cultural attitudes are at the root of the economic evils – not the loss of Empire, not the large sums we must spend on armaments, not the misfortune that the steam-engine was invented by an Englishman. "We are at the moment dying by the mind," wrote Ian Nairn, "it is the mind which must will the change."

That this conviction is a true one must be evident from the way in which Britain transcended her material handicaps at the beginning of the Second World War and strenuously augmented her welfare immediately after it. Nevertheless, a price had to be paid for those exertions, and it was paid during the fifties to such tunes as "I couldn't care less", "I'm all right Jack", and "You've never had it so good". Let us look then at some of the phenomena. In 1951 there was the Festival of Britain, a rather self-conscious, if worthy attempt to revive past glories by invoking the spirit of the Great Exhibition of 1851: perhaps it is not without significance that only now in 1965 is the Festival site beginning to near its final shape.

Then there was the outcrop of "Angry Young Men", novelists and playwrights who voiced contempt for the cautious restraint with which Britain's body politic had been nursed to some kind of health, expressed dissatisfaction about the continuation of class differences and rivalries, and gave vent to indignant alarm at Britain's share in probable nuclear catastrophe. Waugh and Greene were the Roman Catholic antistrophe to Amis, Wain and Osborne, while towering over them all was the Orwellian prophetic nightmare of 1984.

It was during this period too that the theme of the "Establishment" began to be heard; it was a word used to describe our real rulers as distinct from our observable ones – a mélange of the city, Oxbridge, top civil servants and a few scientists congregating for lunch at the Athenaeum, and the upper reaches of a "managerial" class – it was supposedly these who roamed the "corridors of power". Slightly at an angle to the Establishment and more concerned with social etiquette were those things and people who were "U" or "Non-U", a distinction made between those who had made the best of all possible worlds, the old and the new, and those who for reasons of conscience or ineptitude, had not. The spread of affluence to nearly all sections of the population, combined with a lack of clear moral and political objectives acceptable to the younger generation, gave rise to the "teddy-boy", the "beat", and more recently, the "mods" and "rockers". Accompanying all this, part cause and part effect, was the steady erosion of Christian belief, in spite of some renaissance meanwhile in Roman Catholic circles and the attempt to let in some fresh air by means of such publications as the Bishop of Woolwich's *Honest to God*, and the Quaker booklet on sexual morality. The Reith lectures of 1962 by Professor G. M. Carstairs, published in book form under the title *This Island Now*, offer a most clear and penetrating analysis of the psychological condition of our society at the beginning of the sixties.

In the end, however, the best clue to an understanding of the processes of social change in this country since 1945 may be found in education. The 1944 Education Act was the climax of that "silent social revolution" (see Lowndes, *The Silent Revolution*) which had been occurring since 1870. Even though all the clauses of that Act have not yet been implemented, and some of them have been misconceived (particularly perhaps the Religious and the County Colleges sections), its passing undoubtedly set in ferment a whole new concern with the way in which the nation's children were being schooled. During the last half-dozen years education has become news: there have been several governmental Commissions (see Lello, *The Official View of Education:* A Summary of the Major Educational Reports since 1944, Pergamon Press 1964). Of these the most significant were the Crowther, Newsom and Robbins Reports. Dissatisfaction with selection for secondary education at 11 has been leading to its gradual abandonment by a number of educational authorities.

Dr J. W. B. Douglas, Director of the Medical Research Unit, London School of Economics, conducted a "national survey of health and development of children" which showed clearly that our present system of selection for secondary education is seriously biased in favour of middle-class children and against almost all those from poorer families. This is due to lack of encouragement from ill-educated parents and to over-crowding in primary schools, both of which factors tend to lead to a decline of the children's intelligence between the ages of 8 and 11.

A voluntary body, The Association for the Advancement of State Education, has come into existence to bring the pressure of public opinion in different localities to bear on such educational inadequacies as exist there. Yet one curious anomaly remains, namely, the existence and prosperity of the Independent schools; by some these are regarded as our great pride, by others as our greatest curse. The predicament of parents of good will is summed up in the remark: "I am working for the total abolition of independent schools because I think it's wrong to be able to buy educational privilege for one's child, but as long as they exist and are in some cases superior to their state counterparts, I shall continue to buy that educational privilege for my child and not sacrifice person to principle."

The spiritual groundswell of British life since 1945 seems then to have been a compound of fatigue and apathy after exaltation, a steady abandoning of traditional forms of morality and religion, an eagerness for but no great efficiency in the pursuit of material prosperity, and finally a promising concern for educational reform. *Encounter* (Vol. XXIII, No. 6, December 1964) was significantly entitled "New Britain", as though suicide may be succeeded by resurrection.

Looking Ahead

What kind of picture of the contemporary scene emerges as we attempt from the shores of Britain to assess the significance of those world affairs since 1945, which have been the subject of this book?

First, at the political level, there is the existence of a host of sovereign nation-states, for some purposes co-operating with one another, but on many counts ideologically opposed to one another: the only bodies working to relieve their differences and to prevent them from going to war are the adherents of non-governmental organizations and the United Nations Organization. Of the latter it has been said: "The U.N. perfectly embodies in institutional form the tragic paradox of our age: it has become indispensable before it has become effective" (H. G. Nicholas, "United Nations", *Encounter*, February 1962).

Secondly, at the economic level it is evident that within the next decades a policy for controlling world population must be agreed and implemented if there is to be any hope of feeding the growing numbers even at present standards, let alone at desperately needed improved standards of living for over one-third of the total. This means a world authority having the power and resources to produce and distribute food with priority for this work being given over other forms of expenditure.

Thirdly, at the spiritual or psychological level, the fact that there are certain values held in common by the whole human species needs to be acknowledged, for the dynamic proceeding from that acknowledgment must be harnessed to the task of solving the political and economic problems.

By reason of her remote as well as her more recent history, Britain is peculiarly fitted to make modest contributions in all three of these fields. Politically she can witness to the value of compromise in dispute, the acceptance of the fact that "both sides are partly right and partly wrong, and when the rights and wrongs are properly weighed, a third position more adequate than either emerges" (Sabine). An example of this might be Britain's joining of a new, enlarged and outward-turning European Community. Economically she can demonstrate by her domestic example that social democracy is an efficient form of organization, externally she can do her share and more than her share in channelling aid to the underdeveloped countries by means of the United Nations Organization. Spiritually she can uphold in modern conditions the right of individual conscience to absolute respect.

For those who learn and those who teach it may be hoped that the information and reflections contained in this volume will help them to perform their functions as British citizens of one World.

FURTHER READING

From the huge literature on the subject of recent world history, twenty books are listed below: the first five develop many of the ideas expressed in the introduction and Chapter 1; the other fifteen refer to each of the succeeding chapters in order.

BARRACLOUGH, G. *An Introduction to Contemporary History* (Watts, 1964)

BOZEMAN, ADDA, S. *Politics and Culture in International History* (Princeton U.P., 1960)

CROWLEY, D. W. *The Background to Current Affairs* (Macmillan, 1963)

DICKSON, M. *A World Elsewhere – Voluntary Service Overseas* (Dennis Dobson, 1964)

THOMSON, D. *World History from 1914 to 1961* (Home University Library, 1963)

LUARD, E. (Editor) *The Cold War, a Reappraisal* (Thames and Hudson, 1964)

LOWENTHAL, R. *The Disintegration of a Secular Faith* (O.U.P., 1965)

SETON-WATSON, C. *Neither War Nor Peace: the Struggle for Power in the Post-War World* (Methuen, 1960)

NOVE, A. *Was Stalin Really Necessary?* (Allen and Unwin, 1964)

VAN DER POST, L. *Journey Into Russia* (Hogarth Press, 1964)

GOLDMAN, E. F. *The Crucial Decade – And After* (Vintage, 1960)

CLUBB, O. E. *Twentieth Century China* (Columbia U.P., 1964)

THOMSON, I. *The Rise of Modern Asia* (Murray, 1957)

CLARK, W. *India at Midpassage* (London Overseas Development Institute, 1964)

273

Further Reading

KITCHEN, H. (Editor) *A Handbook of African Affairs* (Macmillan, 1963)

KIRK, G. E. *A Short History of the Middle East* (Methuen, 1964)

FERUGUSON, H. *The Revolutions of Latin America* (Thames and Hudson, 1963)

BELOFF, N. *The General Says No* (Penguin, 1964)

SAMPSON, A. *Anatomy of Britain* (Hodder and Stoughton, 1962)

KLINEBERG, O. *The Human Dimension in International Relations* (Holt, Rinehard and Winston, 1964)

INDEX

Addis Ababa Conference, 185
Algeria, 205, 206
"Angry young men", 268
Apartheid, 186
Argentina, 214, 217–23

Baghdad Pact, 88
Bandung Conference, 156, 159
Bay of Pigs, 133
Berlin, Blockade, 83
    Wall, 91
Bolivia, 227–30
Britain: Welfare State, 265–7
    Education Act (1944), 267–70
    Common Market, 267

Caudillo, 212
Chile, 213, 214
Chinese Communist Party, 144
"Civil Rights" (U.S.A.), 113,
    125–31
Cominform, 83
Commonwealth, 262, 267
Congo, 90
Council of Europe, 243
Cuba, 90, 133, 230–4
Czechoslovakia, 83

De Gaulle and Europe, 257, 258
Dien Bien Phu, 87

Egypt, 198–200
"Establishment", 269
European Community: Common
    Market, 243
(ECSC) Coal and Steel Com-
    munity, 244, 245
    Treaty of Rome, 246
    Association Agreement, 256

Festival of Britain, 268
Formosa, 148

General Agreement on Trade and
    Tariffs (GATT), 256
Germany: Occupation of, 57, 58
"Great Society" (U.S.A.), 136
Guatemala, 223–5

Hiroshima, 48, 62
Hiss Case, 116
Hungary: October Revolution,
    102

India: Five Year Plan, 167–9
Iraq, 203, 204
Israel, 207–9

Kashmir, 162, 170
Khrushchev and the Twentieth
    Party Congress, 101–3
Korean War, 86, 121
Kuomintang, 143, 144

Lebanon, 204
Little Rock, 125

Malaysia, 159
Marshall Plan, 81, 111
McCarthyism, 117–20
Mestizos, 212
Mexico, 217
Morocco, 205

Nationalism – Ideas of, 179, 180,
    195
"Non-Alignment", 172, 183
North Atlantic Treaty Organiza-
    tion (NATO), 242

Oder Neisse Line, 56
Organization for European Economic Co-operation (OEEC), 243
Organization of African Unity, 184
Organization of American States, 235

Pan-Arabism, 201
Panch Cheel (Five Principles), 173
Paris Summit Conference, 124
Poland, 55, 72–5
Potsdam, 52, 57

Sino-Soviet dispute, 152
South East Asia Treaty Organization (SEATO), 160
Southern Africa, 193, 194
Stalinism, 92–8
Suez, 88, 198
Sukarno's Indonesia, 158

Teheran, 51
Test Ban Treaty, 91
Truman Doctrine, 81, 111
Tunis, 205

United Nations Educational, Scientific and Cultural Organization (UNESCO), 50
United Nations Organization (UNO), 59, 271
United Nations Relief and Rehabilitation Association (UNRRA), 51
Uruguay, 216

Warsaw Pact, 88
World Trends since 1945, 22–4

Yalta, 48, 52, 54, 64
Yugoslavia, 84

Zionism, 203